IMAGES
*of America*

# SARASOTA COUNTY
# ISLANDS AND BEACHES

**On the Cover:** This image, taken by well-known photographer Joseph Steinmetz in the 1950s, shows a family fishing on Sarasota Bay. (Courtesy of Sarasota County Historical Resources.)

# IMAGES of America
# SARASOTA COUNTY ISLANDS AND BEACHES

Amy A. Elder

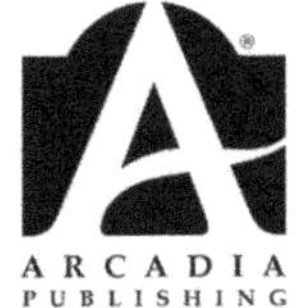

ISBN 978-1-4671-1486-8

Published by Arcadia Publishing
Charleston, South Carolina

Library of Congress Control Number: 2015939476

For all general information, please contact Arcadia Publishing:
Telephone 843-853-2070
Fax 843-853-0044
E-mail sales@arcadiapublishing.com
For customer service and orders:
Toll-Free 1-888-313-2665

Visit us on the Internet at www.arcadiapublishing.com

*To my parents, Betsy and Doug Elder, who make life magical for their family*

# Contents

# ACKNOWLEDGMENTS

I would like to thank my editors from Arcadia Publishing; my proofreaders, including my mother and Rachel North; my Sensitive Women's Writers Salon for critiquing my book for the past year; and my friends and family, my husband, son, and father for taking photographs. Thank you, to my historians Tom Mayers, Connie Davis, Frances "Fluff" Thayer, Dorothy Korwek, James Hagler, and Sydney "Syd" Buffum; the Sarasota County Historical Resources (SCHR), including Jeff LaHurd and Larry Kellerman; and the Venice Museum and Archives (VMA), especially Michelle Harm, Rhonda Rodgers, Carol Bailey, and Chuck Ford for scanning all my pictures. Thanks go to Caroline Reed for her friendship, Dr. Lee Green for her encouragement, and Lois Duncan for her advice and use of pictures. I am grateful to all of the residents whose donated stories and photographs have helped me continue to write about Sarasota's history for the next generation.

# INTRODUCTION

Each of Sarasota's islands is as unique and enchanting as the next. Longboat Key, City Island, Lido Key, St. Armands, Bird Key, Golden Gate Point, Siesta Key, Casey Key, Venice, and Manasota Key all make up the islands of Sarasota. Each provides beautiful beaches, abundant wildlife, lush vegetation, excellent restaurants, marinas and boat docks, exclusive private estates, and accommodating hotels. These are some of the reasons people come here to live or visit.

Throughout this book, we will explore the history of the islands, including the pioneers, developers, and residents who currently enjoy living here. Sarasota's islands are as different as their residents. People who are lucky enough to live or vacation here choose the island that best suits their lifestyle. No two islands are the same, but all the Sarasota islands are a pleasure to visit and a luxury to live on.

Starting at the northernmost island, Longboat Key, which actually extends into Manatee County at its northern end, is manicured, lush, and full of exclusive golf courses. The town of Longbeach, the oldest settlement on the island, is in Manatee County but contains much of the history. The structures are old, the restaurants popular, and the resident flock of peacocks are beautiful. Farther south are mostly residential homes, condominiums, and a few restaurants and stores. The landscaping is immaculately maintained, and beautiful homes and yards abound.

Farther south is City Island, which is owned by the city and home to Mote Marine Shark Laboratory. This island was man-made as a result of dredging channels and disposing of the surplus building materials from John Ringling's Ritz-Carlton, which was demolished on the southern end of Longboat Key and deposited here. This island is also home to some restaurants and the Sarasota Sailing Squadron.

The next island is Lido Key, which has pristine sugar-white beaches. The southern end of Lido Key is a state park where local residents picnic, enjoying the beaches, kayaking, and swimming. St. Armands is an island that connects several nearby islands, mostly dredged together during the building boom of the early 1900s. John Ringling laid it out as a housing development with a circular road pattern and canals. It now has chic and stylish boutiques and diverse restaurants. You can get handmade fudge or ice cream, shop for designer clothes, or enjoy a 1904 salad from the renowned Columbia Restaurant. To the north is City Island, to the south is Lido Key, and to the east, along the causeway to Sarasota, is Coon Key. Most people think it is part of St. Armands, but it was almost entirely dredged from the bottom of the bay. Here, you will find the Sarasota Yacht Club and Plymouth Harbor.

Next along the causeway is Bird Key, which is a gated community with a private yacht club. The Bird Key Yacht Club is a member of the Florida Council of Yacht Clubs (FCYC), as is the Sarasota Yacht Club. This council of about 40 clubs allows visitors from any of the clubs to visit and use the facilities, which brings many other boaters to visit. This is an exclusive residential community, with many illustrious residents.

Golden Gate Point was dredged from the bay floor when much of the present waterfront of the mainland city was filled. The point, earlier known as Cedar Point, was built up as residential lots with a magnificent view of the city and the bay.

Separating the next southern key is Big Pass, a large pass that shifts position often. The next island to the south is Siesta Key, which is more relaxed than its northern sisters, with more natural vegetation and what is widely regarded as one of the top 10 beaches in the world. From the active Siesta Village, with street fairs, shops, restaurants, and nightclubs, to Siesta Beach, with volleyball, sunbathing, and swimming, there is much to do. Locals, tourists, and spring breakers enjoy acres of soft, cool, white sand. South of this area are numerous homes and condos stretching from the public beach to Turtle Beach, another public park. The south end of the island was once Midnight Pass, an opening from the bay to the Gulf of Mexico. This was also the former location of a shark lab used by Eugenie Clark, which later moved to City Island. When their property was threatened by beach erosion, local landowners got permission to "move" the pass by using bulldozers to fill it in with the old Mote Marine Shark Tanks. They promised to keep the relocated pass open, but failed, and the two islands are now connected.

South of the closed pass is Casey Key, a great place to take a Sunday drive to see spectacular homes along a narrow, winding road. This exclusive island is full of a mixture of small older homes and enormous estates. The northern end is a quiet, exclusive residential area, with many mansions replacing the existing cottages. The landscaping here trends toward the use of native plants and an overall natural feeling. The southern end of the island still has some older motels and guesthouses, and south of the Albee Road Bridge, much of the island is a county park. The North Jetty Park, as it is known, features fishing from the jetties, a bait shop, beaches, playgrounds, and picnic and parking areas. Separating this area from the Island of Venice is Venice Inlet, a reinforced set of jetties that keeps the pass open.

Venice is a resort town full of enticing restaurants and shops, sunny beaches, and great community spirit. On the north end is South Jetty Park, with a snack bar, fishing pier, and beach. Along the inlet lies the Crow's Nest Restaurant and Marina. This local institution attracts boaters, who can dock for meals, while others come by car. Nearby is the Venice Yacht Club, a member of the Florida Council of Yacht Clubs (FCYC). Downtown Venice offers food, shops, and stores in a quaint, attractive setting with a large park featuring fairs, markets, and music. The island also boasts its own hospital and airport. Near the airport is a local treasure, Sharky's on the Pier, with a fishing pier as well as casual and fine dining. The southern tip of the island is Casperson Beach, a public park with a very natural appearance, like a step back in time.

Manasota Beach is less traveled and more natural, amassing its culture from plenty of art galleries, treasured shells, and gifts from the sea. The northern end of the island lies in Sarasota County, which is mostly a mix of residential and public parkland. This area also features the Hermitage, an artist's retreat, and the Manasota Beach Club, a private beach and tennis club with dining and activities. The southern end of the island lies in Charlotte County, where hotels, businesses, and commercial properties are located.

This chain of barrier islands from north to south boasts activities and beautiful destinations for locals and tourists alike, and each is its own treasure. Welcome to the islands of Sarasota.

# *One*

# Longboat Key

## Lat 27.3969 N, Long 82.6447 W

Longboat Key was home to Native Americans, then Cuban fishermen for many years. In the late 1880s, Thomas Mann and his family became one of the first permanent nonnative settlers to file for a Homestead Act, thereby farming and living on the north end of the key, which was called Longbeach.

The south end of the island started developing in the early 1900s. In 1904, pioneer Byron Corey homesteaded here, and in 1907, he became the postmaster for the 20-plus residents.

Without any bridges from the mainland, the homesteaders relied on boats for supplies, travel, and communication. In the early 1900s, savvy local businessman John Savarese helped the island grow by providing transportation.

In 1911, Longbeach became a permanent establishment with the filing of the Longbeach plat, then with its own post office in 1914. In the mid-1910s, the subdivision consisted of a large bathhouse, a hotel, and at least 16 homes.

In the 1920s, circus entrepreneur John Ringling owned several acres on Longboat Key, Lido, and St. Armands, as well as the Ringling Estates development company, which he shared with his business partners Owen Burns and Samuel Guptil. He joined the mainland to the islands with a bridge in 1926.

In the 1940s, Longboat Key consisted of a winding two-lane road and lots of vegetation and marshes. Mosquitoes were fierce! According to residents, there were times when a person could grab a fistful of mosquitoes, and sometimes it was so bad people needed handkerchiefs to breathe. The town of Longboat Key, which lies within Sarasota and Manatee County, was incorporated in 1955.

In the 1960s, Arthur Vining Davis opened the Arvida Company, then purchased and developed a large part of Longboat Key, including the Longboat Key Club. He cared greatly about the esthetic beauty of his buildings and the surrounding landscape.

Over the years, Longboat Key has continued to be developed with luxurious homes and condominiums. The speed limit remains a strict 45 miles per hour. Throughout the year, the beautifully manicured roadway plantings are updated to reflect the current season.

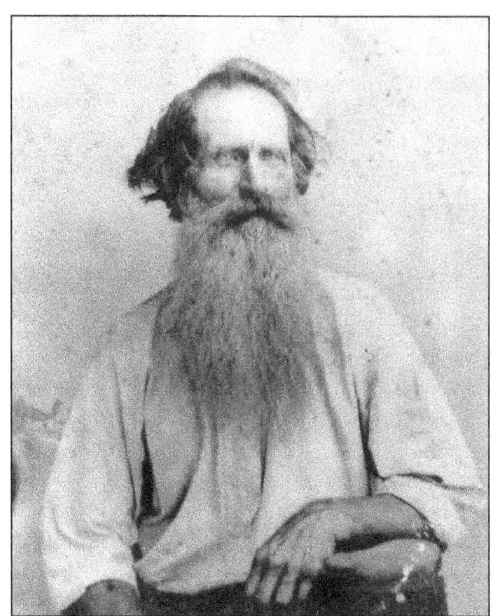

In 1885, Thomas Mann, a Civil War veteran who fought for the North, applied for a homestead application for 144 acres on the north end of Longboat Key. He was not the first to file or be awarded land; however, he was the first to live there. In 1888, Mann first built a palm-frond shelter, then a house for his family, including his wife, Mary Kell, and five children. (Courtesy of SCHR.)

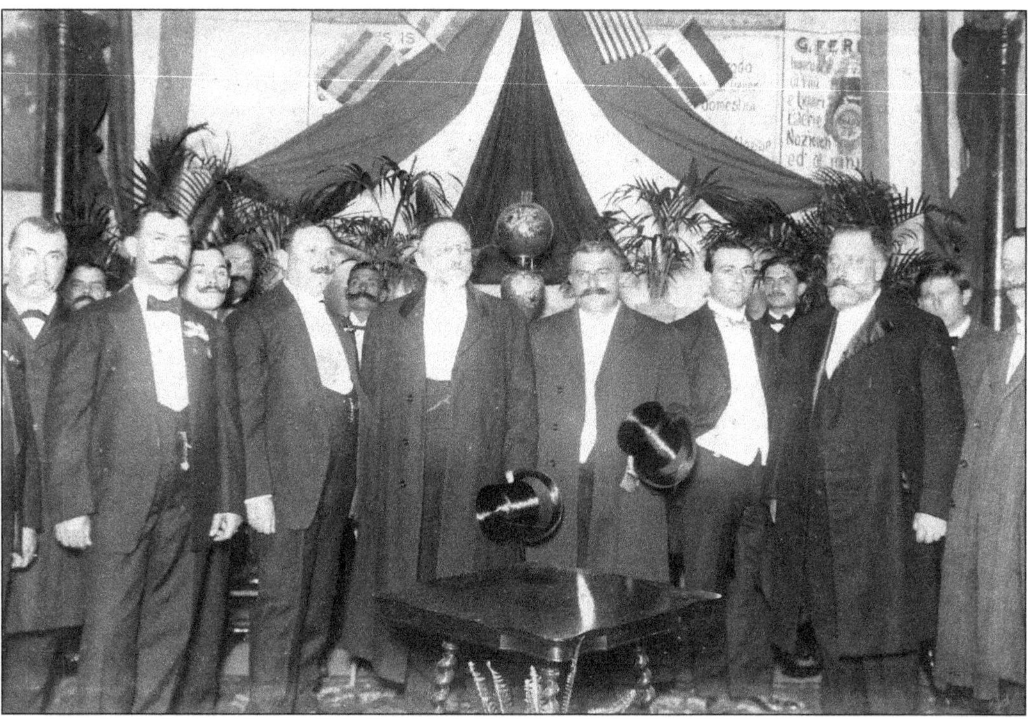

Dating back to the late 1800s, one of the oldest property owners was Capt. John Savarese of Tampa, also known as "Uncle Johnny." He is seen here (fourth from left in the front row) at the Tampa Italian Club, which he founded. He was also knighted by Victor Emmanuel, the king of Italy. In 1885, Savarese started a large wholesale fishing business, which employed 500 people. He built a house on the north end of Longboat Key in 1913, only to have it destroyed in the 1921 hurricane. He owned numerous boats, including the *Mistletoe*, and founded the Tampa Yacht Club. When Savarese died, he left his land to his wife, Nelle Risley, who never had children so she could keep her figure. (Courtesy of Tom Mayers.)

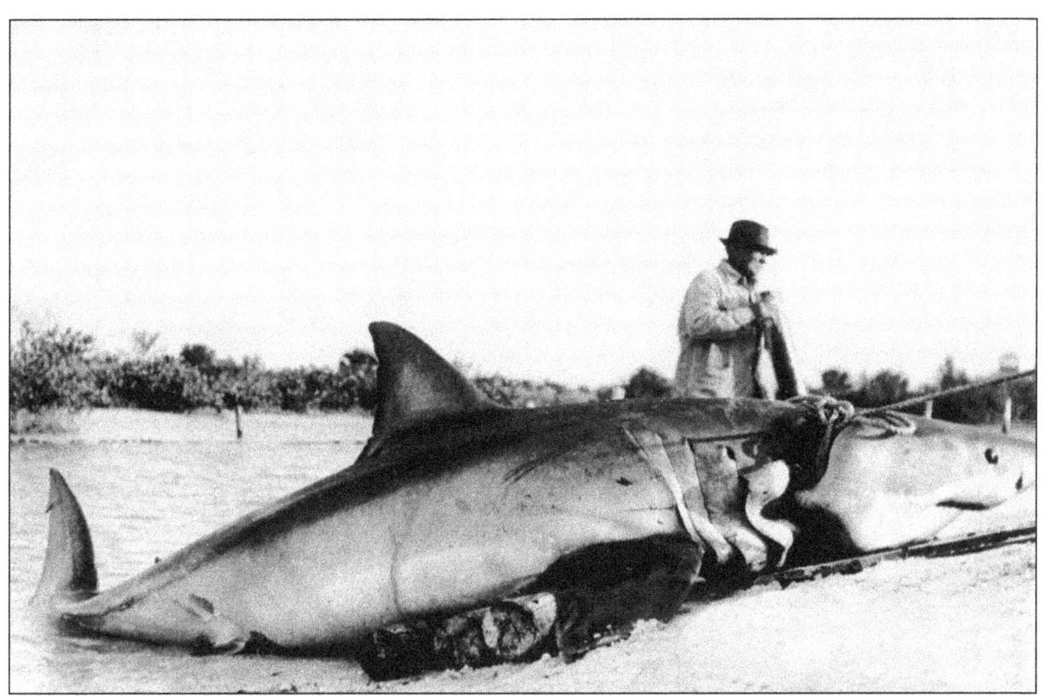

Adolphus M. "Dad" Holbrook started a shark business on the north end of Longboat Key in 1932. Born in Maine, Holbrook was a veteran of the Spanish-American War. He retired to Longboat Key and started catching sharks offshore in the Gulf. He boiled the sharks for oil and sold the fins. Holbrook is pictured here with a 17-foot great white shark that his assistant Edgar Green had just caught offshore near Whitney Beach. (Courtesy of SCHR.)

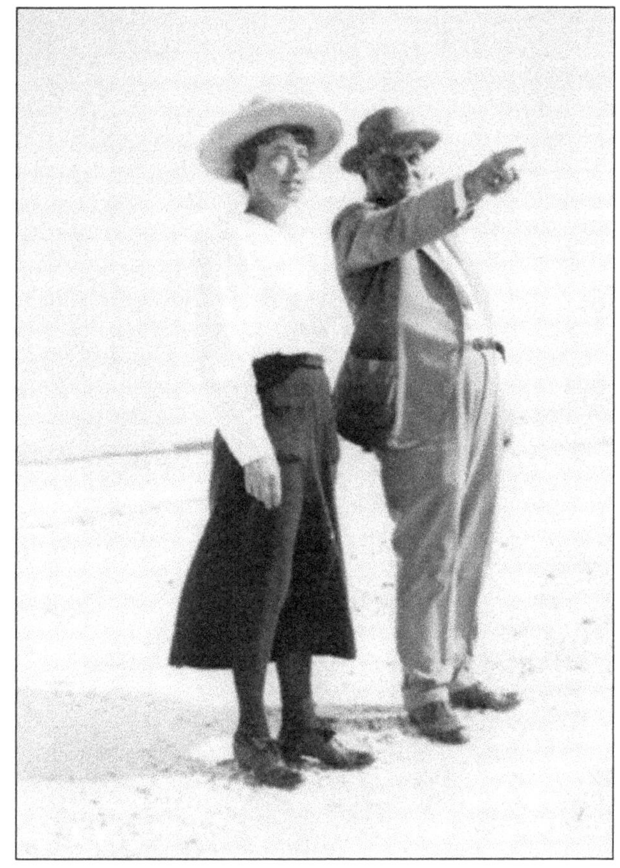

In 1939, Nelle Savarese offered her niece Francis "Fran" and husband Frank Mayers the land at the end of Longboat Key as a wedding gift, with the stipulation that they would pay 10 years of back taxes. After chasing off a shark fisherman named Holbrook, they built their vacation cottage and called it Lands End. Pictured here are Nell and John Savarese. (Courtesy of Tom Mayers.)

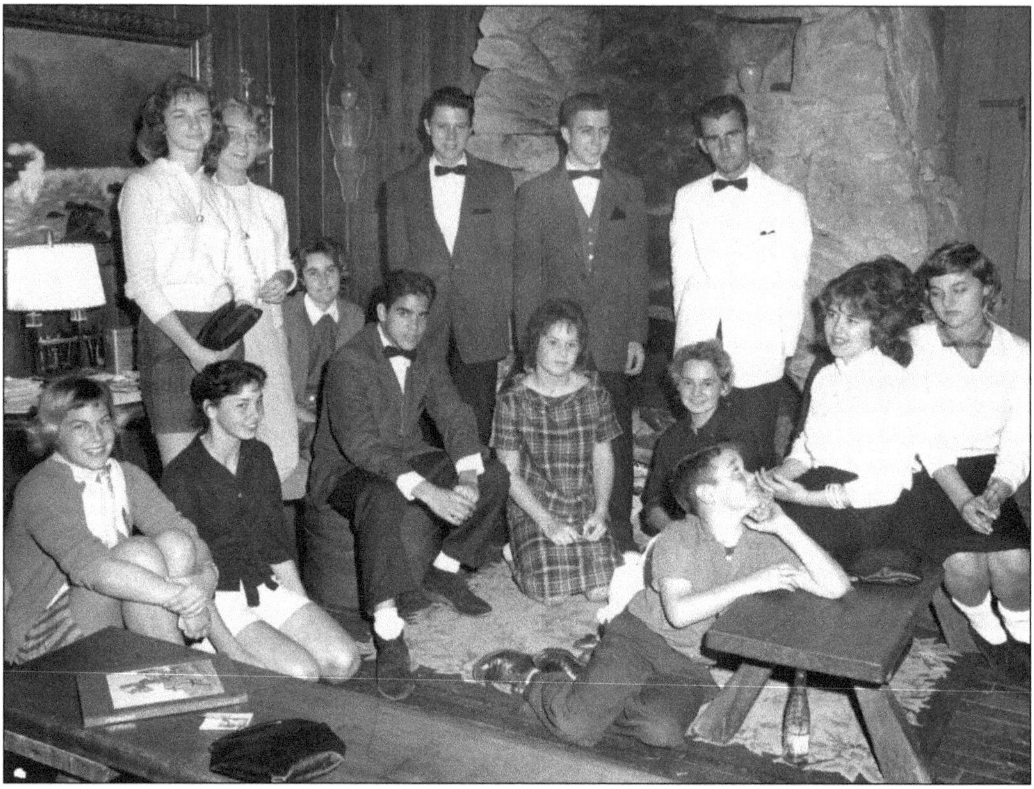

The Mayers family built Lands End in 1940. When they moved to Florida as permanent residents in 1959, they brought their three children—Michael, Joan, and Tom. Taking advantage of the Longboat Pass Bridge that opened in 1958, the Mayers family started and operated Land's End Marina. They also sponsored dances for the local youth. In the front of the picture is a young Tom with the older attendees of a dance. Note that the band members are wearing tuxedoes. (Courtesy of Tom Mayers.)

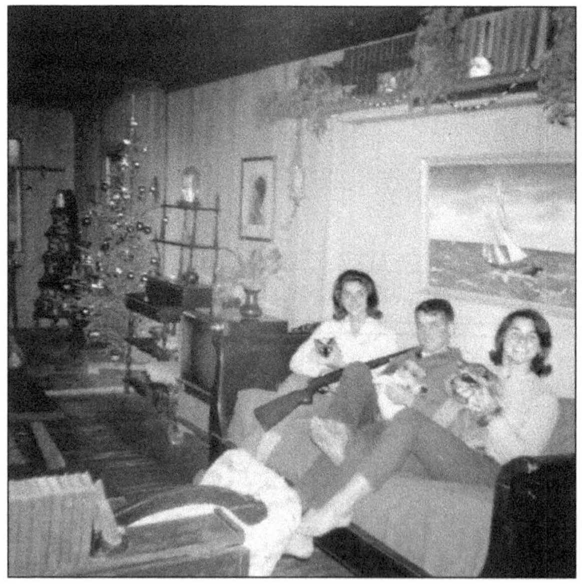

Sometimes, the family would spend Christmas on the island. Pictured here inside Lands End cottage are Michael (holding a cat), Tom (holding a dog), and Joan (holding a raccoon). According to Tom Mayers, it was common for children to raise raccoons as pets on the island. (Courtesy of Tom Mayers.)

Lands End cottage is still owned and enjoyed by the Mayers family. Eldest daughter and realtor Michael Saunders is the current owner. Lands End started as a weekend cottage, then transformed over the years into a restaurant and later a bait and tackle shop. The restaurant served sandwiches, burgers, and smoked mullet fish, which are abundant in the pass and Gulf. Fishermen see mullet jumping out of the water daily. (Courtesy of Tom Mayers.)

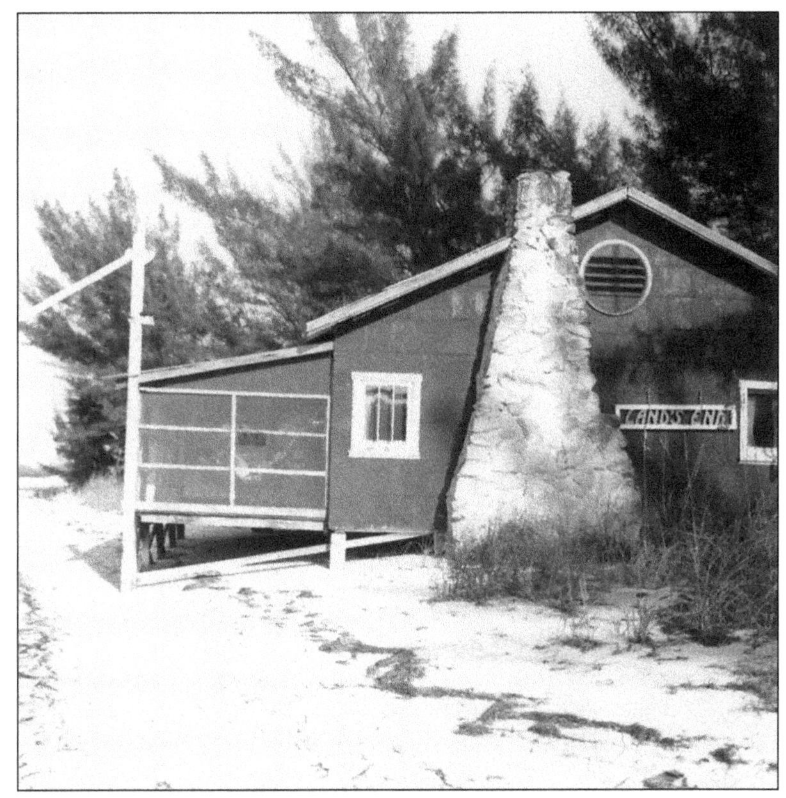


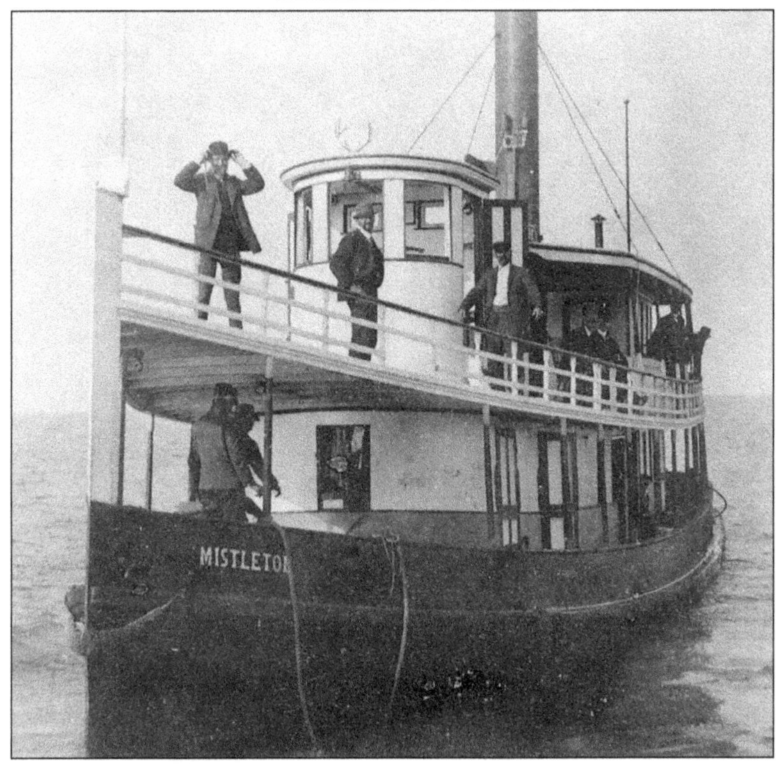


John Savarese used his fleet of boats, including his steamer the *Mistletoe* (pictured), to run between Tampa, Sarasota, and stops along Longboat Key. This allowed the pioneers to sell and receive produce, lumber, and fish, as well as travel to the mainland. The Longbeach dock was too shallow, so small sailboats would help to load and unload the steamship. (Courtesy of SCHR.)

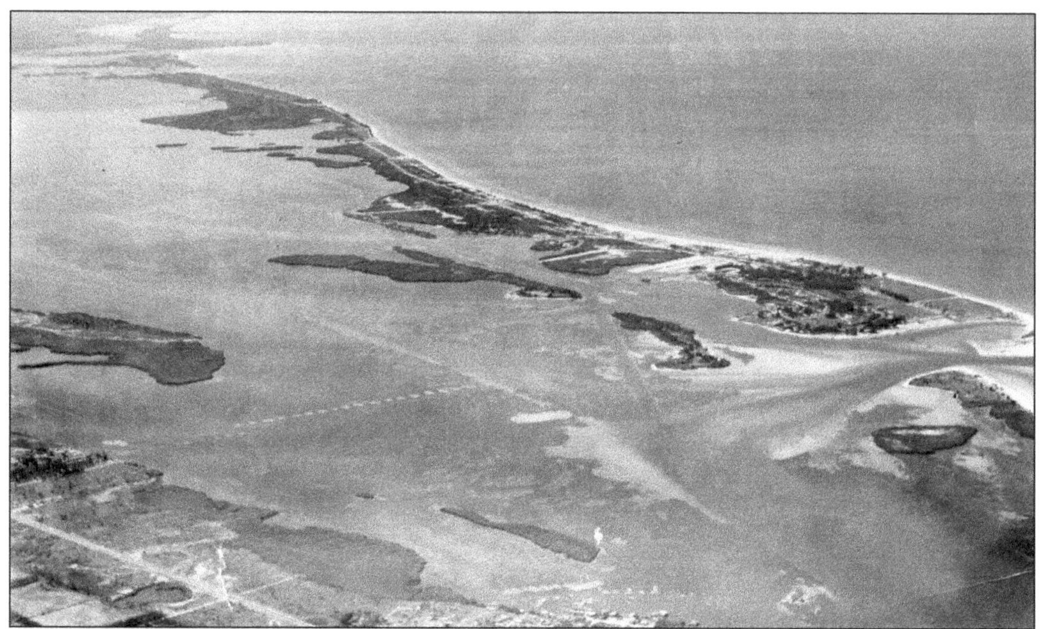

Longboat Pass is located at the northernmost tip of Longboat Key and the southern tip of Anna Maria Island. It has grown and shrunk over the years due to storms, erosions, and tides. In the 1930s, Longboat Pass was a single channel to the bay. Today, locals enjoy beaching their boats on a small island near the pass that is referred to as "Beer Can Island." (Courtesy of SCHR.)

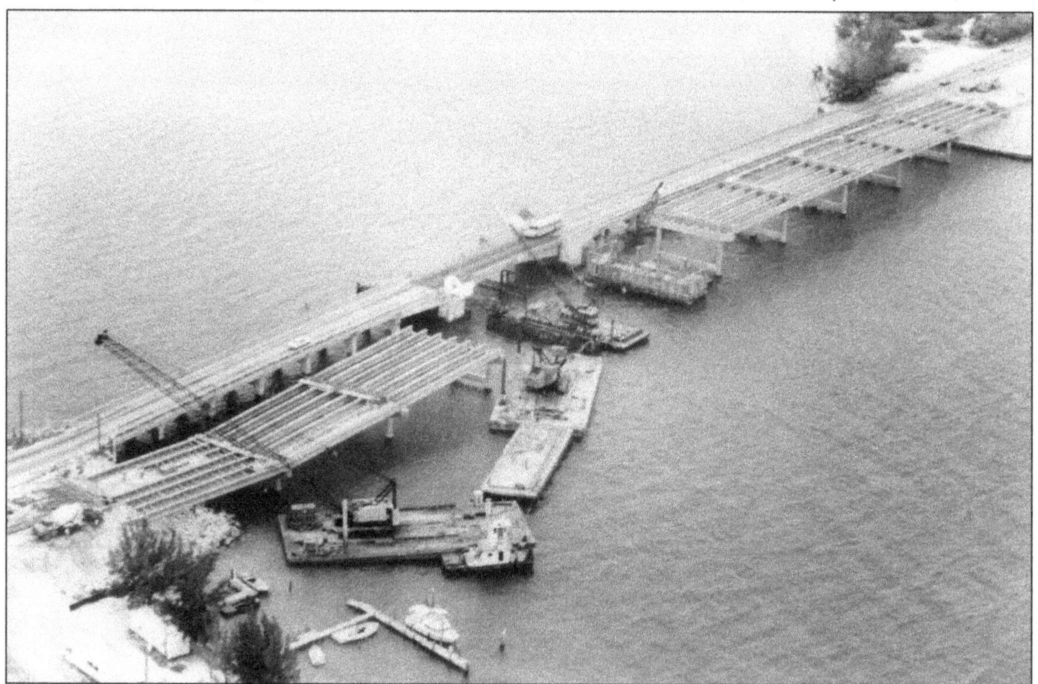

There were a couple of bridges between Longboat Key and Anna Maria Island that were destroyed by weather or con men. A bridge was built in 1926, only to be washed away by high tides in 1932. Part of the bridge ended up on Jewfish Key and was towed to Palmetto to be used as the first bridge to Sneed Island. Seen here are the remains of the 1926 bridge. (Courtesy of SCHR.)

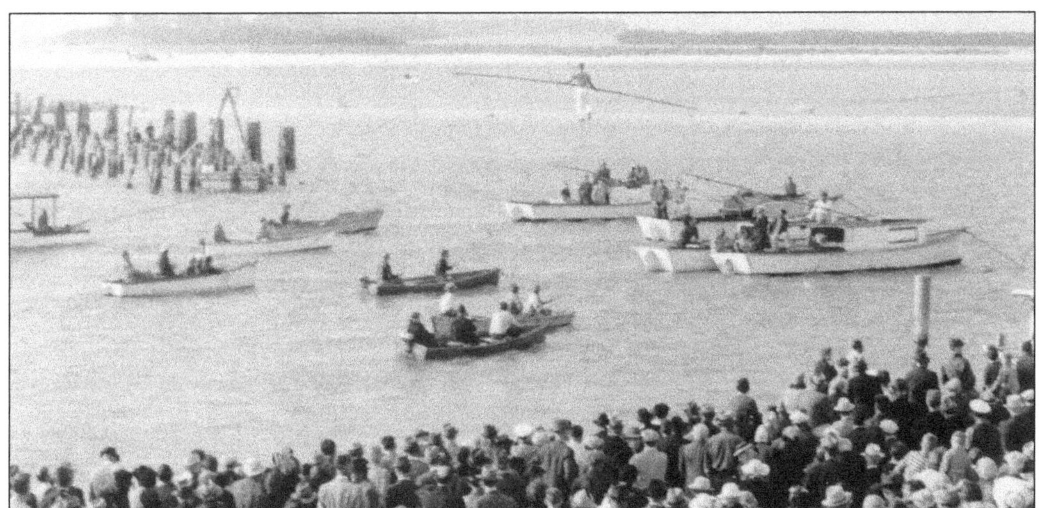

In 1940, a group of con men sold stocks to residents to build a toll bridge between Longboat Key and Anna Maria Island. The newspaper stated 17,000 people came to the celebration to promote a phantom new bridge. The Gulf Coast Cracker Band played at the event, where "the Great Arturo" is seen crossing the pass on a high wire. (Courtesy of SCHR.)

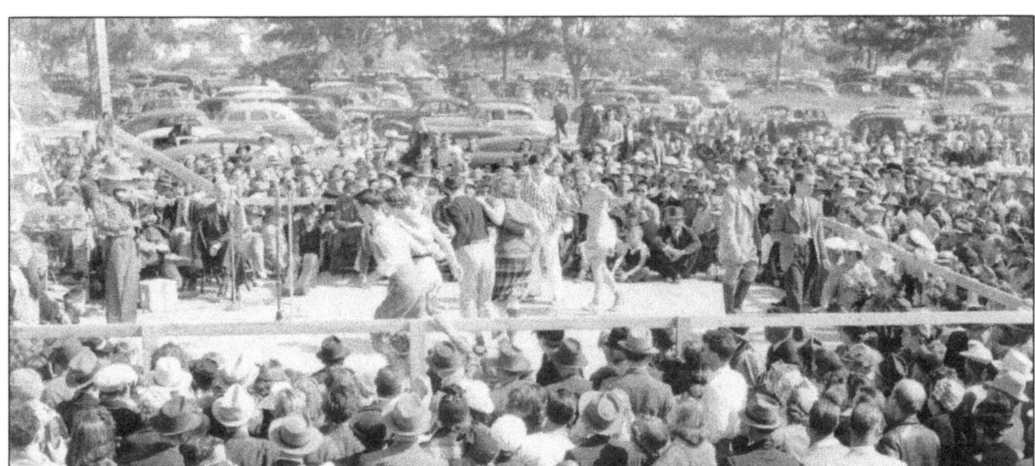

There were many fun activities at the bridge celebration. Fishing, dancing, and, of course, free barbecue brought the community from both sides of the pass together. Bill Carmichael fed 4,500 people by cooking on an open fire. The next day, the promoters and money were gone, and a bridge was not built until 1958. Pictured here are locals enjoying a jitterbug dance contest. (Courtesy of SCHR.)

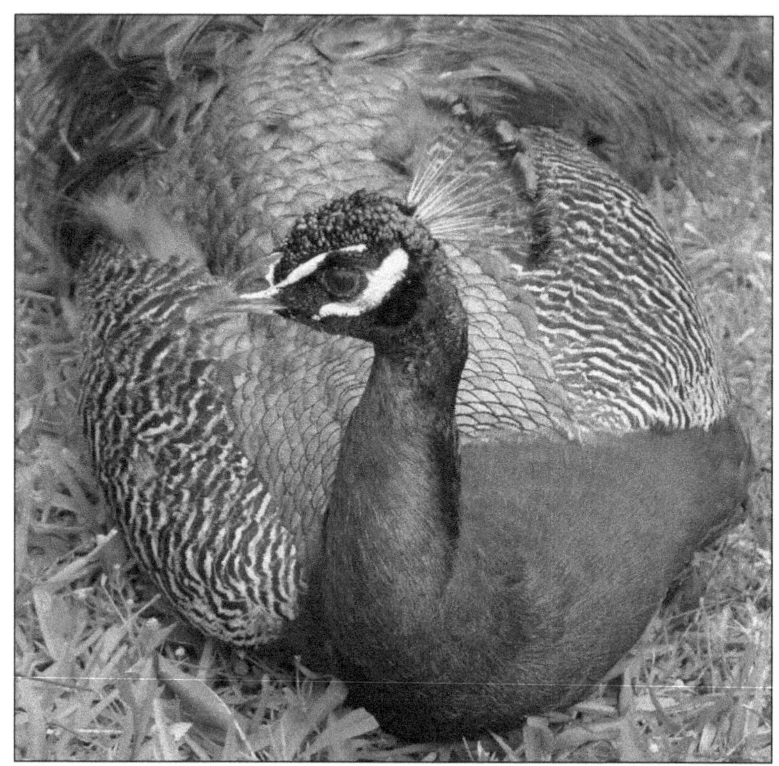

In the late 1970s, Ginny Pier, along with a group of residents, purchased a flock of peacocks and donated it to the village on the north end of Longboat Key. Tourists love to drive by and watch them, and are often surprised when a male shows off his colorful feathers to the female birds. Not all residents like the mating calls and squawking, however. (Courtesy of SCHR.)

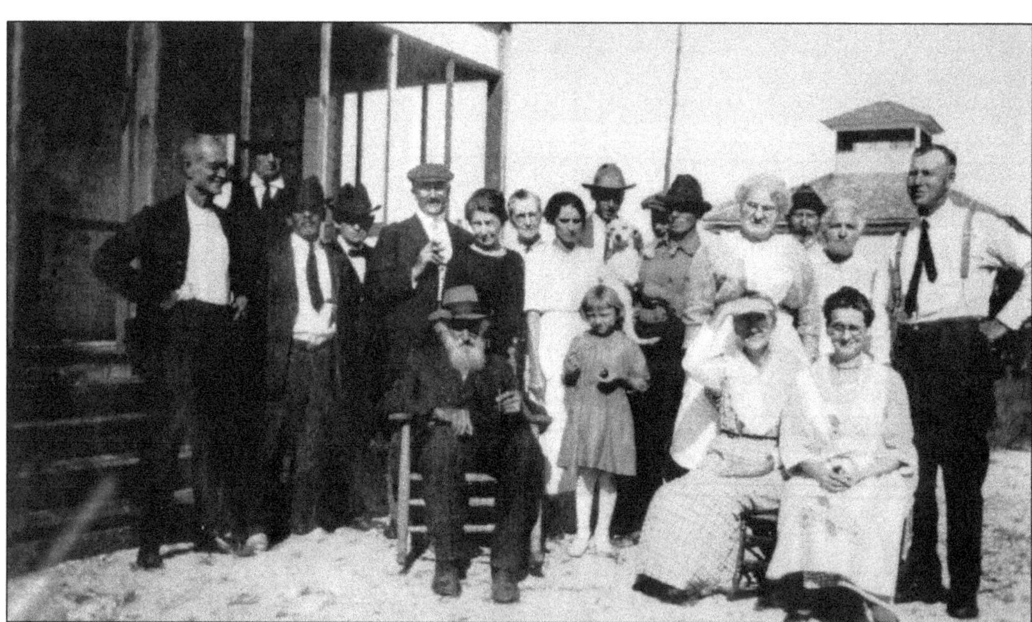

Henrietta Tallman, the postmaster, owned Jordan's Longbeach Hotel with her husband, Denver. The entrepreneurial couple ran a store and the post office out of their hotel. Built in 1912, the hotel welcomed tourists arriving on the *Mistletoe* or private boats. Employees would meet guests at the dock and use wheelbarrows to carry their luggage. (Courtesy of SCHR.)

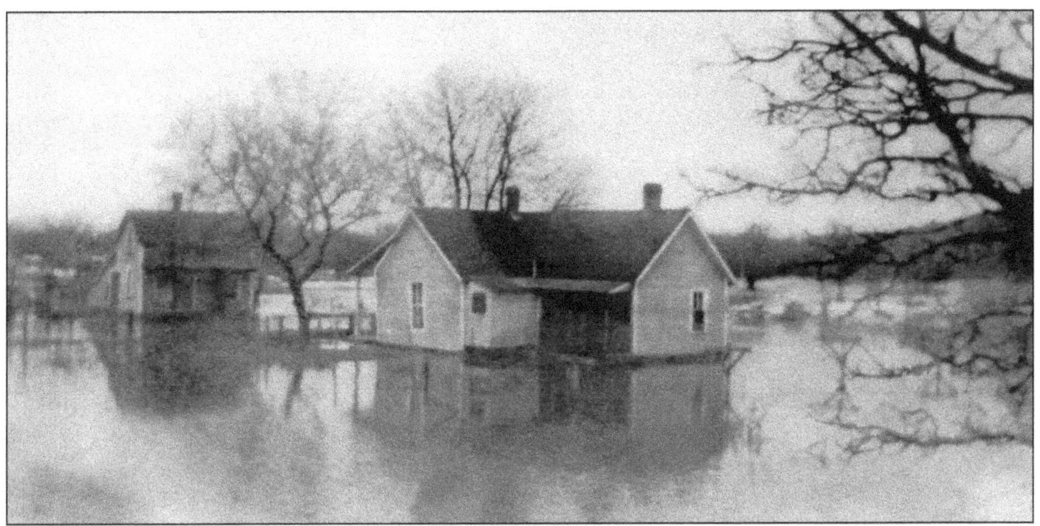

Bryon Corey developed the area and built his house and post office on a long pier that was also used to dock the *Mistletoe*. Unfortunately, in 1921, a large hurricane flooded the crops and animals in this community. Most residents were forced to move, and as a result, the post office was closed. (Courtesy of SCHR.)

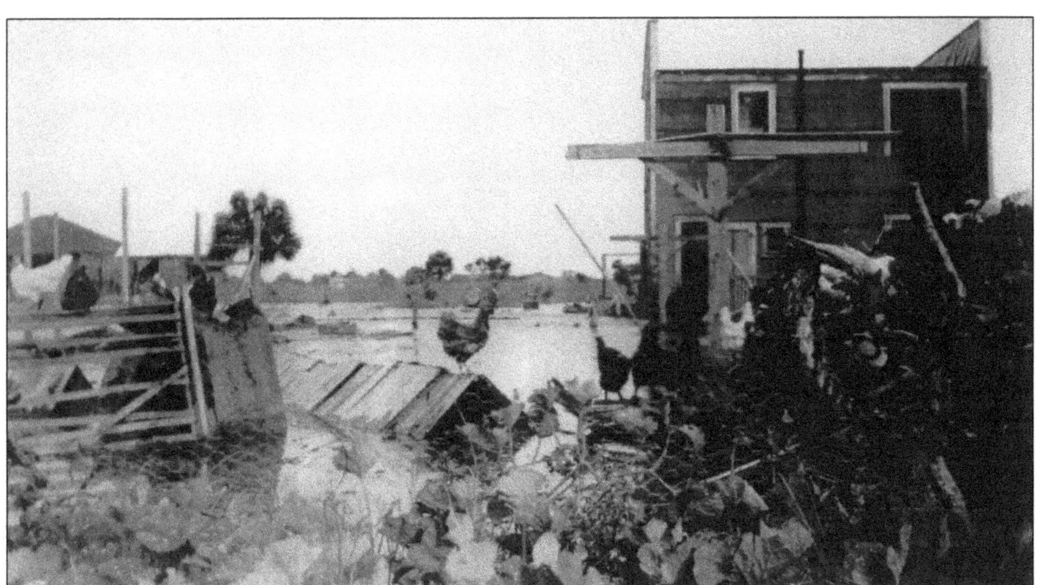

The flood destroyed the south end of the island. This haunting picture in which a rooster attempts to find high ground after bad flooding tells a story of survival. The level where the tide came up to is also visible. The exact location of the houses is unknown. (Courtesy of SCHR.)

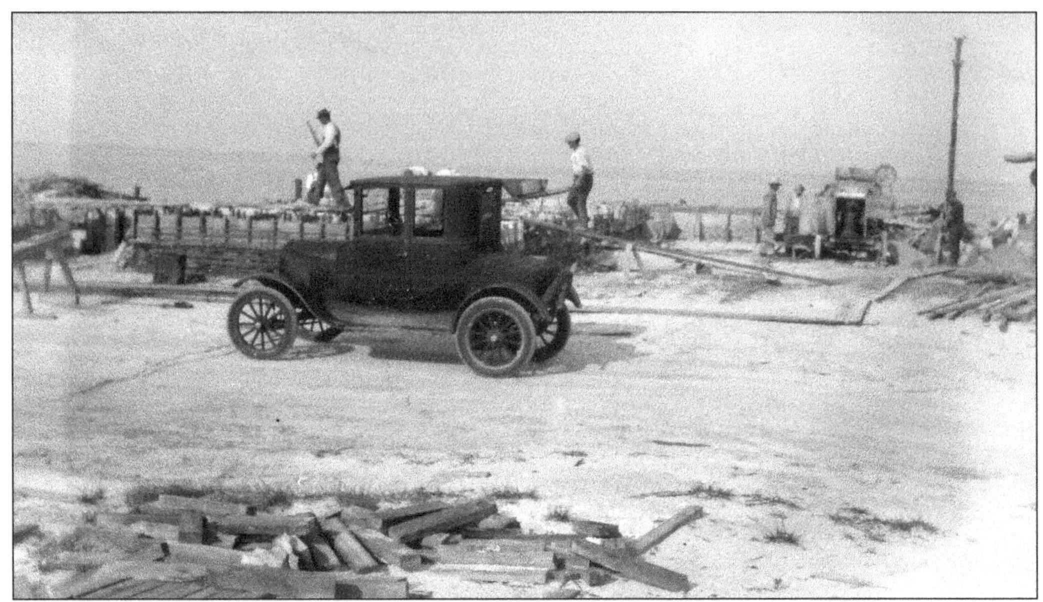

John Ringling hired the Tampa Dredging Company to build a bridge starting at Golden Gate Point and ending at St. Armands. A 7,000-pound steam hammer with 35-foot leads was used to drive two oyster-shell concrete piles a day into the bedrock. On January 1, 1926, the Ringling Causeway Bridge was completed, and Ringling drove his green Rolls-Royce over the new bridge. The bridge was opened to the public in February. For marketing purposes, Ringling offered free bus service. After investing $750,000 to build the bridge, he gave it over to the city as a gift in June 1927. (Courtesy of SCHR.)

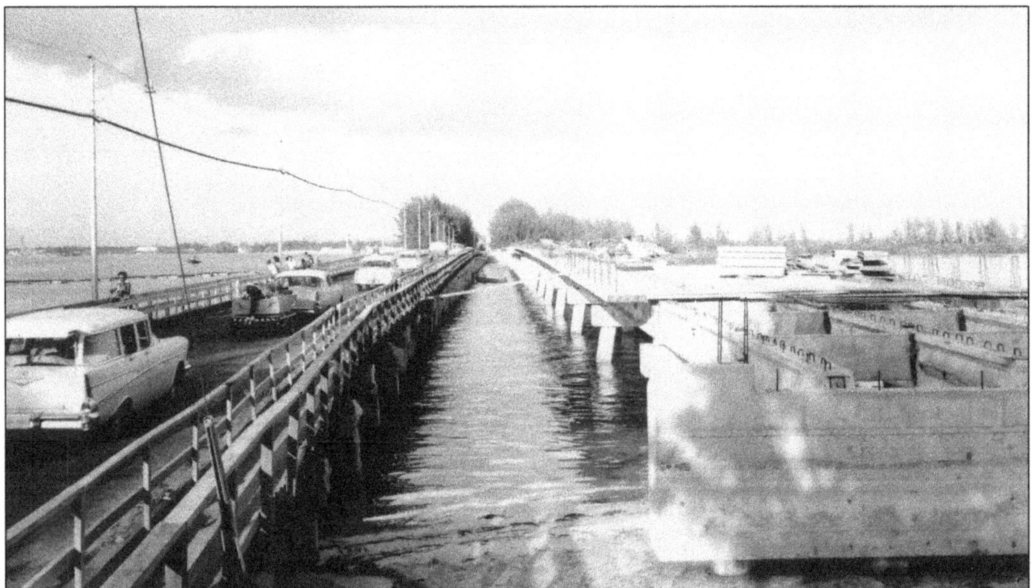

In return, the city gave Ringling a dollar for the bridge and agreed to operate and maintain it, while making it available for the residents to use free of charge. The bridge was built to last 20 years but actually lasted 34. The engineer James A. Moreland revealed it was the largest project in this area to use oyster-shell concrete. This material was used because large amounts of concrete were hard to obtain at the time. (Courtesy of SCHR.)

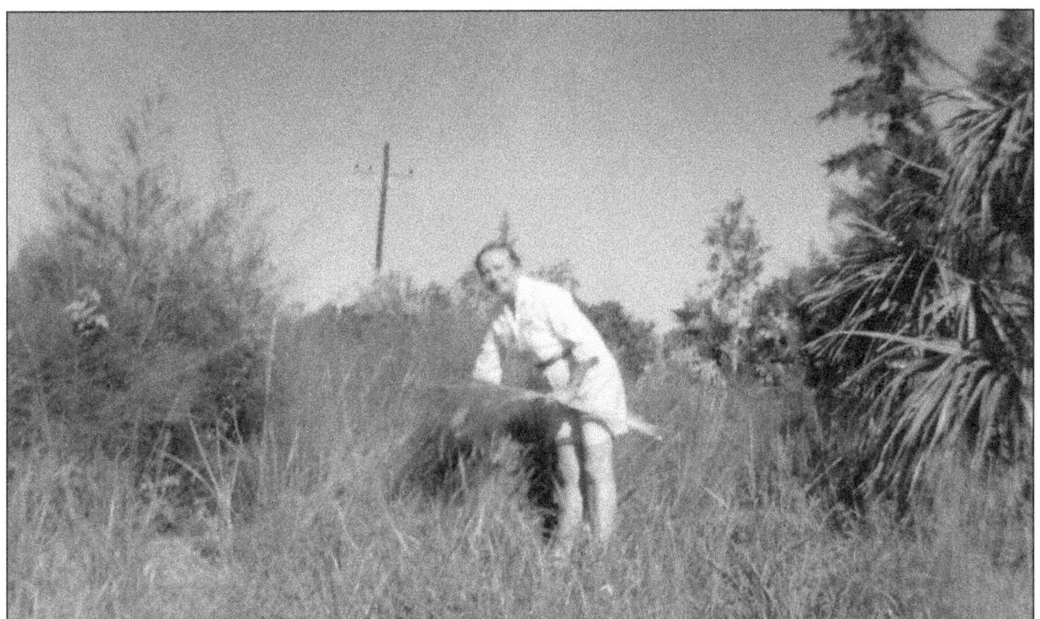

To attract tourists, a group of civic organizations voted for mosquito control and campaigned to have a mosquito control district for Sarasota County. This initiative was delayed during World War II, then restarted in 1946. Surplus equipment was purchased from the local army air base to clear the island. Longboat Key resident Thaida Holmes is pictured on the key in the 1940s. (Courtesy of SCHR.)

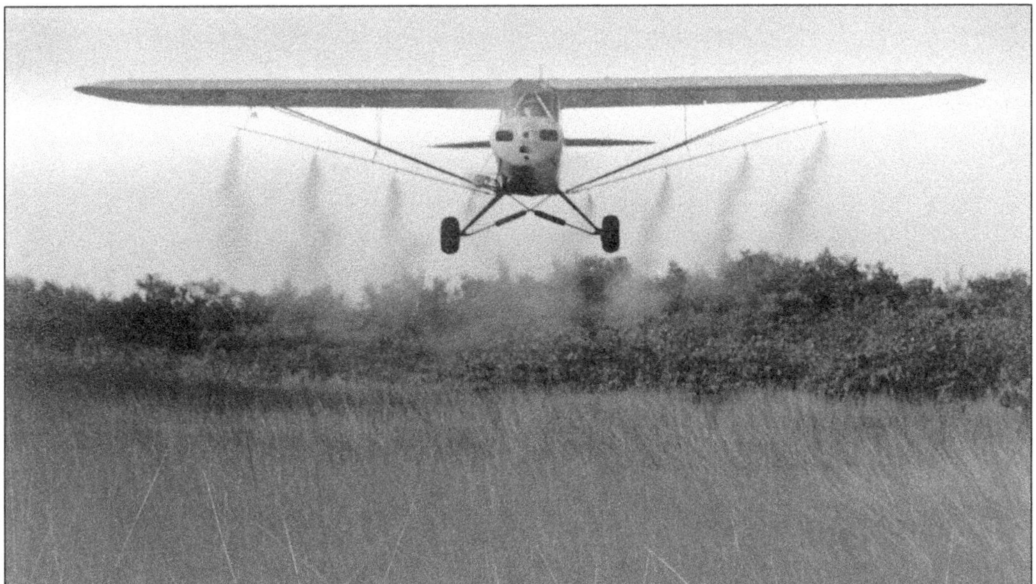

Workers used a backhoe, bulldozers, and machetes to clear their way through the unclaimed wilderness. They wore hip boots, long-sleeve shirts, and pants to navigate around the numerous rats, snakes, and other animals that fled from construction. Foreman Omar Casey was in charge of mosquito control for 22 years, and the island became more pleasant for people. Airplanes or trucks were used to spray the area with pesticide until 1999, but now the larvae are treated directly to help keep the mosquitoes at bay. (Courtesy of SCHR.)

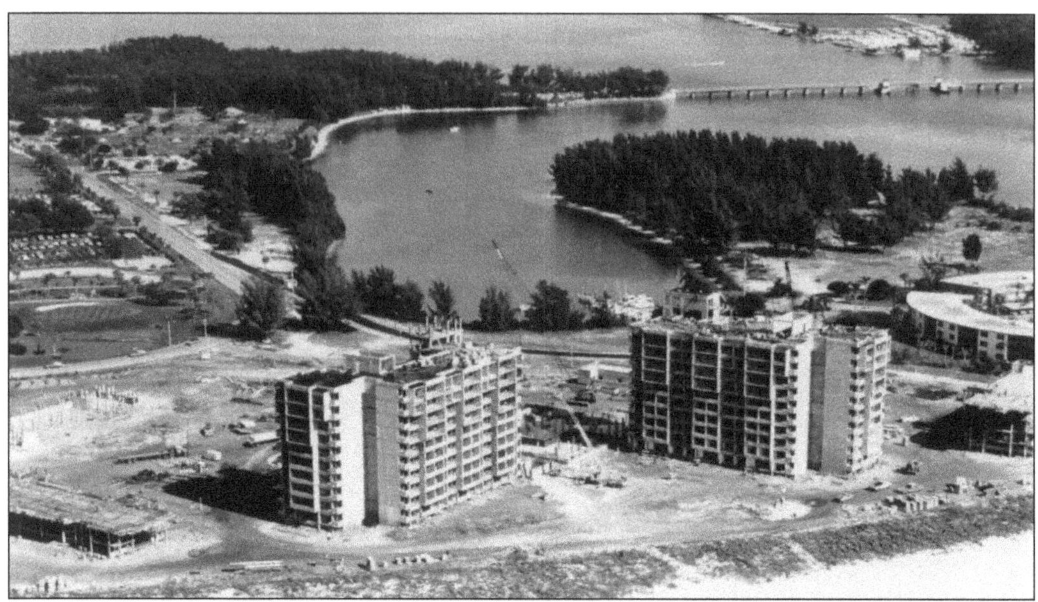
At age 91, Arthur Vining Davis purchased 2,000 acres of land on Longboat Key, Bird, Coon, Lido, and Otter Keys, and St. Armands from the Ringling interests and others in 1959. He developed luxury housing, golf courses, and a shopping mall. According to his company's motto, "Every community we build, every facility we operate, and every service we provide, should be the finest of its kind." Some of the properties that Arvida Corporation developed were Seaplace (1973), Bay Isles (1975–1976), the Bayou section (1977–1978), Beach Place (1981), Inn on the Beach (1982), Fairway Bay (1981–1986), and Sunset Beach (1983). (Courtesy of SCHR.)

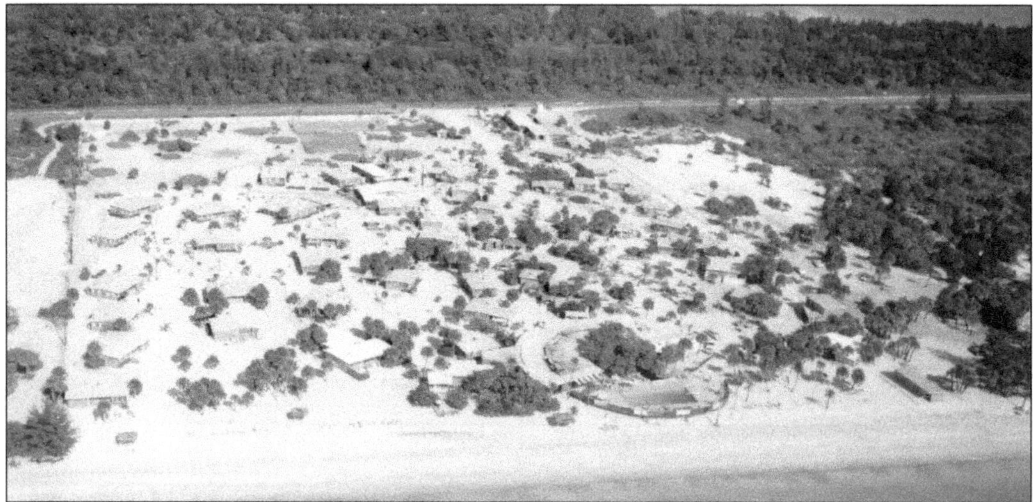
In 1949, restaurateur Herb Field and family discovered Longboat Key and decided to relocate from Chicago. They bought land on the key to build the Colony, a development with cottages and a restaurant that opened in 1954. When Murray "Murf" Klauber visited from Buffalo, New York, he too liked the area and bought the Colony in 1969, extending its name to the Colony Beach and Tennis Club. With his vision, the property grew to over 230 luxury condos, 21 tennis courts, multiple conference and meeting rooms, and a gourmet restaurant. Over the years, many important people have stayed there, including Al Gore and Pres. George W. Bush, who was there during the 9/11 terrorist attacks. (Courtesy of the SCHR.)

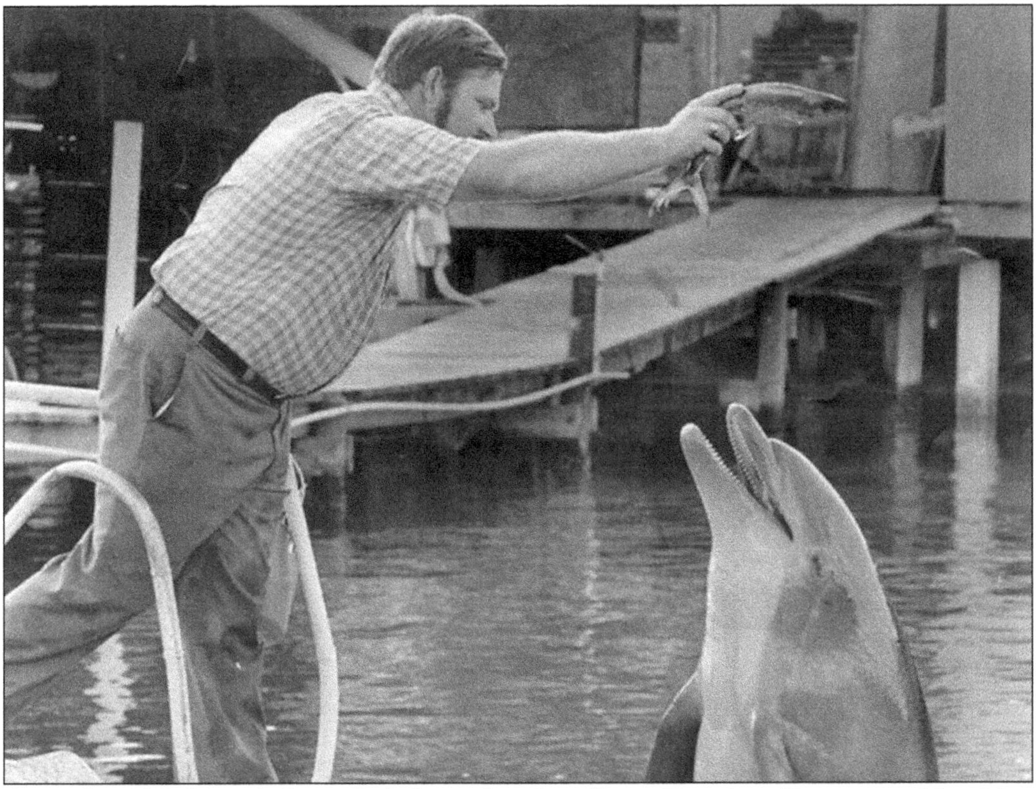

Opened in 1967, Moore's Stone Crab, located in the village of Longboat Key, is one of the oldest restaurants on the island. Tourists and locals come for the fresh seafood and view of the sparkling turquoise water. John "Pete" Moore and brother Hugh opened the restaurant along with Robert Hicks, who is seen here feeding Jackie, the resident dolphin. (Courtesy of Robert Hicks.)

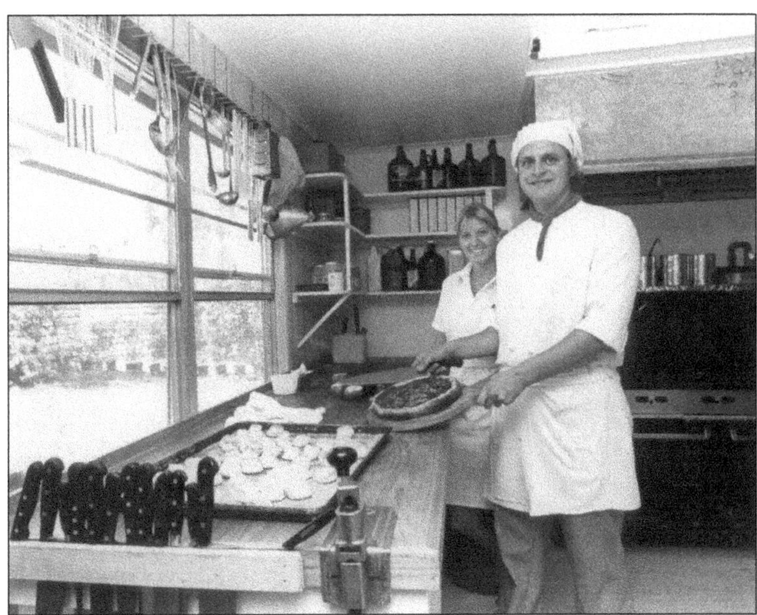

Elizabeth Arnold, a lively resident of Longboat Key, said when inviting guests that the first call was to the guests, the second to Harry's. Owners Lynn and Harry Christensen are pictured here in the kitchen making delicious recipes and fulfilling their passion for gourmet cooking. (Courtesy of Harry's Continental.)

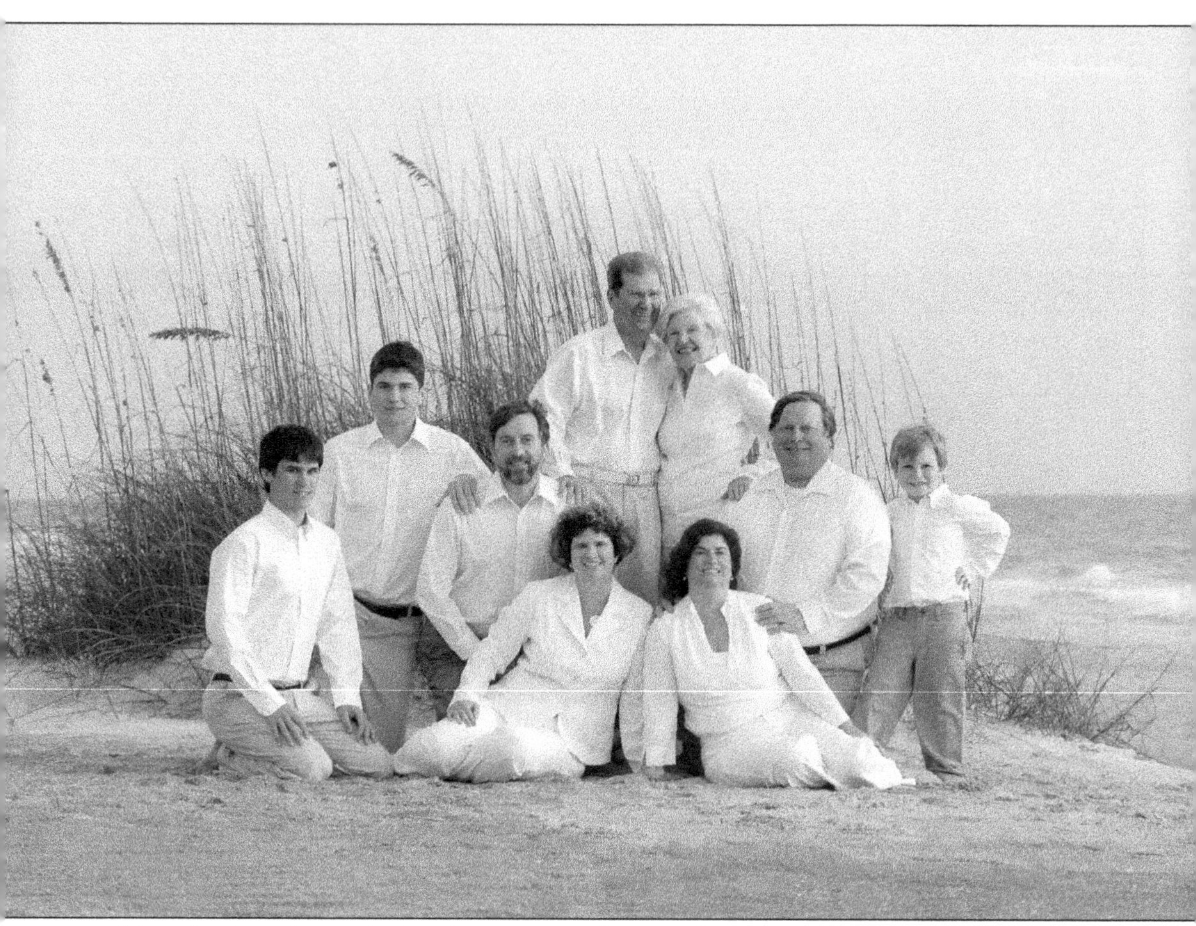

Many families choose the beach as a setting for a family portrait. This photograph was taken in the 4000 block of the beach on Longboat Key. Three generations are represented here for Betsy and Doug Elder's 50th wedding anniversary. Photographer Scott Hime has documented families in Sarasota since 1981. Hime moved to Sarasota and hung his portraits in the local mall, from which his business grew, and he opened a studio in 1982. Hime is now one of the most sought-out photographers in Sarasota County. According to Hime, there are only two times a day to create beautiful portraits, sunrise and sunset, when the light is softer. (Courtesy of Scott Hime.)

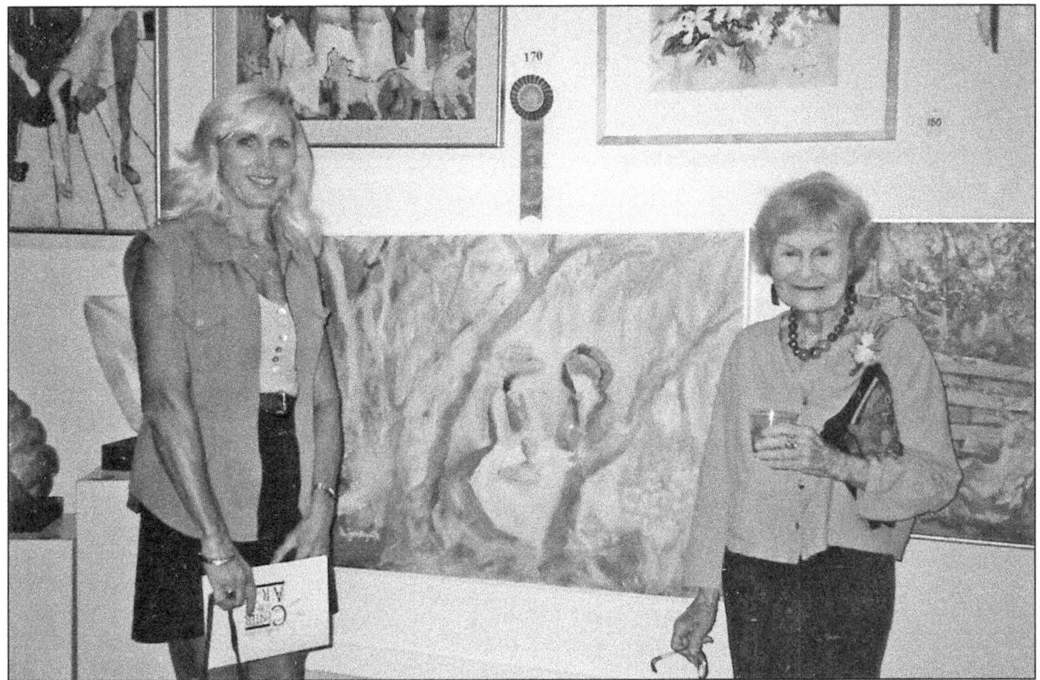

Pictured are Longboat Key artists Barbara Jendrysik (left) and Leona Sherwood from the National League of American Penwomen at the Longboat Key Art Center in 2000. Lora and Gordon Whitney, Allis Ferguson, and Grace and George Yerkes asked Sarasota architect Werner Kanneberg to design the center, which first opened in 1952. Over the years, there have been art classes of all kinds, as well as lectures and community gatherings. (Courtesy of Barbara Jendrysik.)

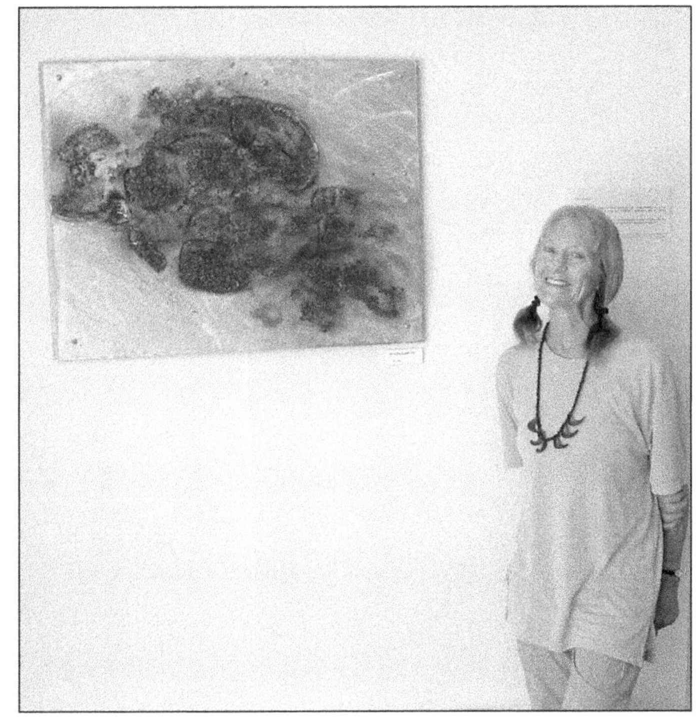

Artist and Longboat Key resident Barbara Harrison first came to the island with her husband in 2001. They were enchanted by the natural beauty of the area. Harrison is known for her wall sculptures in welded brass. A book of ancient maps inspired her series of wall pieces consisting of burned acrylic sheet placed over aluminum to give the impression of geographic features. In describing her artistic process, Harrison explained, "My blowtorch was my paintbrush!" (Courtesy of Barbara Harrison.)

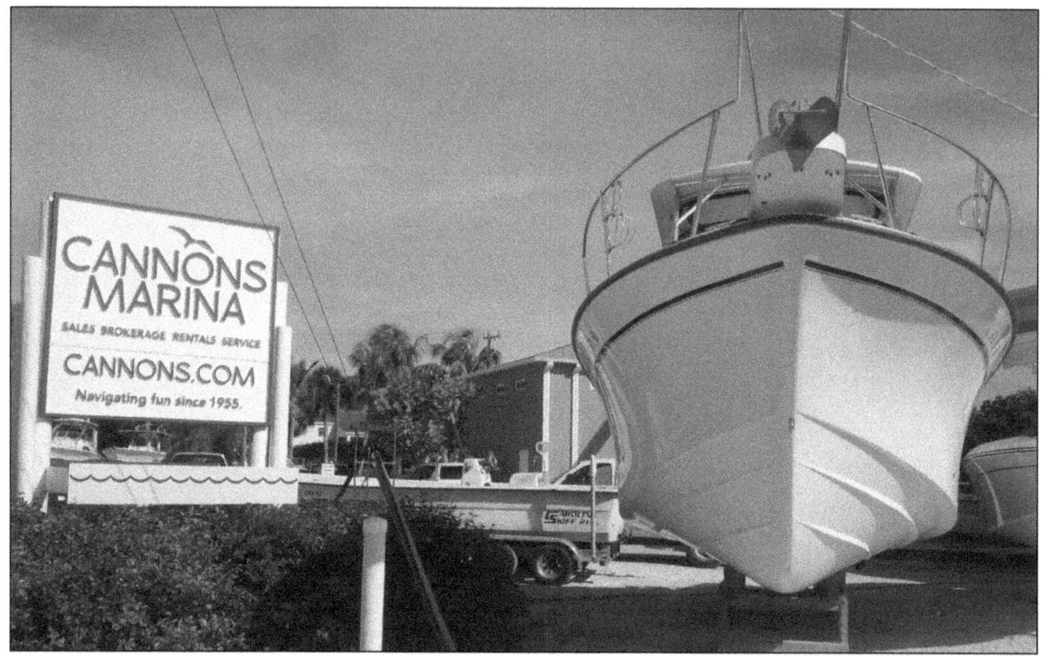


Cannons Marina is the oldest family-run business on Longboat Key. The marina was started and owned by Ernie Cannon, who sold it to Dorothy and Paul Miller in 1955. In addition to a repair and bait shop, the marina sells new outboard motors and boats and offers rentals for locals and tourists who want the chance to be on the water and enjoy Sarasota Bay. (Author's collection.)

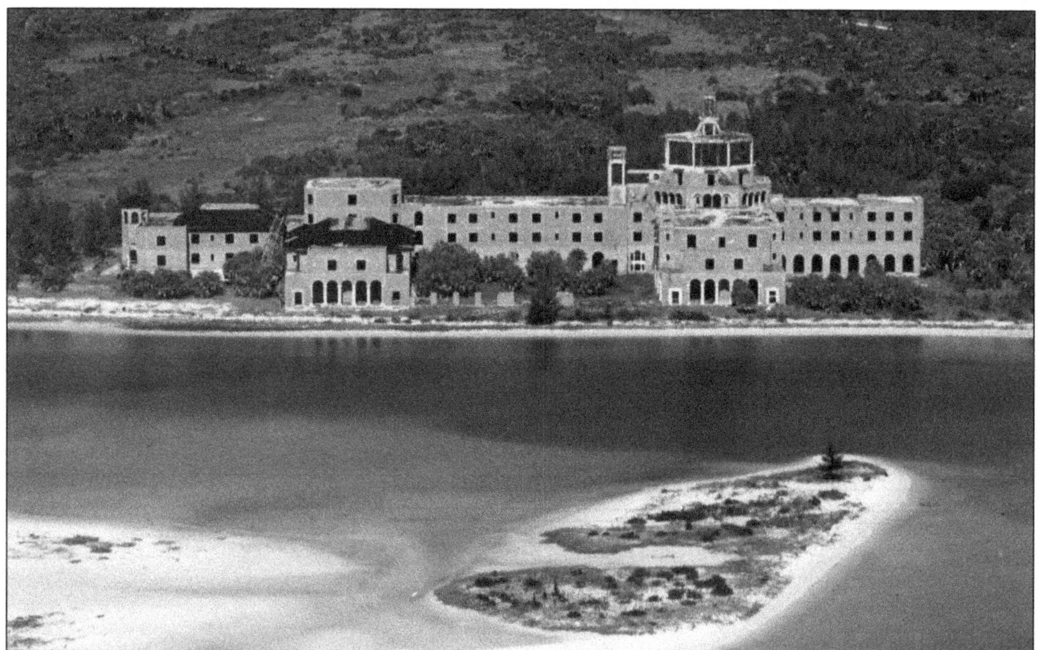

In the 1920s, John Ringling initiated the construction of a Ritz-Carlton on Longboat Key. He had great plans to provide luxurious accommodations for visitors. With the Great Depression, he was unable to bring the project to fruition, and the unfinished hotel was finally torn down in the 1960s. (Courtesy of SCHR.)

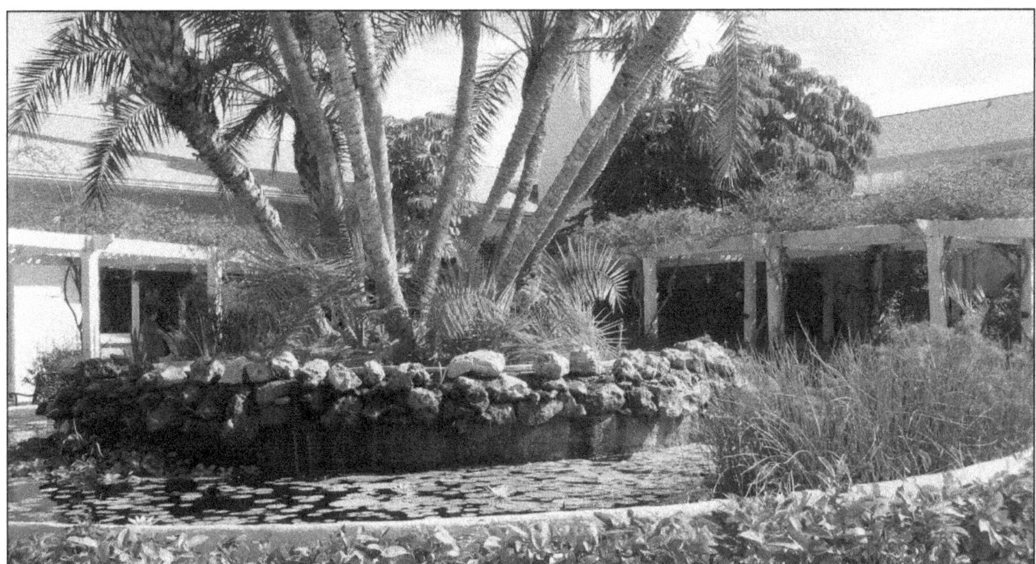

Places of worship on Longboat Key include St. Mary Star of the Sea Catholic Church, Christ Church Presbyterian, Temple Beth Israel, and Longboat Island Chapel, which became a reality in 1956 thanks to Melanie and Guy Paschal. The Paschals hosted church members of all denominations in their studio/barn according to the philosophy "a place where thinking people can worship God." Visiting ministers and/or residents were asked to give a sermon. (Author's collection.)

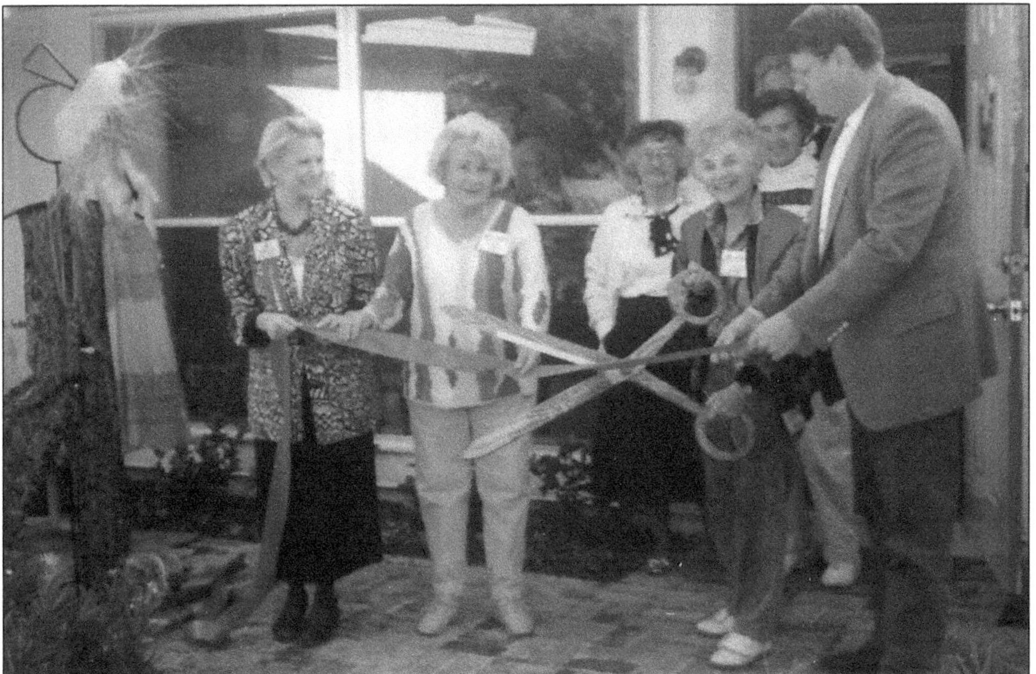

When the Longboat Key Chapel congregation started to multiply, services were moved to the Longboat Key Art Center until a home was found to build an interfaith church. Over the years, the church and its surroundings have continued to grow, including lush gardens and a thrift store called the Lord's Warehouse. The opening of the Lord's Warehouse is pictured. (Courtesy of Sue Reese.)

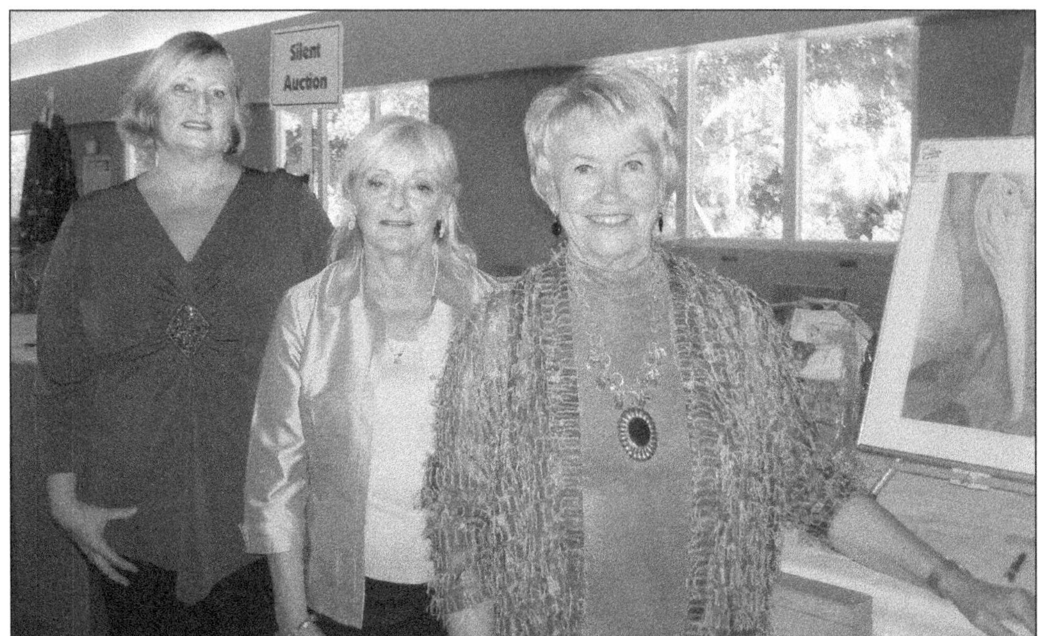

Church volunteers from the Longboat Key Chapel organized the 16th annual fashion show. The sold-out event featured clothing from the consignment store. From front to back are commentator Sue Reese and cochairs Miriam Russell and Jan Herman. (Author's collection.)

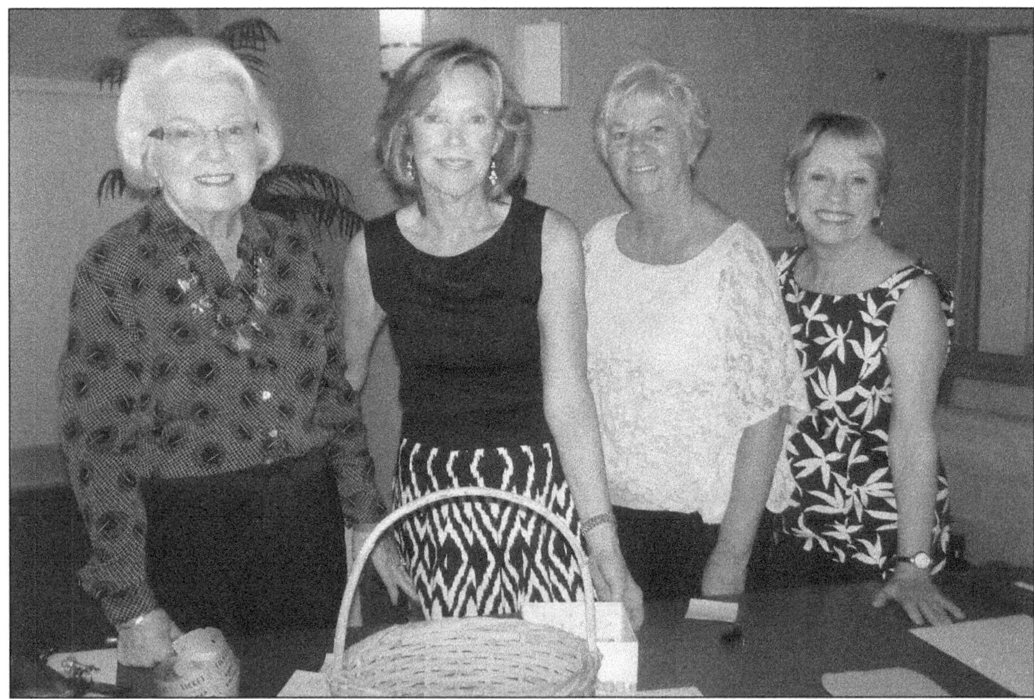
To raise money for the church during the 16th annual fashion show, church volunteers sold raffle tickets and conducted a silent auction. Local businesses donated gifts and services for the event. From left to right are Dorothy Gordon, Alice Dzenitis, Barbara Koetsier, and Anne Summer. (Author's collection.)

# *Two*

# Small Islands

## Lat 27.3187 N, Long 82.5767 W

In 1890, a cluster of small islands was located off the shore of Sarasota. There was cedar point, then Bird Island in the bay, and beyond that were a dozen or so small sandbars and islands beside the Gulf of Mexico. In the 1900s, the development boom resulted in dredging and filling that created the islands as they are now known: City, St. Armands, Lido, Coon, Bird, and Golden Gate Point.

City Island was created indirectly to satisfy the demand of Sarasota's electrical power needs. In 1914, an eight-foot channel was dredged from the Gulf to the bay. It was not until 1926 that the city dug a deep-enough port, and in that year, Sarasota sold its power plant to Florida Power & Light to pay for the dredging. As a result, the power company acquired half of City Island.

St. Armands has grown into a wonderful place to dine and shop. John Ringling, in partnership with Owen Burns, had a real estate office on St. Armands Circle.

Lido Beach lay quiet for many years after the Great Depression. As part of a Works Progress Administration project, the Lido Casino was built in the 1940s. In the 1950s and 1960s, visitors wanted to stay on the beach and not the trail, as was previously done.

Coon Key was dredged from the surrounding waters and is now home to the Sarasota Yacht Club and Plymouth Harbor Retirement Facility.

Bird Key is a small island near downtown Sarasota. John Ringling purchased Bird Key in the 1920s, providing a bridge for car access. In the late 1950s, the Arvida Corporation purchased Bird Key, and its development continued.

Golden Gate Point was once known as Cedar Point and Sunset Park. The island was first platted in 1899 and recorded in public records in Manatee County as an addition to the town of Sarasota. The narrow strip of land was divided into three blocks for building. It is no wonder people enjoyed parking their cars to watch the sunset from this island. They also enjoyed watching fireworks there until the late 1940s.

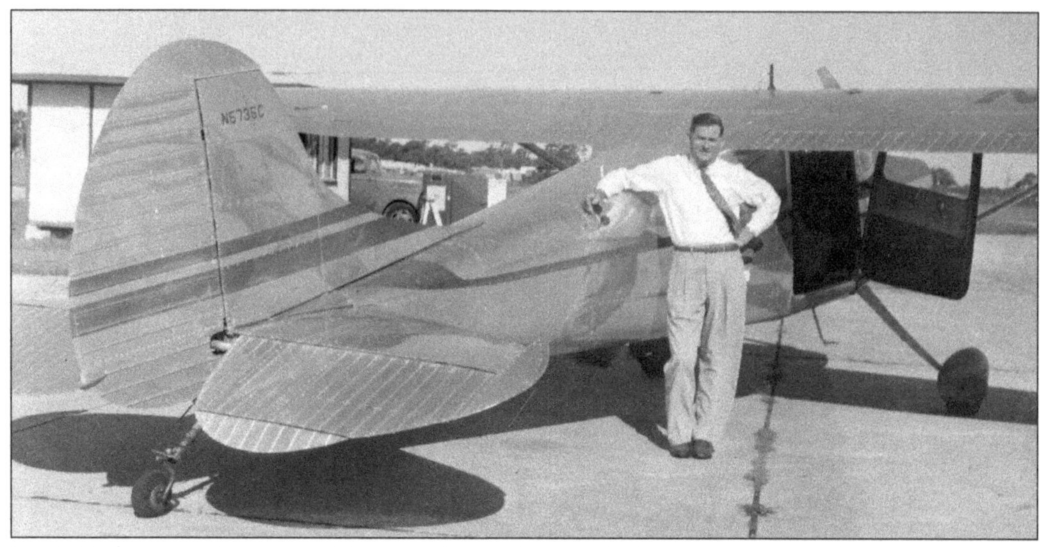


In 1989, the commissioners of Sarasota held a formal dedication ceremony for Ken Thompson Park on City Island. Thompson, a remarkable man and citizen, was a captain in the US Air Force, city manager of Sarasota for 38 years, and past president of both the Florida City and County Managers Association and the Florida League of Cities. Fish houses and bait shops supplied the local fishermen, and New Pass Bait Shop still does. When John Ringling's unfinished Ritz-Carlton Hotel was demolished in the 1960s, it provided building materials to help construct City Island, which was created to indirectly satisfy the demand of Sarasota's electrical power needs. Pictured here is Thompson with his plane. (Courtesy of SCHR.)

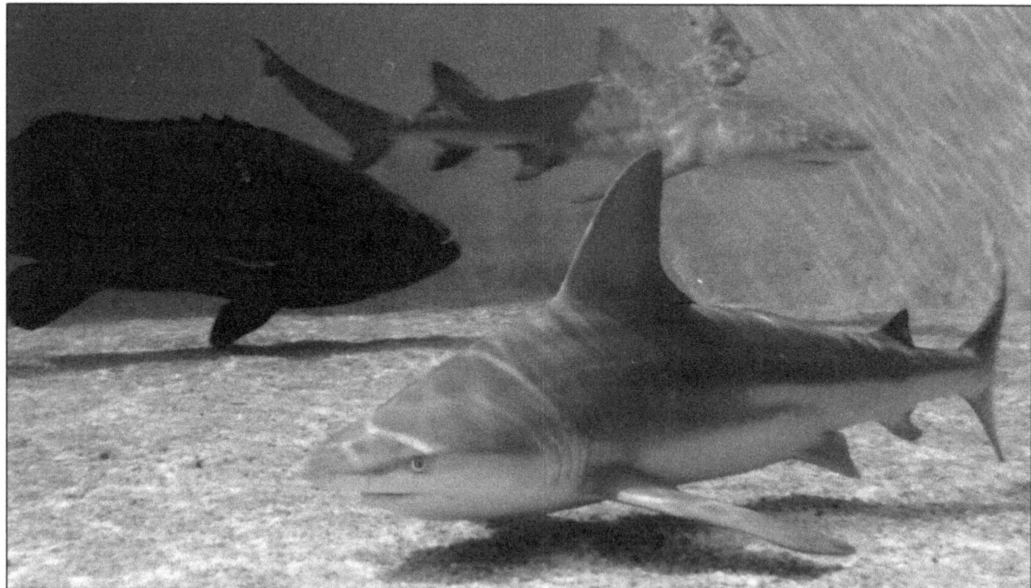

Eugenie Clark, known as "the Shark Lady," lived a full life as a scientist who studied sharks. Clark first started at the Cape Haze Laboratory. There were also shark tanks located at Midnight Pass, which was close to Clark's home on Siesta Key. When the lab started to outgrow its humble beginnings, it moved to City Island and became the Mote Marine Shark Laboratory. Mote Marine is a world-famous laboratory, and its research library is open to scientists. There are great school programs available to the public as well. (Courtesy of Mote Marine.)

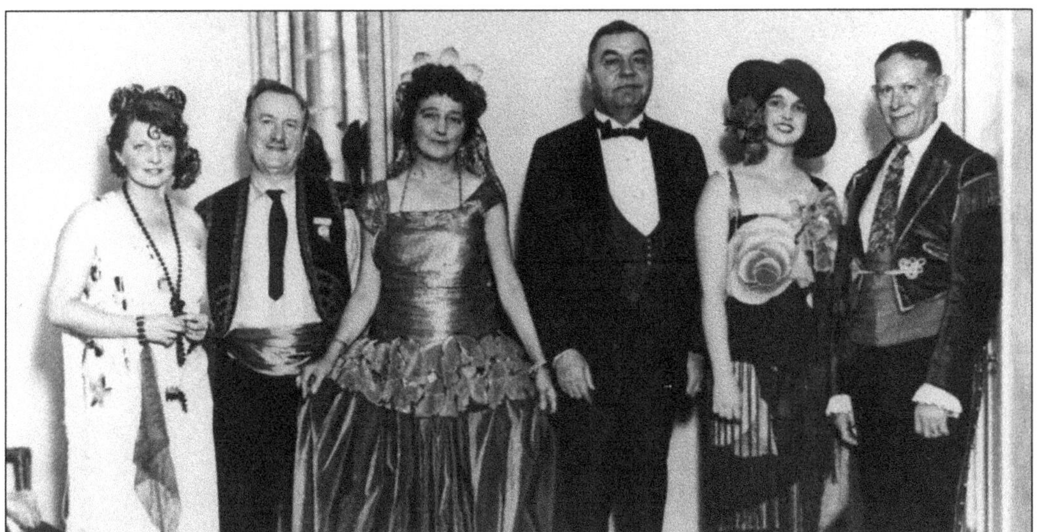

In 1928, John Ringling attended the Coronation Ball, held during the Sara de Soto Pageant. The attendees pictured here are, from left to right, Frances Booth, J.W. Burns, Mrs. A.E. Cummer, John Ringling, Frances Edwards, and Samuel Gumpertz, Ringling's good friend and business associate. (Courtesy of SCHR.)

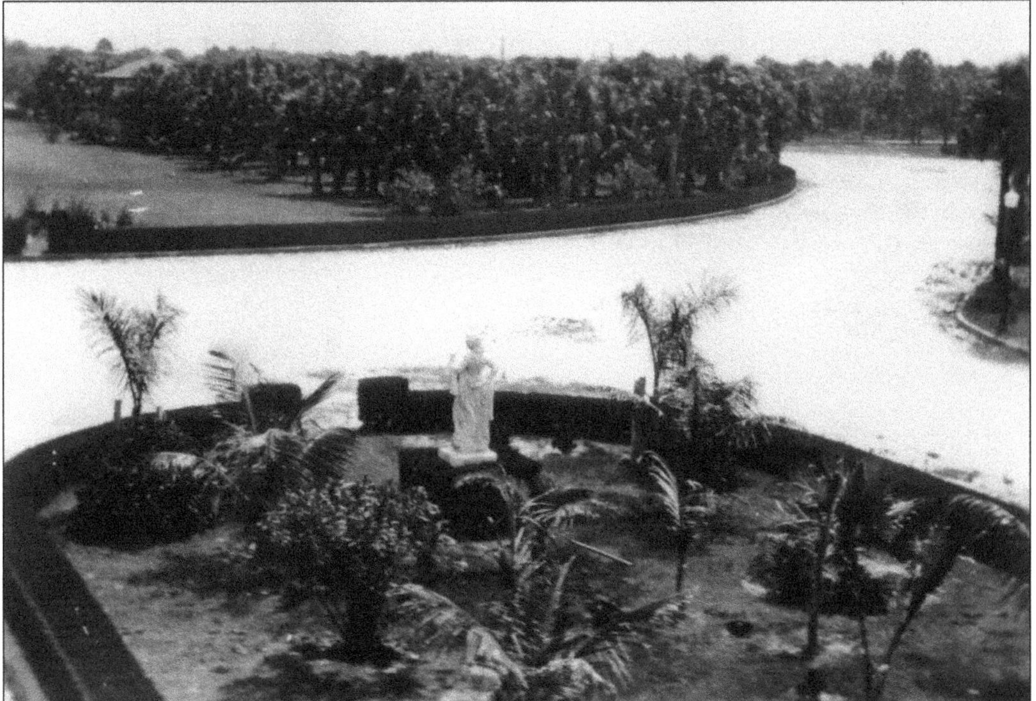

In the 1920s, John Ringling had a vision of what St. Armands could be. He purchased several acres and planned to develop them with his associate Owen Burns. They called the development Ringling Isles, pictured here under construction. Ringling, in partnership with Burns, had a real estate office on St. Armands Circle. Together, they developed some of the islands in Sarasota Bay. Ringling brought statues from around the world, mostly from Italy, to decorate Ringling Isles and give it the international flair that it still has today. (Courtesy of SCHR.)

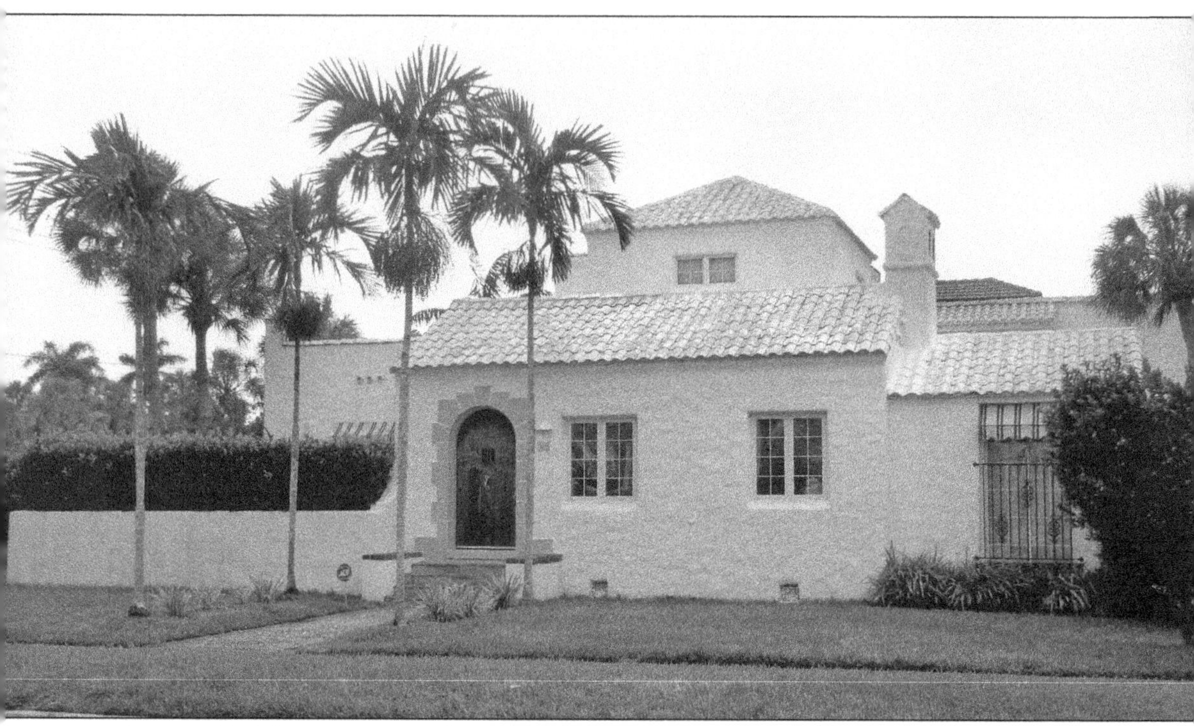

Joyce and Jeff Hart's home on St. Armands Key is one of the two houses left that John Ringling built as speculation homes to promote Ringling Isles in the 1920s. Joyce's parents first owned the house for many years. When they decided to sell, the Harts did not want to see it go, so they sold their house and moved in. Joyce and her family have lived in the house for 47 years and hope to pass it on to their daughter. The tile around the fireplace was also used in some of the guest rooms in the Cà d'Zan mansion. Their house takes constant upkeep, but the history and charm make it worthwhile. (Courtesy of Joyce and Jeff Hart.)

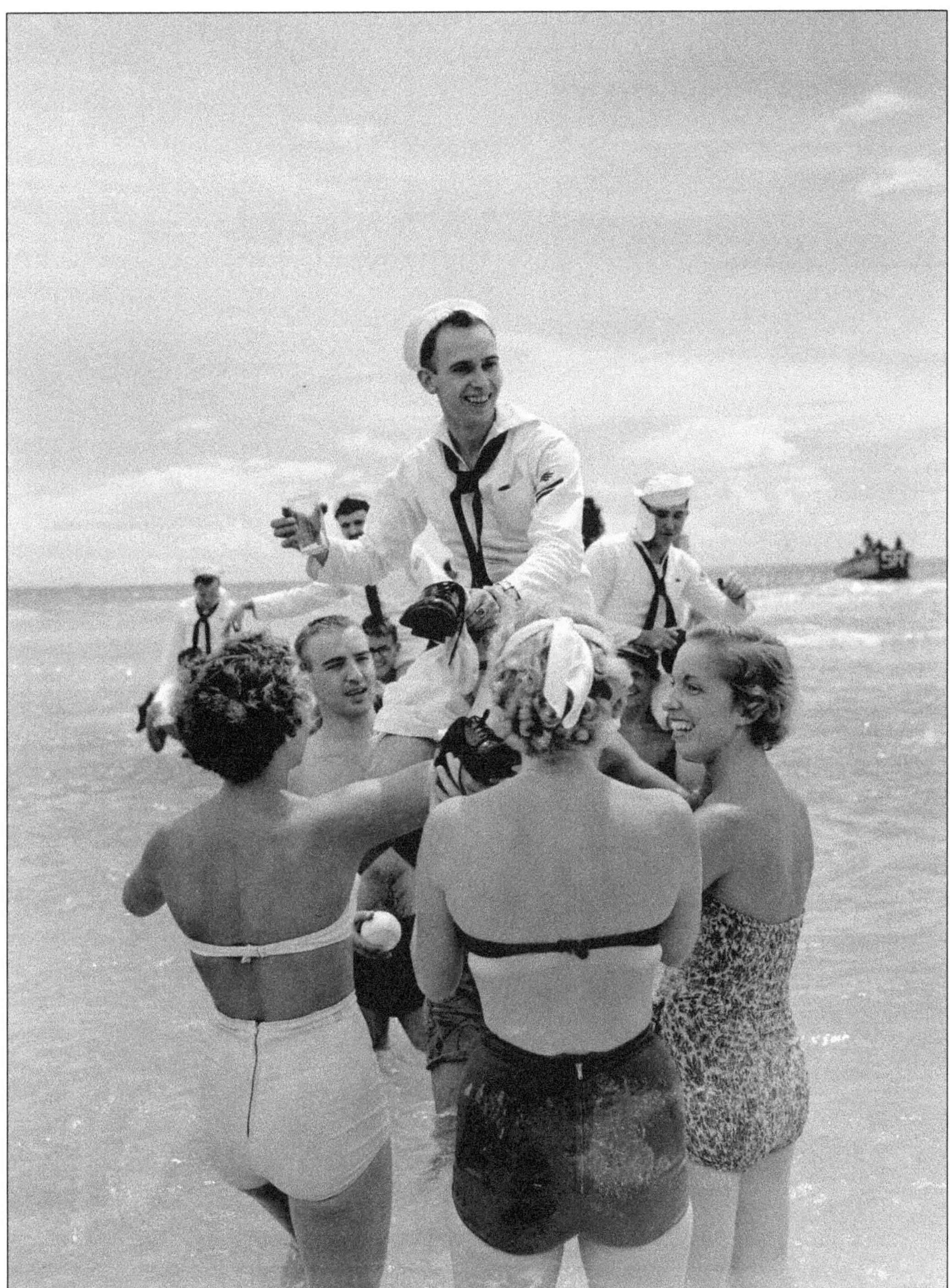

This photograph was taken on Lido Beach in the 1950s. Young sailors come to shore off the USS *Sarasota*, which is anchored in deeper water. Residents help them celebrate their leave with a glass of cheer. In the 1950s, Phillip Hiss opened a development office and hired Paul Rudolph, Ralph Twitchell, and William Zimmerman to build modern homes designed to be compatible with the natural elements of Florida. (Courtesy of SCHR.)

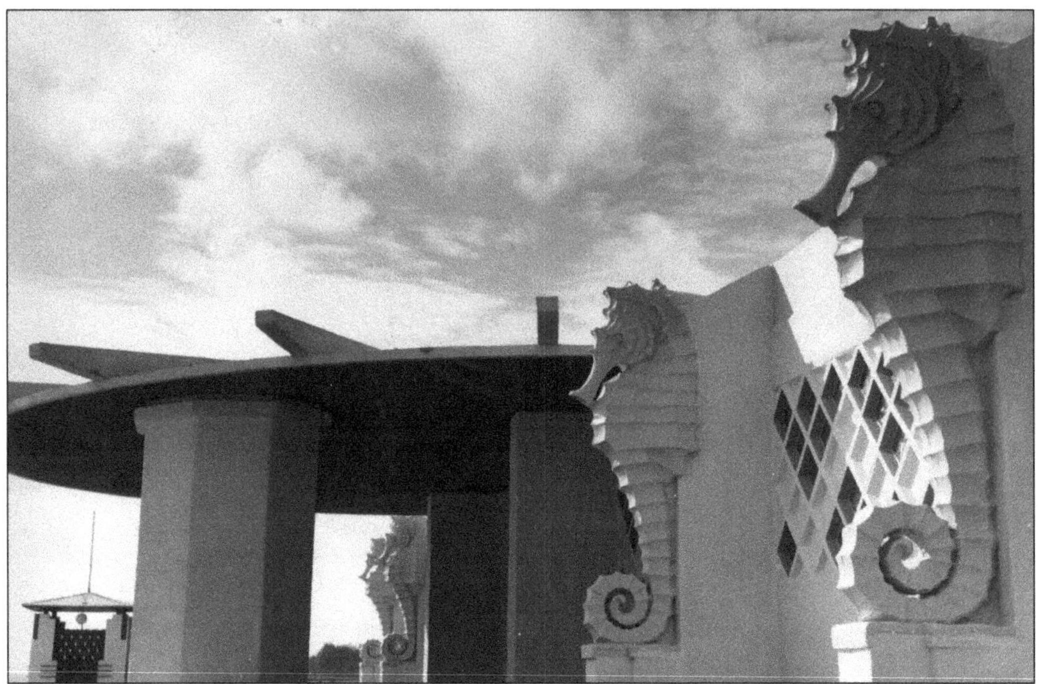

Many longtime residents of Sarasota remember the Lido Casino as the place to go. Built as part of the Works Progress Administration project, the casino brought people together to swim or dance. Servicemen stationed in Sarasota and Venice would fill in as dancing partners for the locals. Designed by Ralph Twitchell from the Sarasota School of Architecture, the casino offered restaurants, a pool with high dive, beach cabanas, and even a ballroom. (Courtesy of SCHR.)

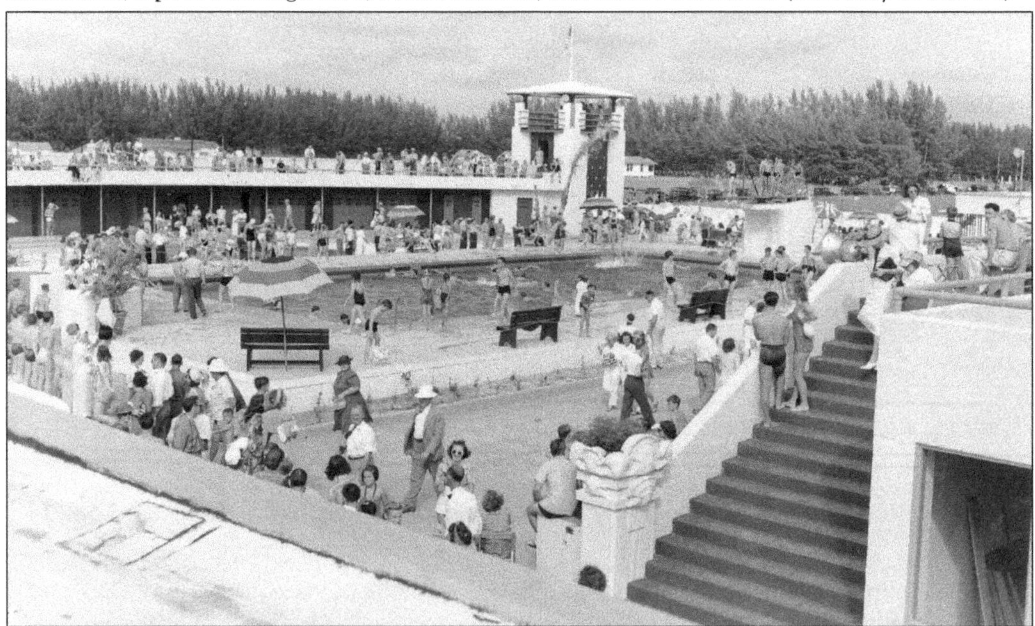

People from all over would come to socialize at the Lido Casino, a great place to spend a hot day at the pool or attend dances held in the ballroom. Pictured here are tourists and locals relaxing at the pool and beach. (Courtesy of SCHR.)

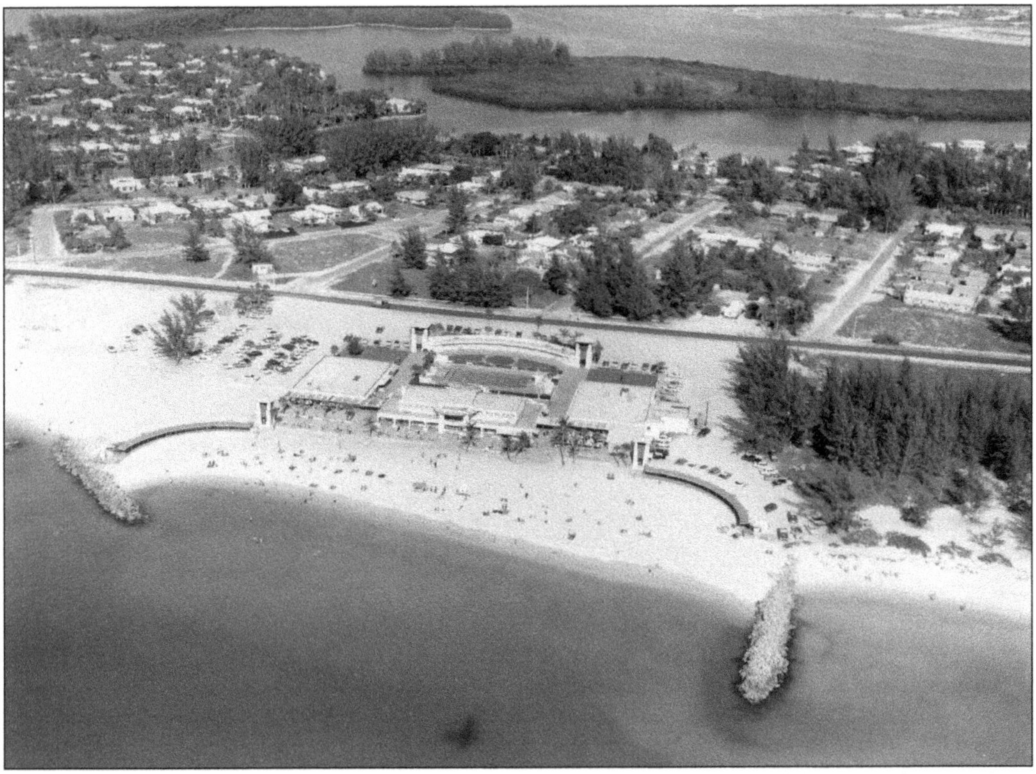

This is an aerial photograph of the Lido Casino. Residents regret not fighting to keep it from being torn down, as many people spent time there. (Courtesy of SCHR.)

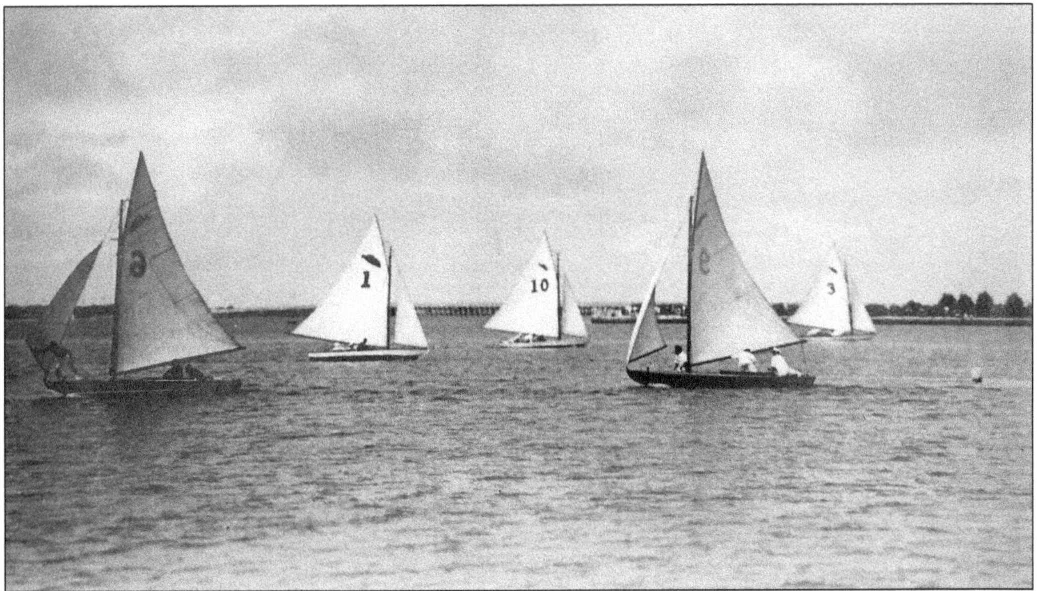


Pictured here is group of small sailboats from the Sarasota Yacht Club. These wooden boats are racing on Sarasota Bay. Founded on June 21, 1926, Sarasota Yacht Club had a fleet of sailboats called "Fish Class," which won the 1938 Florida West Coast Fleet Championship. (Courtesy of the Sarasota Yacht Club.)

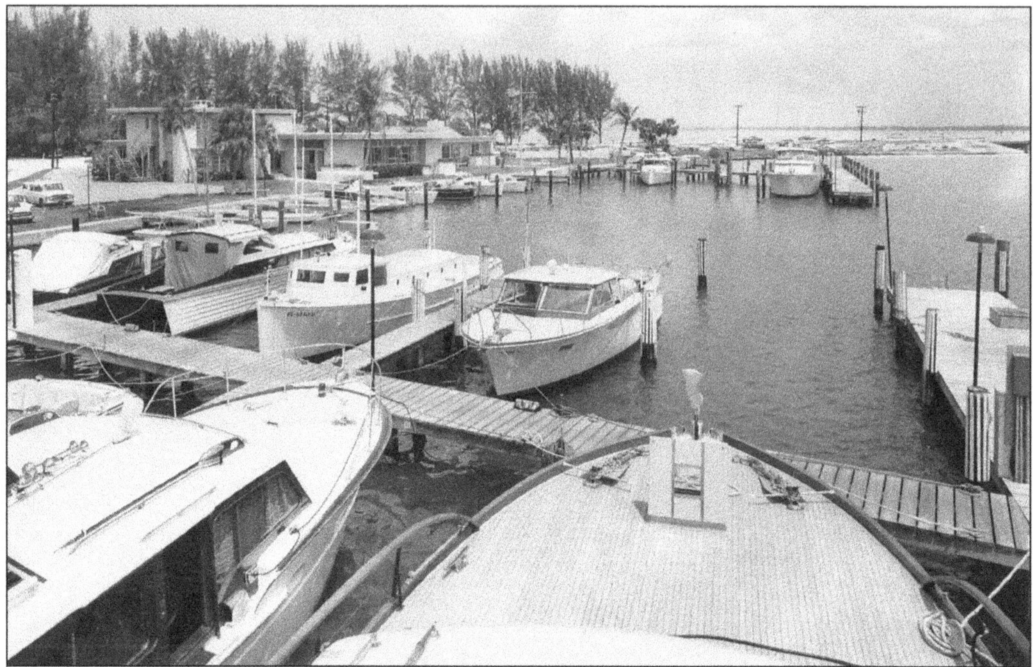

At its start, the Sarasota Yacht Club consisted of one building and one dock. As interest increased, a main dining room, private rooms, a sail loft, restrooms, and dockmasters' quarters were added to the club. F.S. Love Boatways built additional dry storage for 60 small boats on Whitaker Bayou. This photograph was taken in 1958. (Courtesy of Sarasota Yacht Club.)

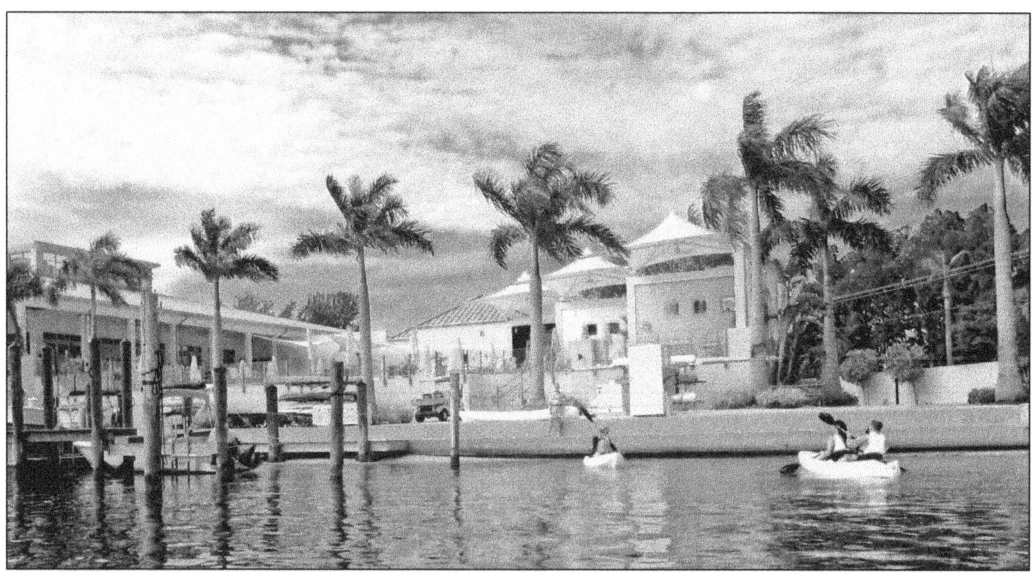

The majestic new Sarasota Yacht Club opened on April 3, 2010. Since the old clubhouse was torn down and rebuilt, the facilities have been booked by club members, as well as other community members and organizations. (Courtesy of Sarasota Yacht Club.)

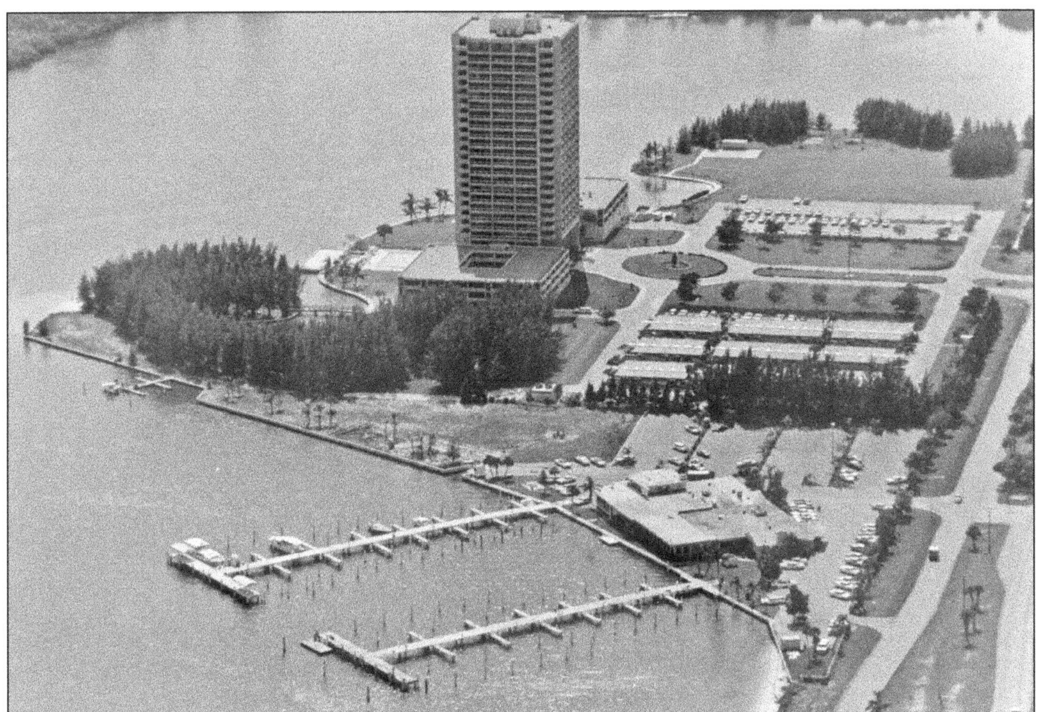

Plymouth Harbor was built on faith. Before the funding was available to construct the 25-story retirement home, the First Congregational United Church of Christ put an option on the land in hopes of building. Rev. John Whitney wanted to create a retirement home that would encourage a sense of community. Designed by architects Frank Folsom Smith and Louis S. Schneider, the building had nine colonies that each surrounded a common area. It was a community effort, and several competing local banks worked together to fund the project. (Courtesy of SCHR.)

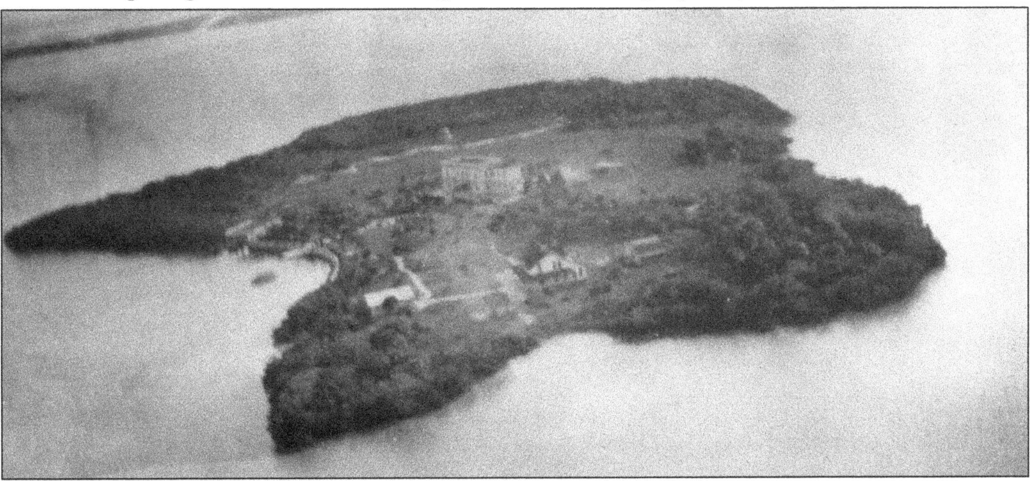

When John Ringling bought Bird Key in the early 1920s, he had ambitious plans for the island. He wanted to turn Worchester's home, New Edzell, into a winter home for Pres. Warren Harding. Unfortunately, Harding died in 1923, and Ringling's big plan did not come to pass. Ringling's sister, Ida Ringling North, lived at the Worchester estate until she died in 1950. When Ringling built the bridge and causeway to St. Armands, he provided a bridge to Bird Key, which made it accessible for residents and visitors to access by car. (Courtesy of SCHR.)

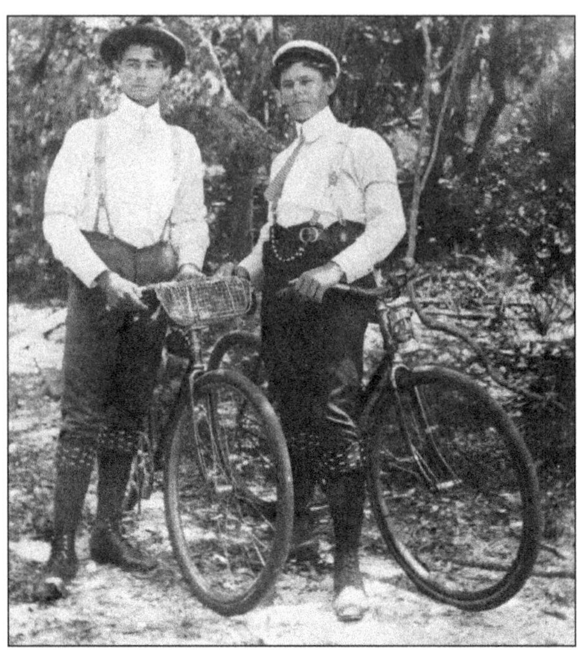

Back in 1902, young people used bicycles to explore the islands. Pictured here are two unidentified boys with their bicycles. (Courtesy of SCHR.)

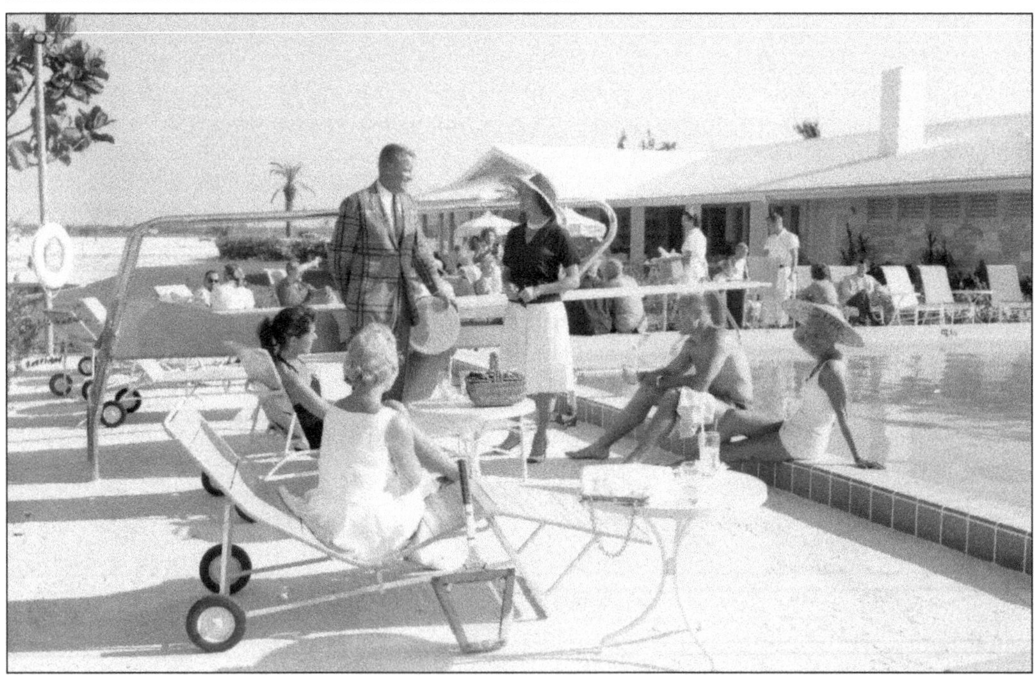

The Arvida Corporation purchased Bird Key from Ringling corporations and interests in the late 1950s. Effecting the most change to the island, Arvida tore down Worchester's mansion and built a yacht club, planned for 500 building sites, and expanded the island to 10 times its original size. Extensive dredging and filling was done to enlarge the natural grass flats of Bird Key to develop the island. On Coon and Otter Keys (both named after local animals) and South Lido Key, fill was limited to the mangrove lines. On Bird Key, however, the Arvida Corporation got permission from the city to fill out to the edge of the flats. Pictured here is the Bird Key Yacht Club, located on the former site of the Edzell mansion. (Courtesy of SCHR.)

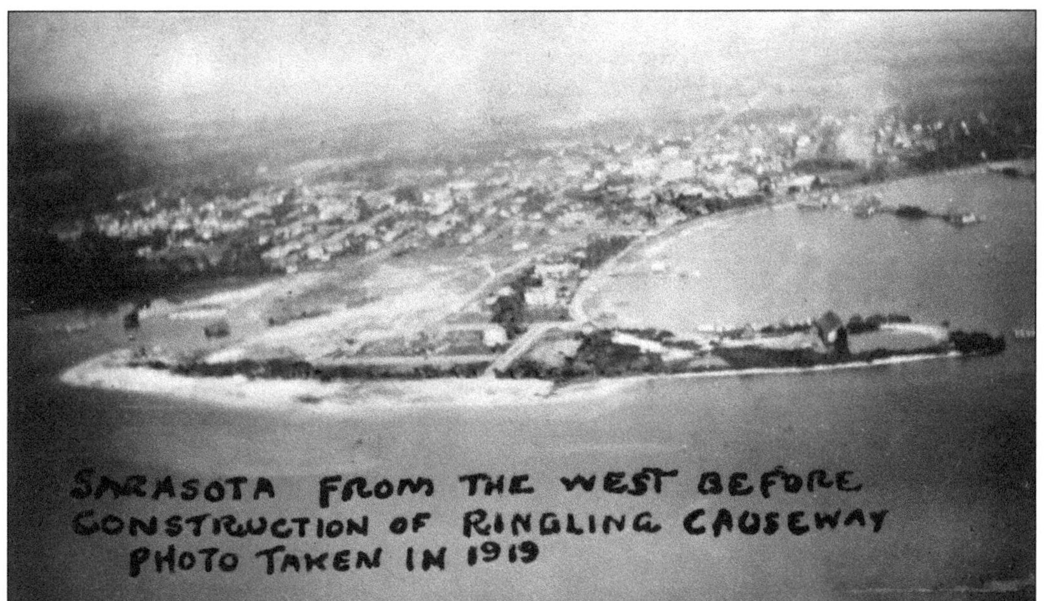


This photograph of Golden Gate Point was taken in 1919. It shows the island before the construction of the John Ringling Causeway Bridge. In 1922, Owen Burns expanded the island by dredging, filling, and adding a 3,500-foot seawall. (Courtesy of SCHR.)

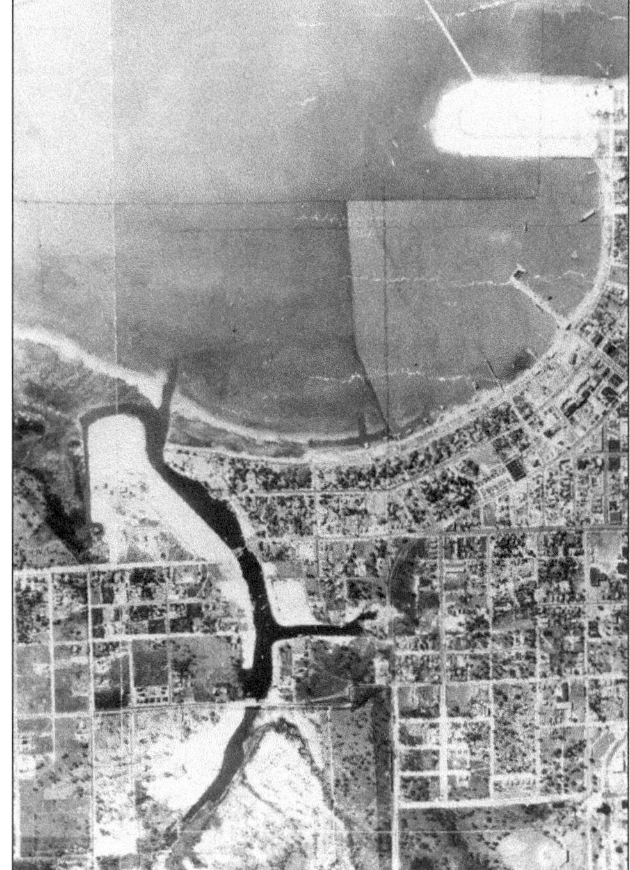

Golden Gate Point, pictured here in 1926, has been enjoyed by many over the years. In 1913, the Sarasota Auto and Yacht Club relocated from Siesta Key. As commodore, Owen Burns hired local architect Alex Browning to design a clubhouse, which boasted a 360-degree view of the city. (Courtesy of SCHR.)

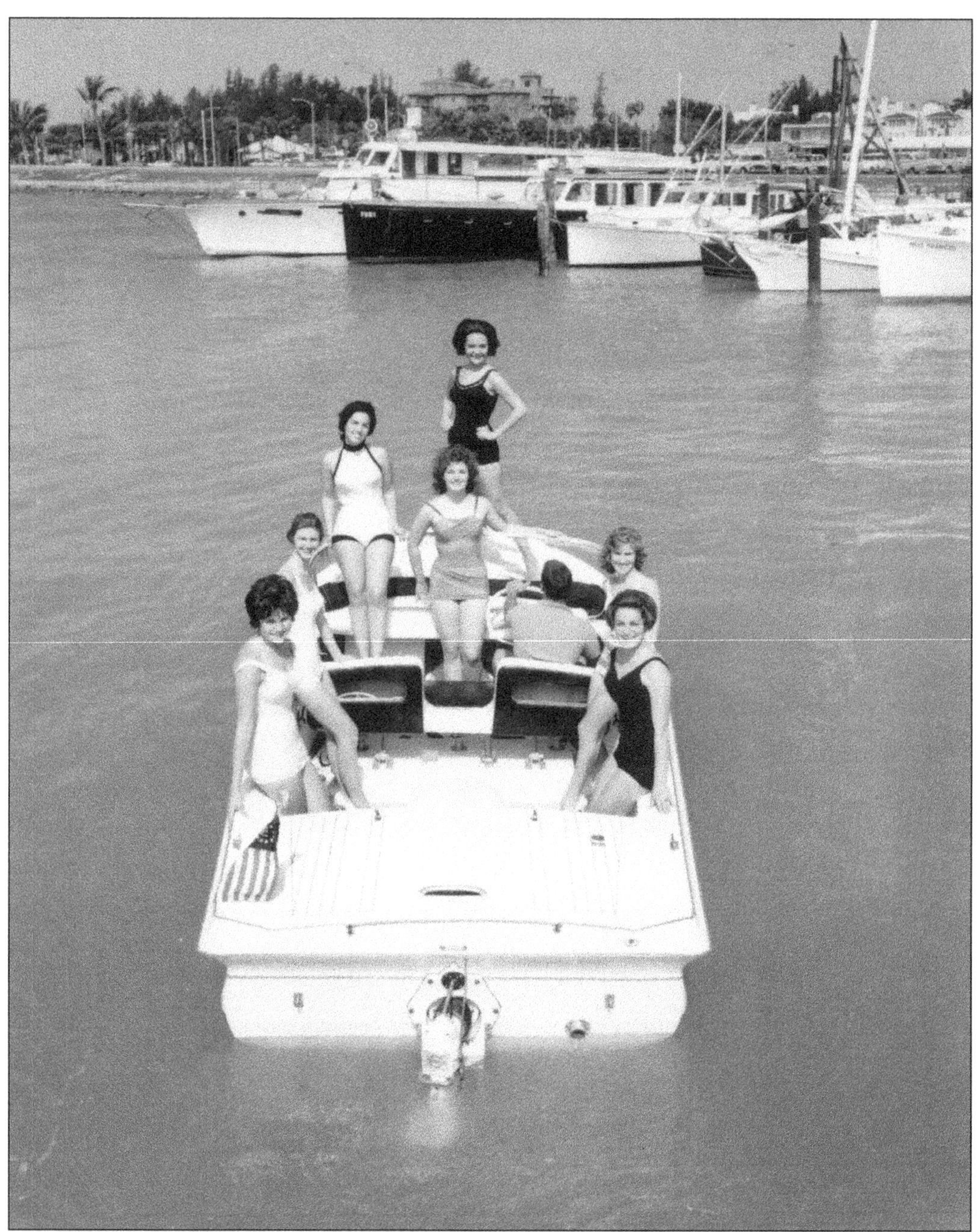

John Ringling purchased the yacht club in 1917 when the club defaulted. During World War II, the Sarasota Naval Militia used the club facilities. Pictured here is a boatful of hopeful Miss Floridas who were visiting the area. Classes on how to walk, among other talents, were taught on local beaches. The boat pictured here is located off Golden Gate Point, near the Marina Jack Restaurant. (Courtesy of SCHR.)

# *Three*

# Siesta Key

## Lat 27.2753 N, Long 82.5525 W

Siesta Key is a popular tourist destination with beautiful beaches and other hidden shores. With its powder-soft sand, Siesta Key Beach is ranked in the top 10 beaches of the world according to *National Geographic* magazine. Siesta Key has also been called Sarasota Key, Clam Island, Muscle Island, and Little Sarasota Key. Harry Higel and his partners, Louis Roberts and E.M. Abogast of Siesta Land Development, developed the north end of the key in the early 1900s. Higel built the Sarasota Yacht Club in 1907 and the luxurious Higelhurst Hotel in 1915, then became postmaster of the Siesta Key Post Office. He provided a ferry to Siesta Key from the mainland since there were no bridges. In 1913, Higel Avenue was named in his honor for his efforts to develop and improve Sarasota and Siesta Key.

Other pioneers who moved to Siesta Key were Louis Roberts, Sophie and Peter Crocker, and Mary Hook. In 1906, Roberts extended his house and made a guest hotel known for its tasty clam chowder and scenic views. The Crockers were the postmasters of the Crocker Post Office and lived on the key with just a few neighbors. Hook started a boardinghouse on Sandy Hook at the northern end of the island.

There were many popular places to eat on Siesta Key. James Alonzo "Lonni" Blout and his wife, Ida Mims, owned a little fish house called the Siesta Key Fish Market. In 1932, they moved a small bungalow to the north end of the island to use as their home. Then Lonni built a market for his retail business and a small smokehouse, which used seasoned hardwood for the smoking process. Lonni bought fresh fish from local fishermen to sell, until he sold his business in 1955. This fish house was a popular place for residents to meet during the 1930s and 1940s, and it has been said that a hungry person in need could go there and work for food. The Blout family reported that Eleanor Roosevelt visited in the 1940s. She enjoyed the smoked fish and had it sent to the White House.

Many artists enjoyed living on Siesta Key, including painter Syd Solomon, photographer Joseph Steinmetz, and writers MacKinlay Kantor and John D. McDonald. With funding from the Vanderbilts, Eugene Clark started Cape Haze Marine Laboratory in Placida, Florida, in 1955, then later moved it to Siesta Key in 1960. While it was on Siesta Key, there were shark tanks located on the north shore of Midnight Pass. In 1967, its name was changed to Mote Marine Laboratory after William R. Mote. The lab was moved to City Island in 1978.

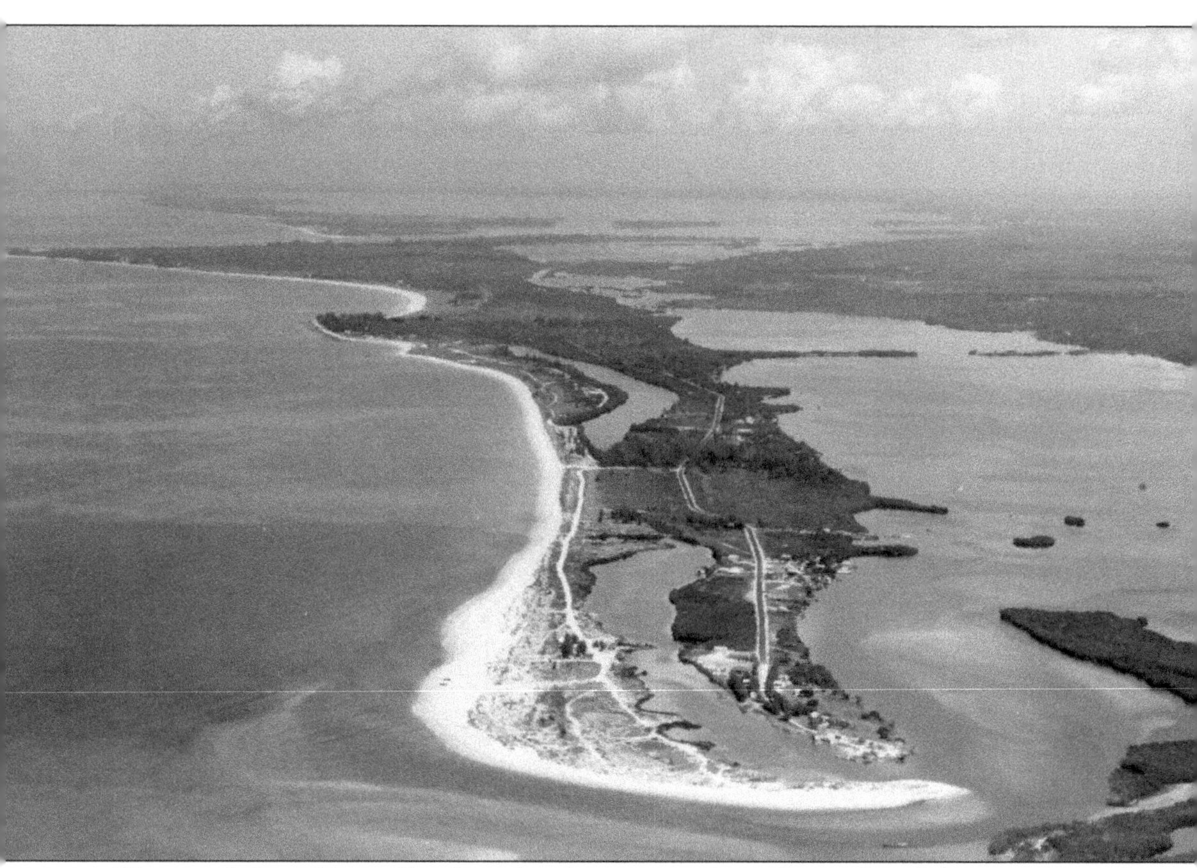

This aerial shot of Siesta Key shows beaches running from the north end down to the south. Even though the island now has a continuous beach, there are three distinctive beaches: Siesta Beach, Crescent Beach (formerly Mira Mar Beach), and Turtle Beach. Starting at the north end is the Siesta Bridge, which provides access to the north end of the island. There are two bayous off Sarasota Bay on the north side of the island. (Courtesy of SCHR.)

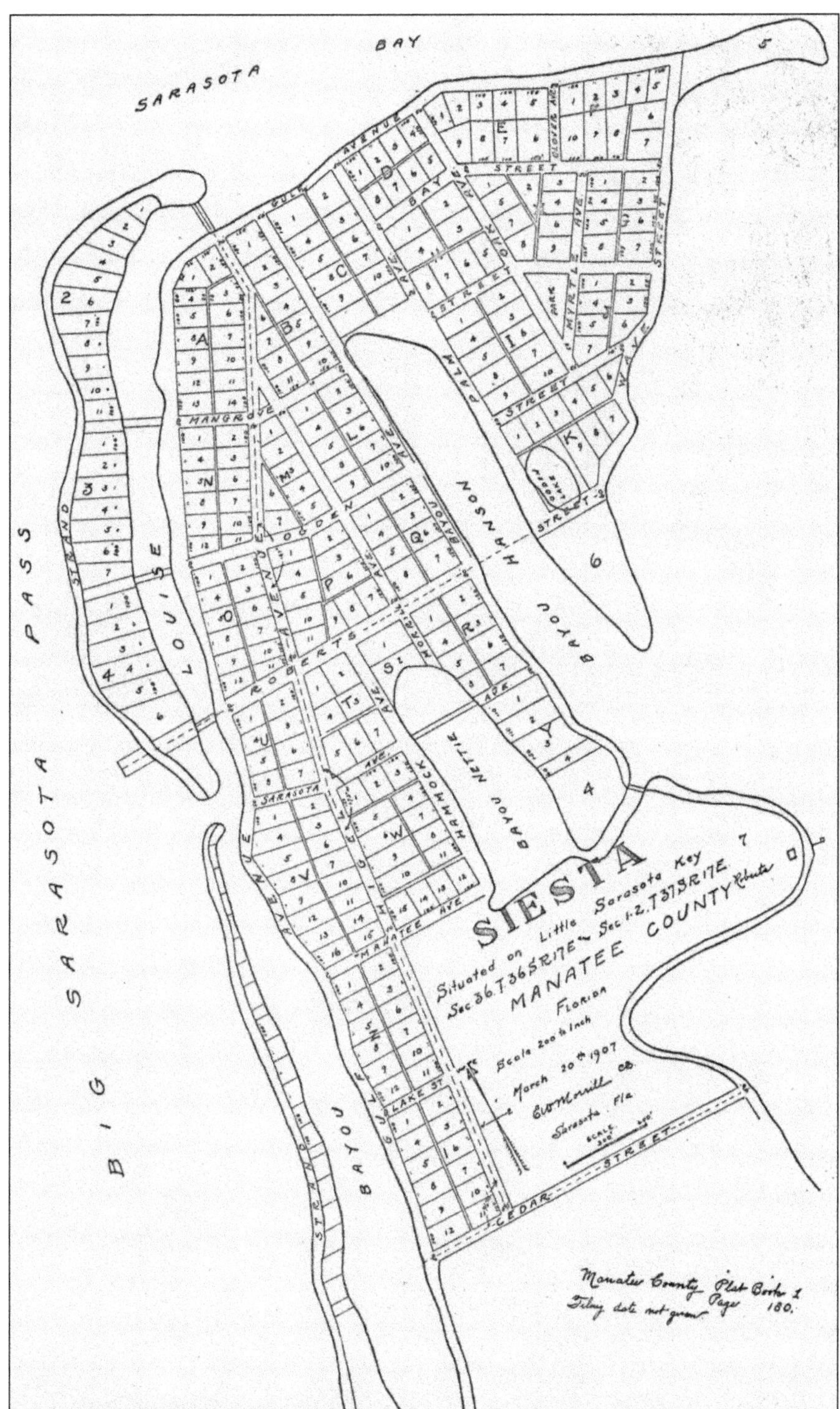


This map of Siesta Key is dated 1907. Before Sarasota became a county in 1921, the island was part of Manatee County, which demonstrates how the north end of the island was platted near Hanson and Louise Bayous. (Courtesy of SCHR.)

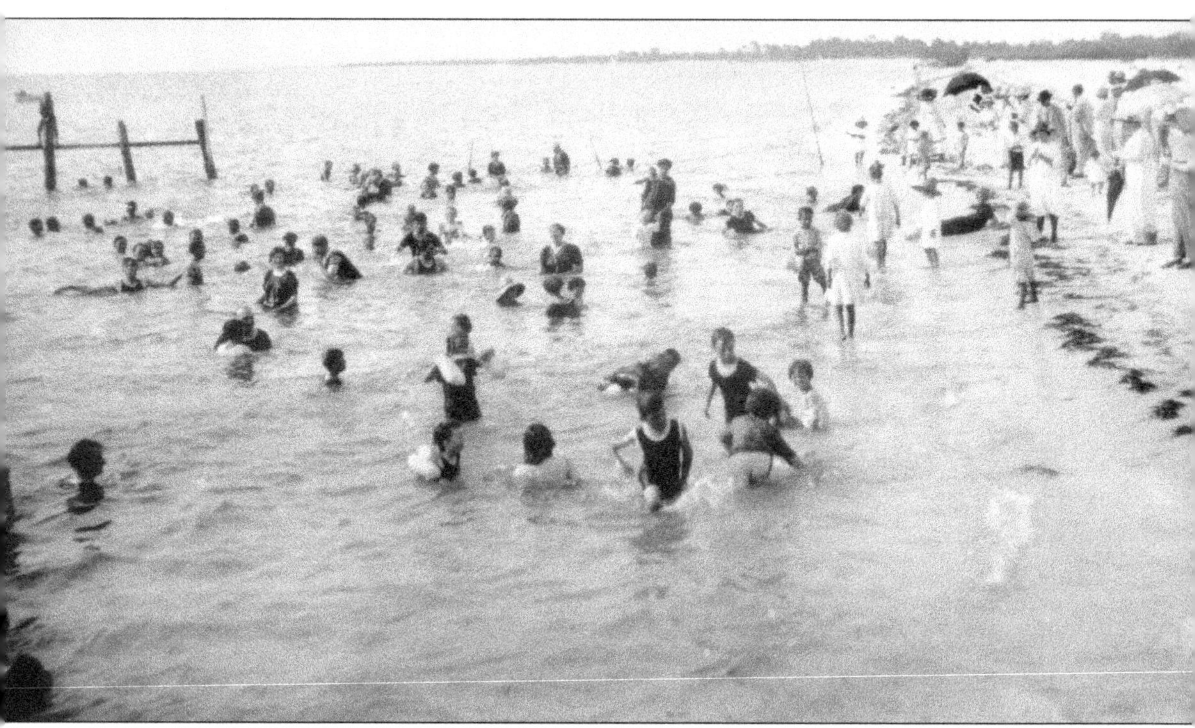

Bathers swim in the warm, clear water and stroll on the cool, powder-soft sand of Siesta Key. The long, deep beach extends for miles. People enjoy walking, running, and bicycling on the beach. The lifeguard stations are painted in several colors so children and adults can use them to identify their location on the beach, as the current can force swimmers to drift down the shore. (Courtesy of SCHR.)

Harry Higel was a pioneer and early developer in Sarasota. He purchased the dock at the end of Main Street and served as a local agent for businessman John Savarese's Tampa steamship line. He also worked with others to install phone lines and dredge canals. Higel was murdered in 1921, but his killer was never found. (Courtesy of SCHR.)

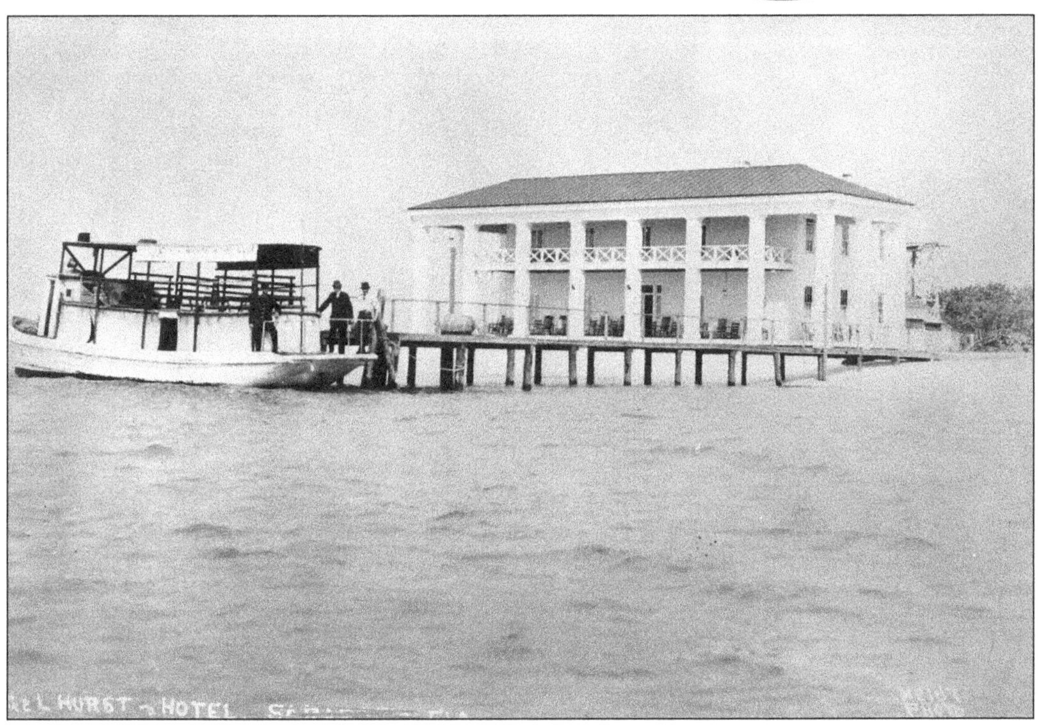

In 1915, Higel built the glamorous Higelhurst Hotel, which had a 150-seat dining room. Unfortunately, it burned down in 1917. In order to get people to the island, he purchased and ran the steamship *Vandalia* in 1907 when the steamship SS *Mistletoe* could not afford to continue. (Courtesy of SCHR.)

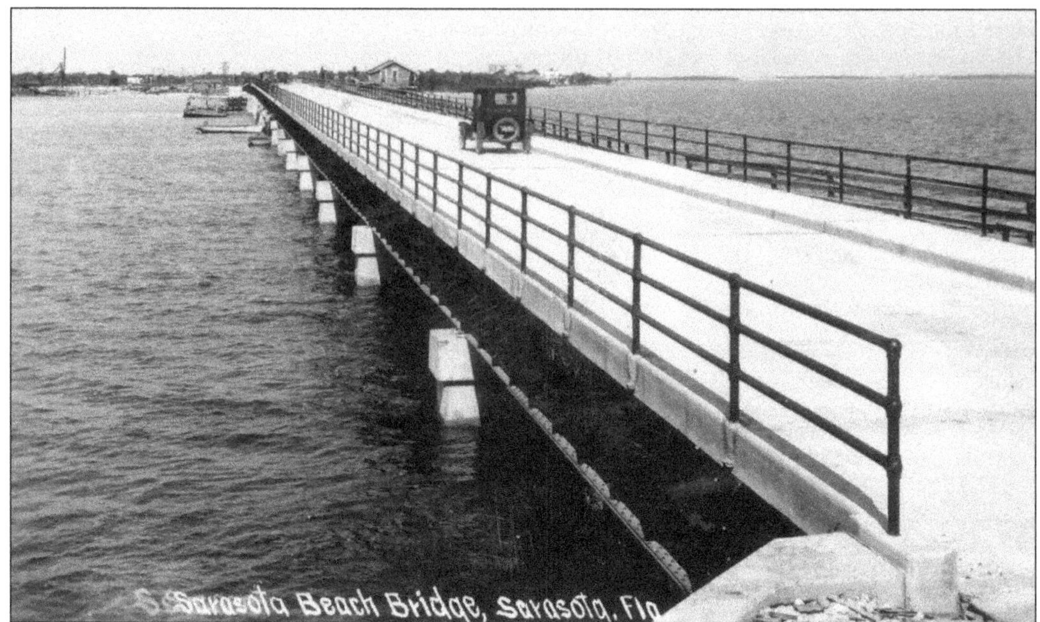


The Bay Bridge was the first thoroughfare connecting Siesta Key to the mainland. Then, in 1917, the Siesta Key Bridge was built. Today, it is a four-lane, dual-opening bridge that runs on schedule every half hour. Before bridges were built, pedestrians could get to the island by crossing through "the Meadows," or "the Narrows." A navigational passage was made in the early 1900s to allow travel between Roberts Bay and Little Sarasota Bay. (Courtesy of SCHR.)

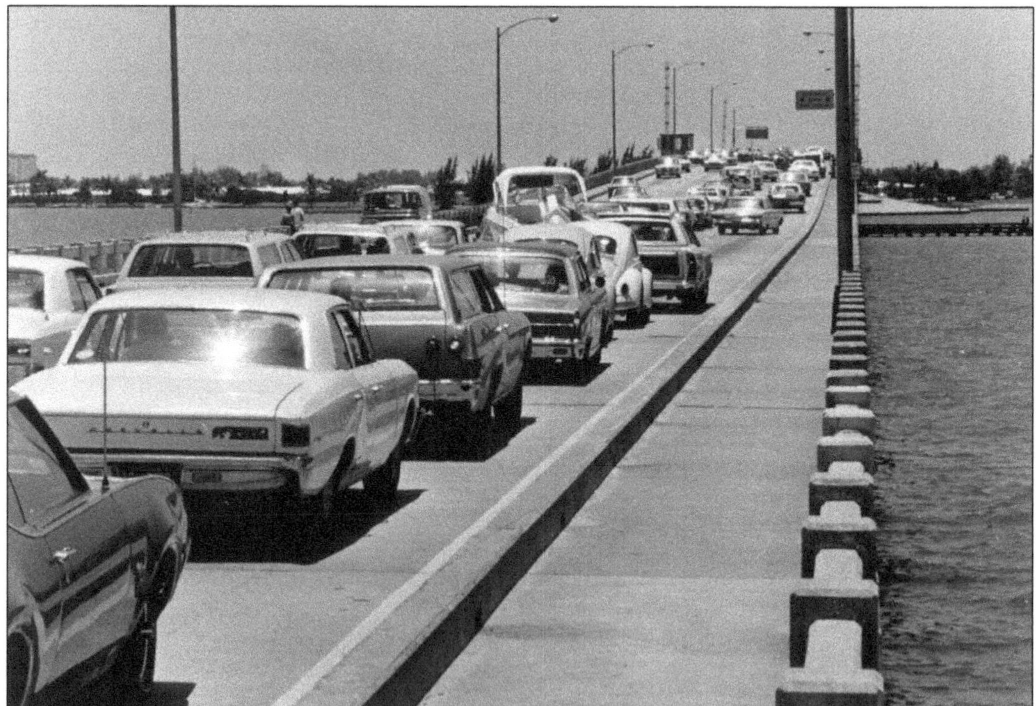

By the 1960s, people were flocking to Siesta Key. As seen here, a traffic jam occurs when the Siesta Key Bridge opens on schedule for passing boats. (Courtesy of SCHR.)

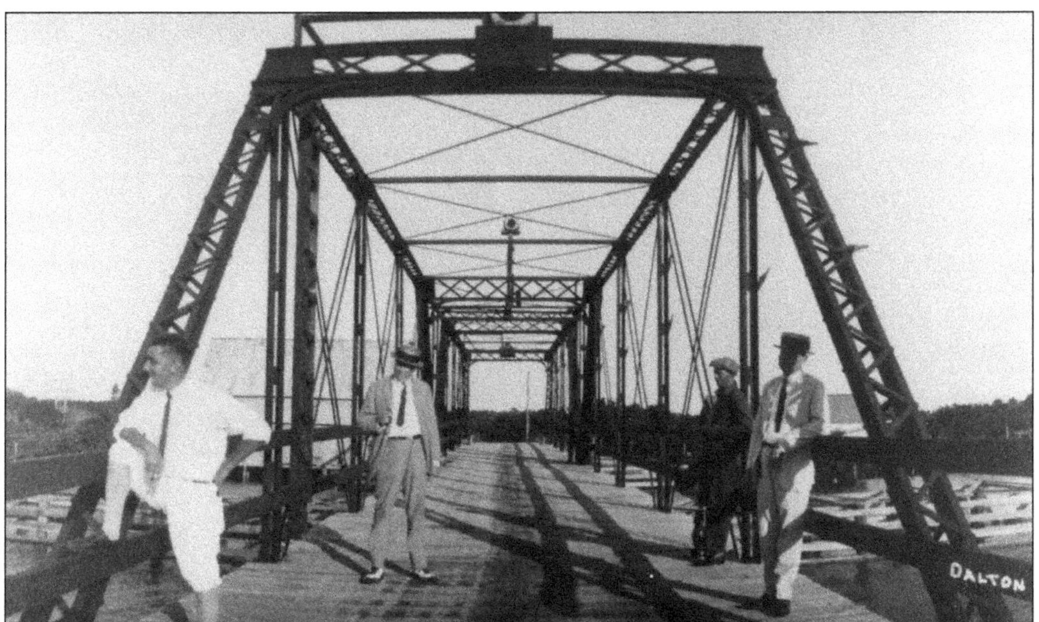


In the early 1900s and 1920s, the bridges to Siesta Key were built with private funding. When Sarasota County was created in 1921, the residents wanted funding for the island that was not provided while still part of Manatee County. In 1924, a bond was issued for Stickney Point Bridge, named for "Uncle Ben" Stickney, who came to Sarasota in 1894 and lived south of the bridge on the island. The cost of the bridge was $25,000. Built in 1925, the one-lane, six-ton bridge lasted until the new Stickney Point Bridge was built in the mid-1960s. The four-lane, machine-powered bridge was constructed for $250,000. (Courtesy of SCHR.)

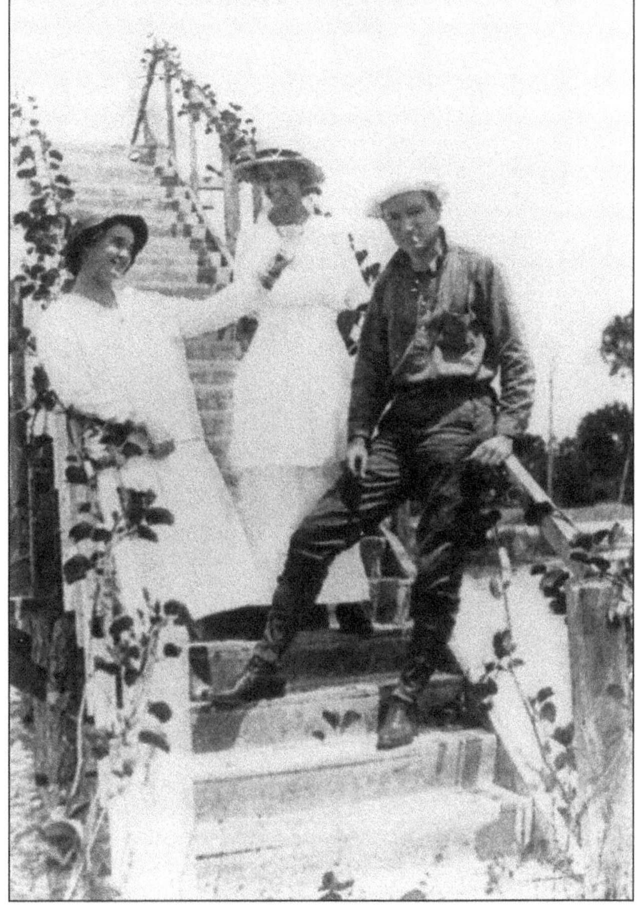

Spanning Bayou Louise, the rustic Siesta Key Foot Bridge was believed to have been built around 1915 to ease resident travel within the island. After other bridges and roads were built, the footbridge fell into disuse. (Courtesy of SCHR.)

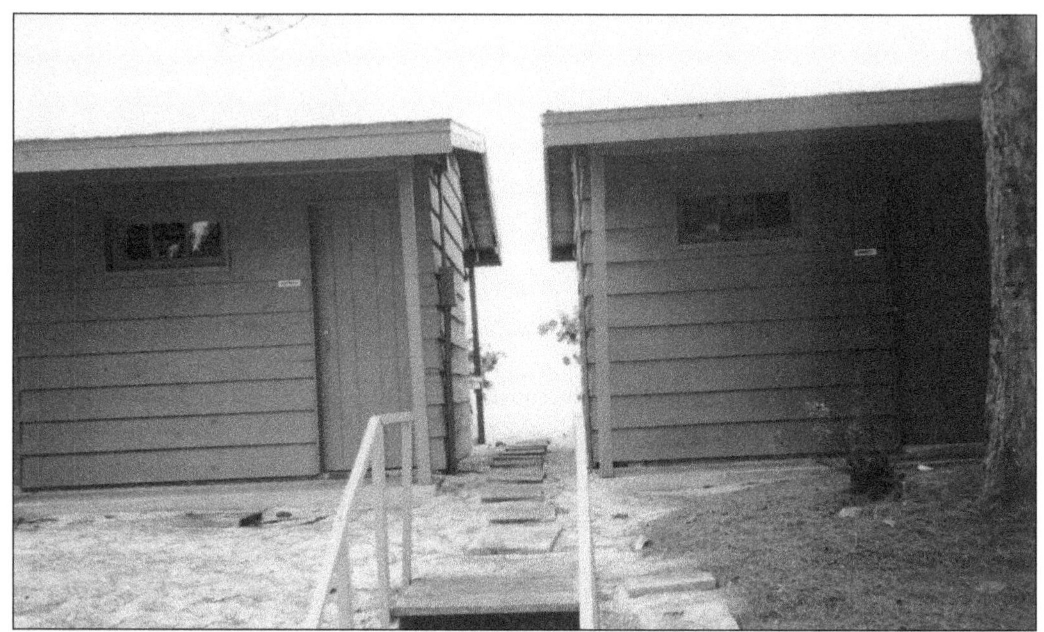

Developer Eldridge S. Boyd built the Turtle Beach Cabanas for Sarasota residents as a private place to change and gather while at Siesta Key. Along with the cabanas was a common area called the Centrale for large parties. In 1952, some of the members sold their shares to start the Siesta Key Club, which is now known as the Sanderling Club. Boyd's plan was to build 32 ten-foot-square cabanas to entice "like-minded people" to invest in Siesta Key. (Courtesy of SCHR.)

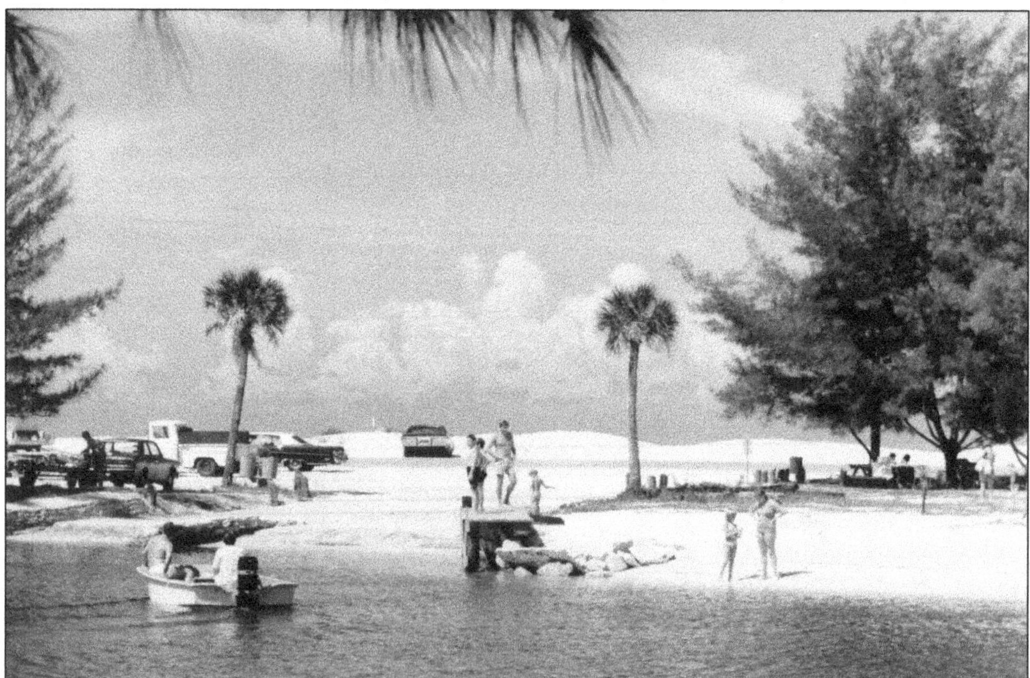

Turtle Beach is a nice option to spend the day. It is not as big as Siesta Key Beach, but it has a charm of its own. Turtle's and Ophelia's are two popular restaurants near Turtle Beach. (Courtesy of SCHR.)

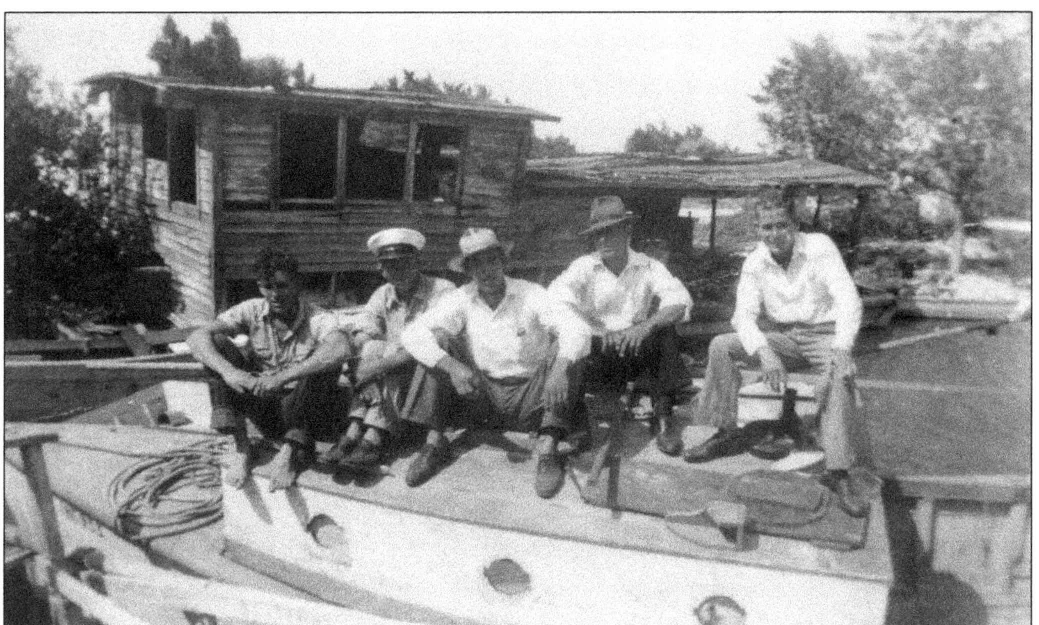

Established in 1932, the Siesta Key Fish Market was located on the north end of Siesta Key. James Alonzo "Lonni" Blout and his wife, Ida, sold smoked or fresh fish, and other seafood that they caught or purchased from local fishermen, some of whom are pictured here. (Courtesy of SCHR.)

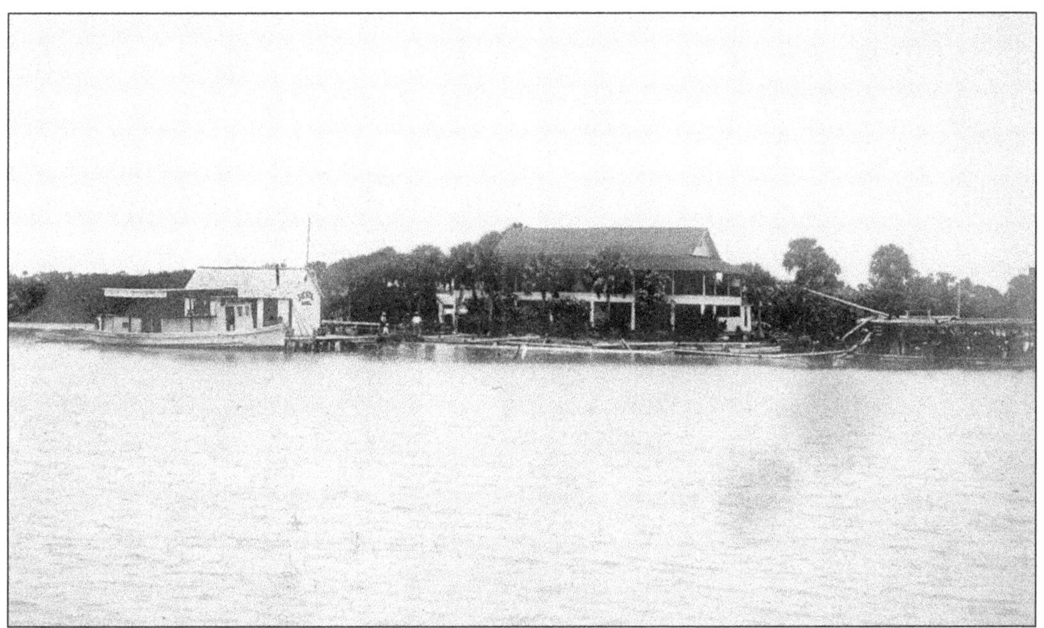

"Captain" Louis Roberts was an early developer and businessman. He moved to Siesta Key from Key West in the 1870s and married Ocean Hansen, the namesake of Ocean Boulevard. Roberts opened the Roberts Hotel, which became an important fixture on Siesta Key. He also worked with the Siesta Key Land Company, which platted the north end of the island in 1907. (Courtesy of SCHR.)

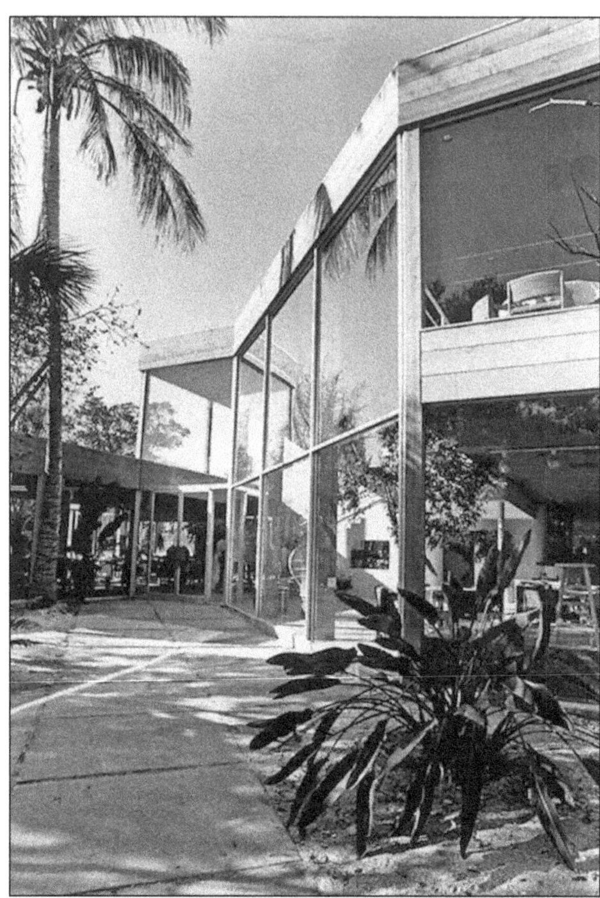

In 1991, chef Paul Mattison opened the Summerhouse Restaurant on Siesta Key. He received his early training in cooking and gardening from his Italian grandmother in New York, followed by formal education at the Culinary Institute of America, both of which helped him succeed as a local celebrity chef in Sarasota. Residents fondly remember celebrating special occasions at the Summerhouse Restaurant or listening to live music at the upstairs piano bar. The property was sold and became luxury condos. Meanwhile, Chef Mattison started Mattison's Catering Company and a line of restaurants with partner Jason Sago in 2001. (Courtesy of SCHR.)

The first Sarasota Yacht Club, built by Harry Higel in 1907, was located at the north end of Siesta Key. The yacht club was just one piece of Higel's overall plan for the island. Higel and A.B. Abogast also developed the Sarasota Yacht and Bay Isles Hotel. (Courtesy of SCHR.)

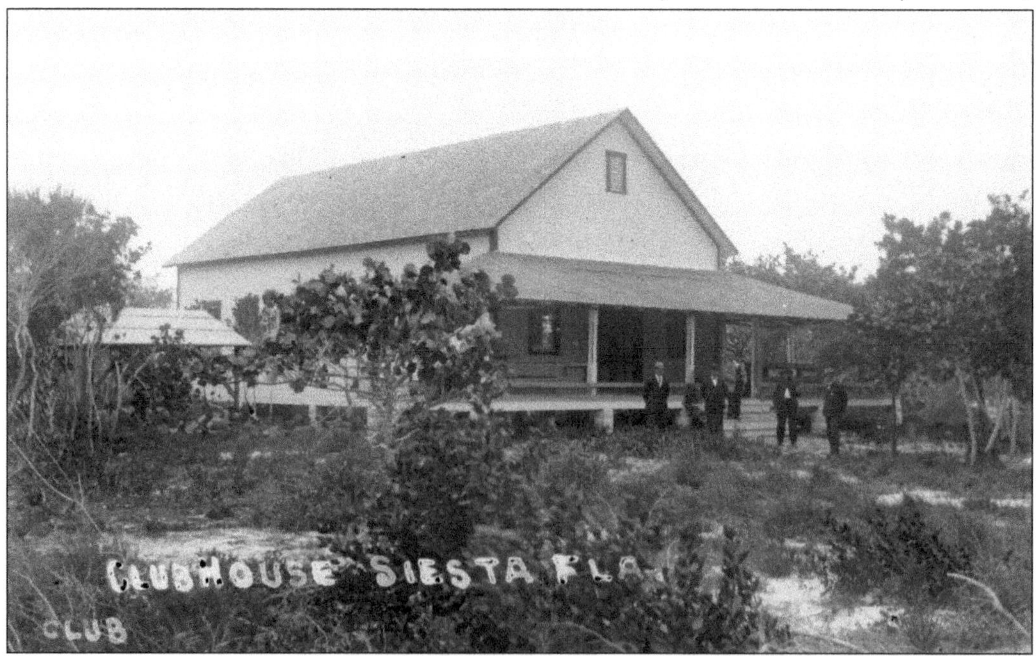

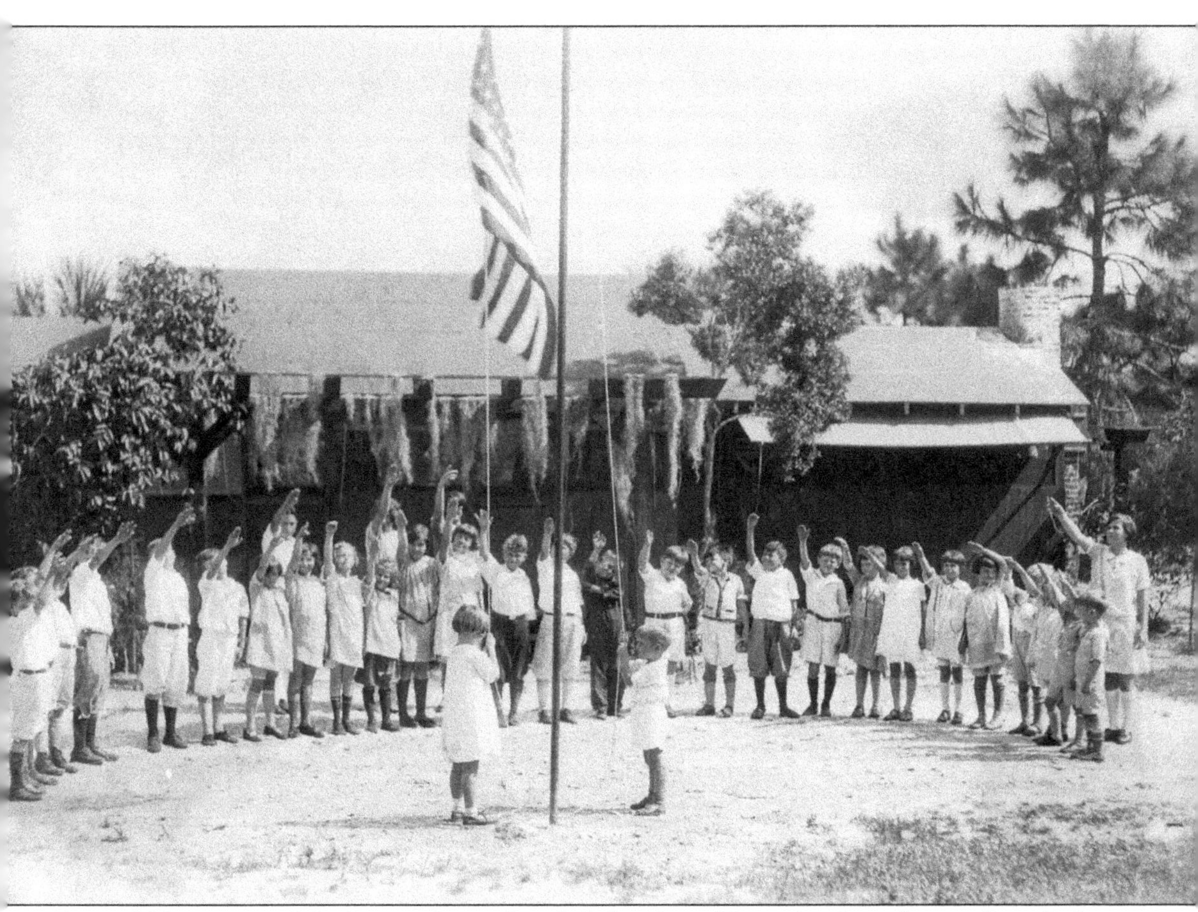

Fanneal Harrison and Catherine Gavin founded the Out-of-Door Academy (originally called Out-of-Door School) on Siesta Key in 1924. The school was based on the theory of Dr. Ovide DeCroly, who was a pioneer of progressive education in Europe. DeCroly believed that a school's function was to promote children's healthy bodies, minds, and spirits and to let students learn in an environment of self-discipline and freedom. Children swam in Big Pass on the north end of Siesta Key, learned to speak French, and engaged in construction. (Courtesy of SCHR.)

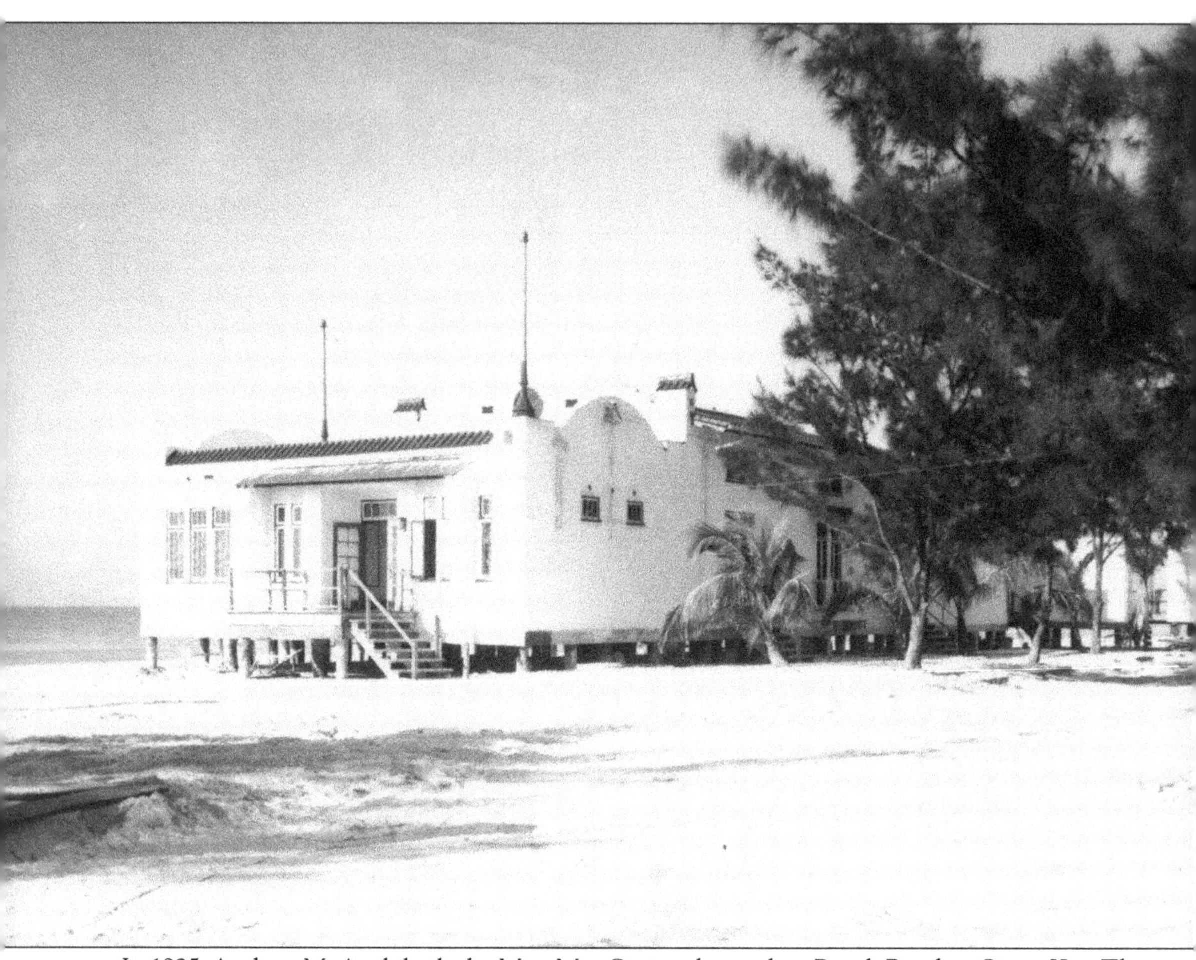

In 1925, Andrew McAnsh built the Mira Mar Casino, located on Beach Road on Siesta Key. The Mediterranean-style casino was intended to be an "amusement center" for residents and included a lounge, dance floor, private club rooms, and a dressing area for bathing. He used a red-tile roof and coquina-shell stairs. In 1934, the casino was sold and transformed into a private club called the Beach Club of Sarasota. (Courtesy of SCHR.)

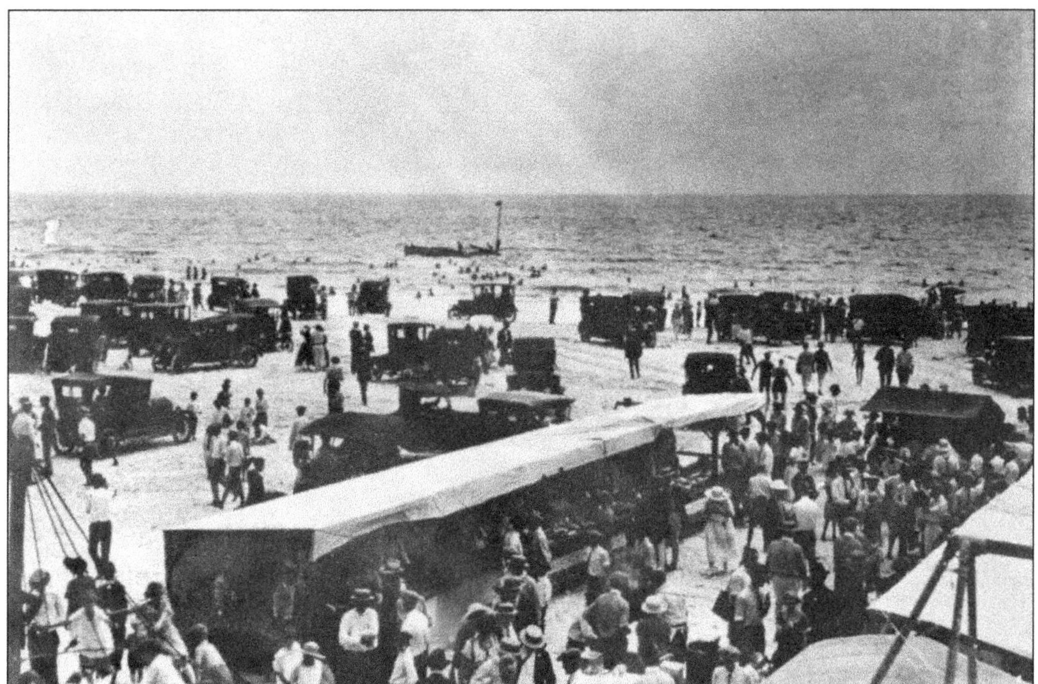

Venice and Sarasota saw value in Sarasota's beautiful beaches and reserved beach property in the 1920s and 1930s. In the 1950s, there was renewed interest in developing Siesta Key. In the 1970s, *National Geographic* magazine first rated Siesta Key as one of the top ten beaches in the world. Pictured here is the First American Legion picnic on Siesta Key Beach in the 1920s. (Courtesy of SCHR.)

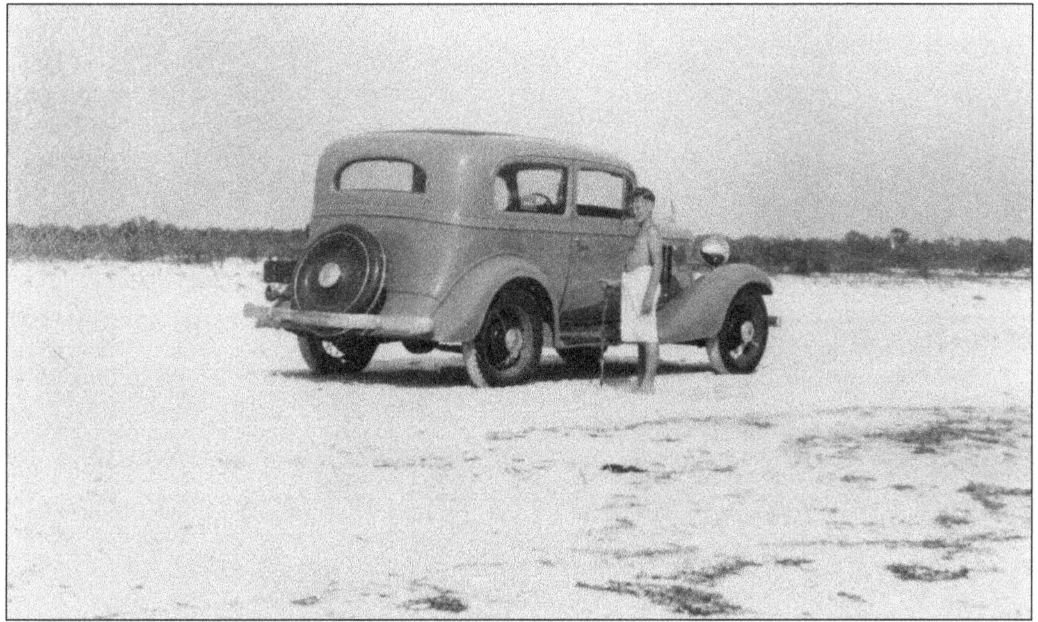

Initially, there were many names for Siesta Key, including Little Sarasota Key or Sarasota Key, and finally, in 1952, it received its official Siesta name. Pictured here is a boy next to an old car parked on the beach. (Courtesy of SCHR.)

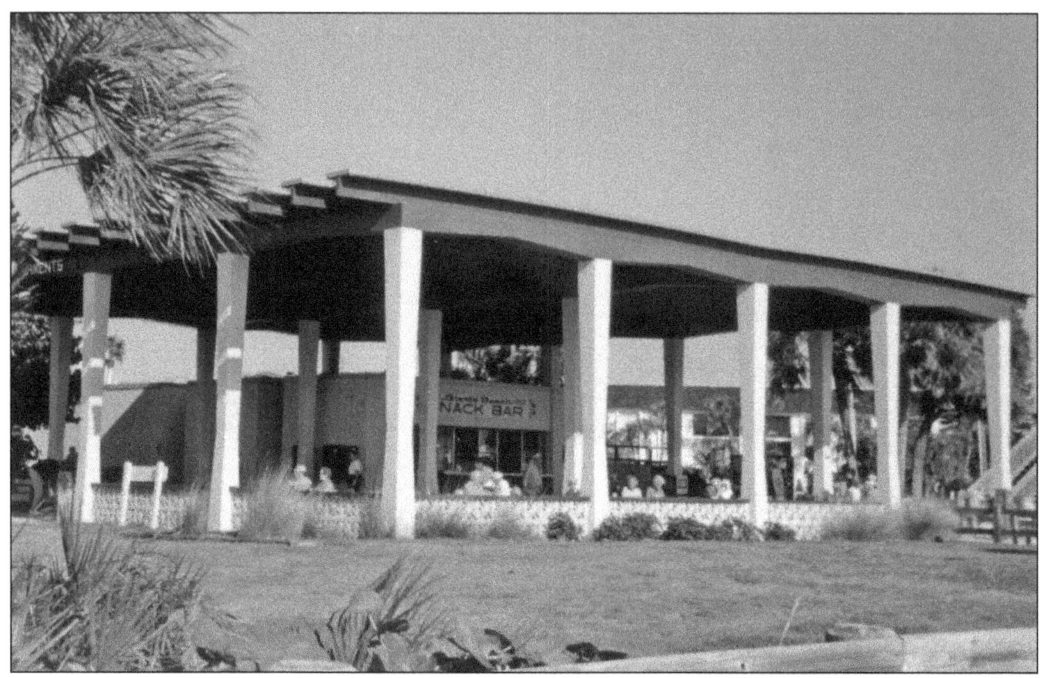


The development on Siesta Key slowed down until after World War II. With the use of DDT insecticide, mosquitoes were kept under control. Architect Edward "Tim" Siebert, from the Sarasota School of Architecture, was hired to build the Siesta Key Beach Pavilion, which opened in 1959. (Courtesy of SCHR.)

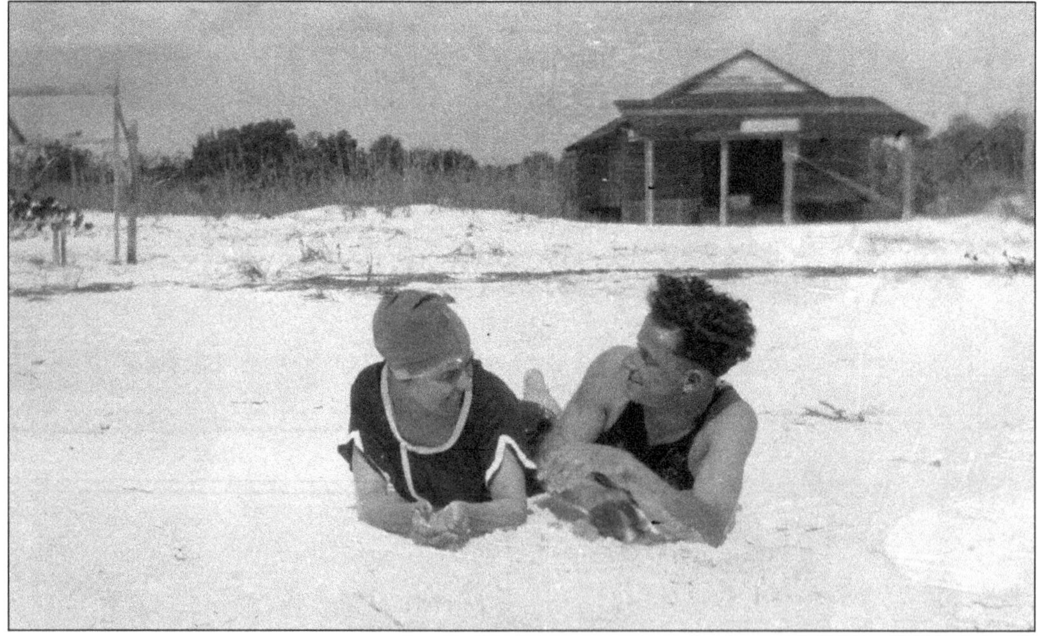

After the first bridge was built on Siesta Key in 1917, footpaths became basic roads. In the 1920s, C.I. Archibald built a bathing pavilion on Crescent Beach, providing bathers with a civilized place to change into proper swim attire. This image shows a couple enjoying a tête-à-tête on Siesta Key Beach. (Courtesy of SCHR.)

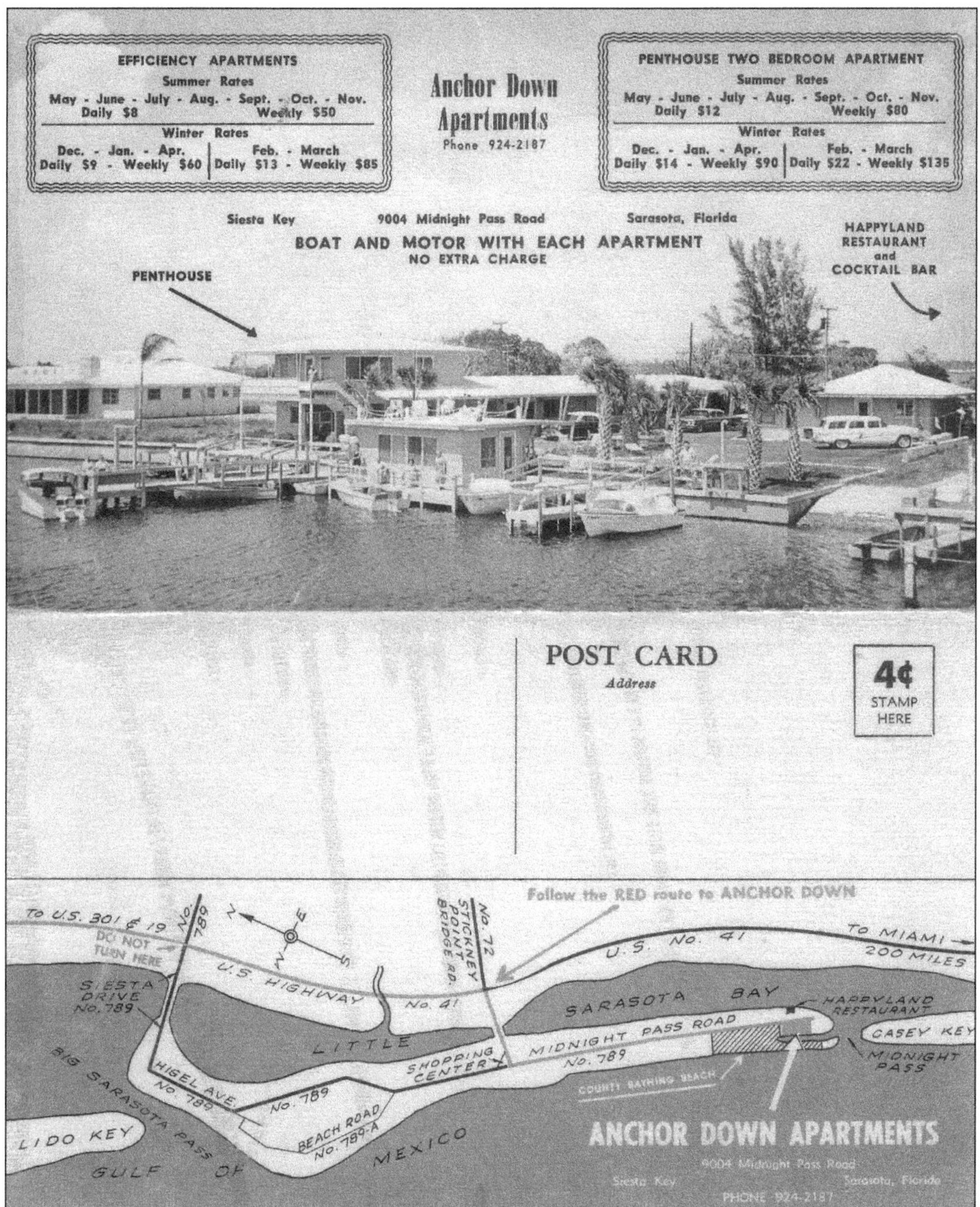


Mr. and Mrs. Hamilton of Michigan opened the Anchor Down Apartments on Siesta Key as an economical place to stay and fish. A 16-foot motorboat was provided for each room at no extra charge. The apartments were located on a deep lagoon at Midnight Pass and "air conditioned by nature." Guests, who returned yearly, could look forward to an "all-you-can-eat" buffet for $2.25 at the Happyland Restaurant located across the street. (Courtesy of Jimmy Von Hubertz.)

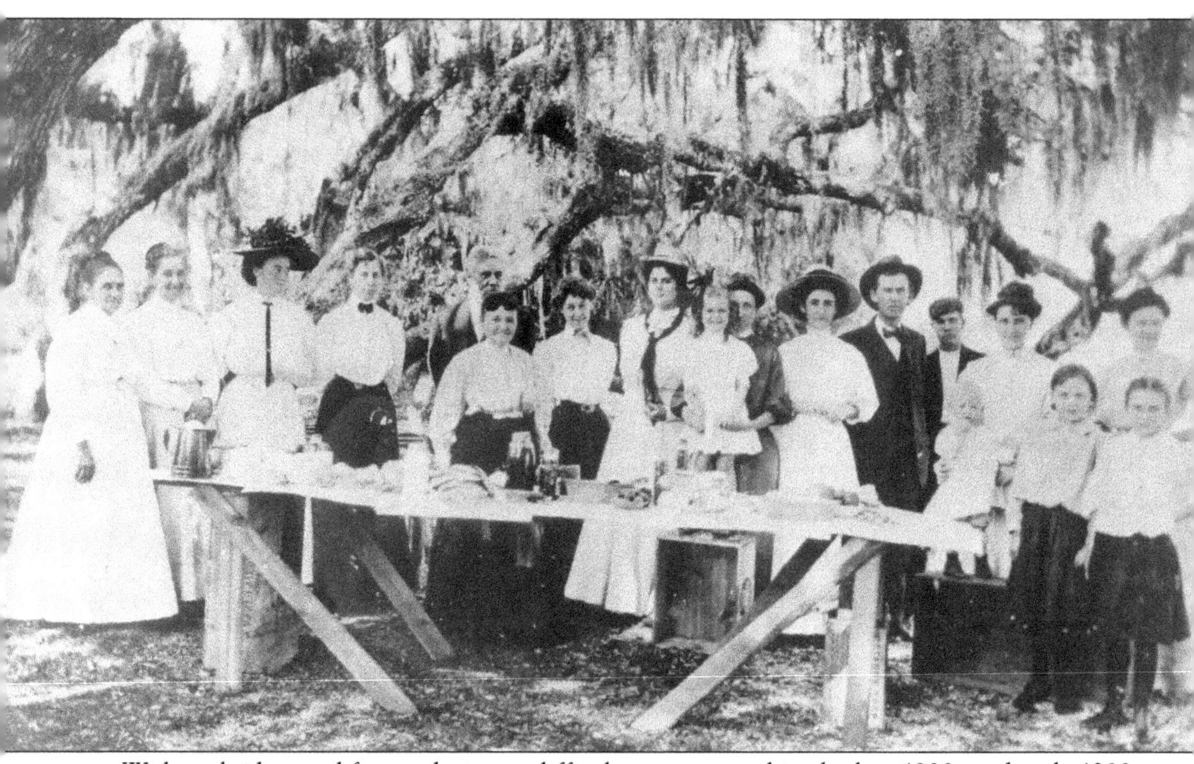

With no bridges and few roads, it was difficult to get around in the late 1800s and early 1900s. "Uncle Ben" Stickney let visitors picnic on his property, as seen here. (Courtesy of SCHR.)

Joseph Steinmetz was born in Philadelphia, Pennsylvania, in 1905. His family was in the insurance business and hoped he would carry on. After receiving a graduate degree in English from Princeton, he fell in love with photography. On a trip to Egypt, he purchased a Leica camera and captured his trip on film. He later started taking wedding pictures for friends and, through word of mouth, became a popular photographer. Here, he is holding a few of his nature photographs. (Courtesy of Lois Duncan.)

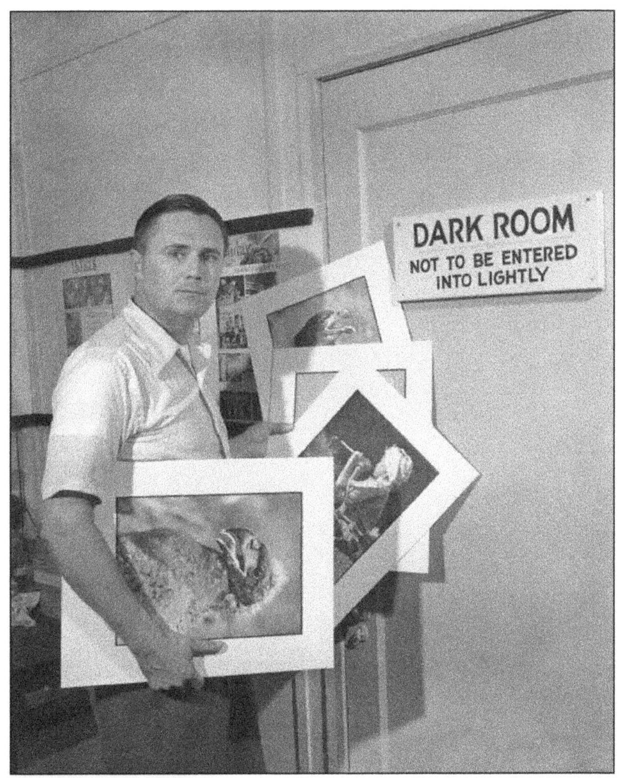


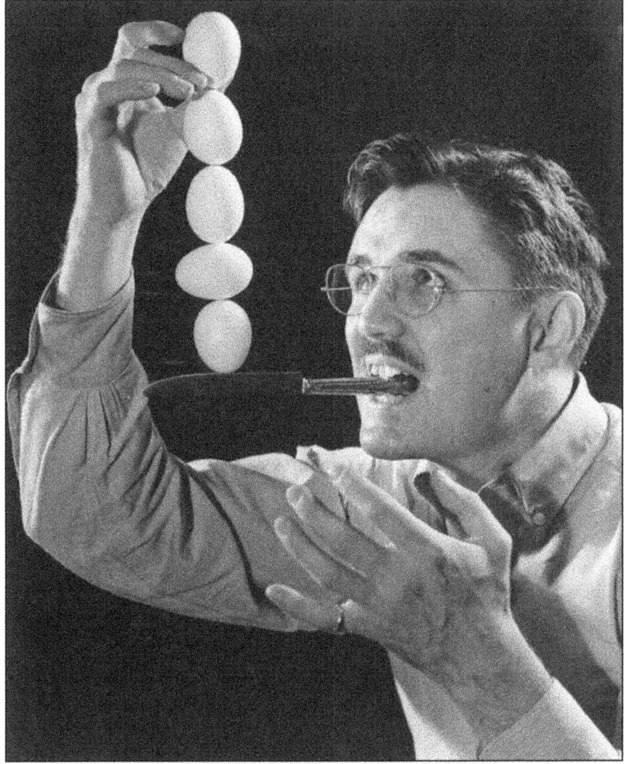

Both Joseph Steinmetz and his first wife, Lois, were local photographers whose work was published in national magazines. His second wife, Louise, was a watercolorist. Together, they specialized in photojournalism for illustration and advertising. Joseph was considered the "unofficial town photographer" of Sarasota. He enjoyed taking aerial photographs of Sarasota. He displays his sense of humor in this picture while balancing eggs on a knife. (Courtesy of Lois Duncan.)

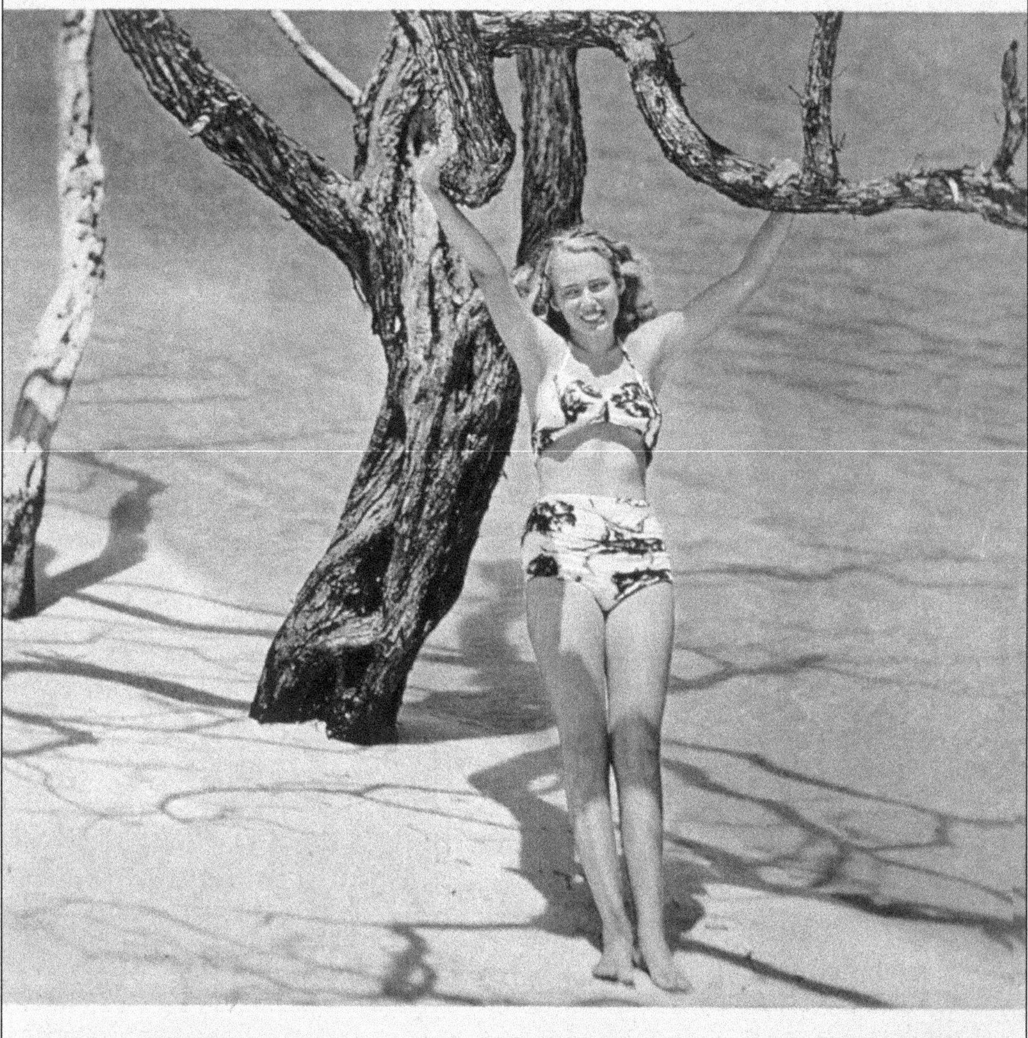


Joseph Steinmetz took this picture of his daughter on Siesta Key, and it was used for the cover of *Collier's* magazine in 1949. His daughter Lois Duncan, a resident of Sarasota, is an award-winning writer. A few of her books, including *Hotel for Dogs*, have been made into movies. (Courtesy of Lois Duncan.)

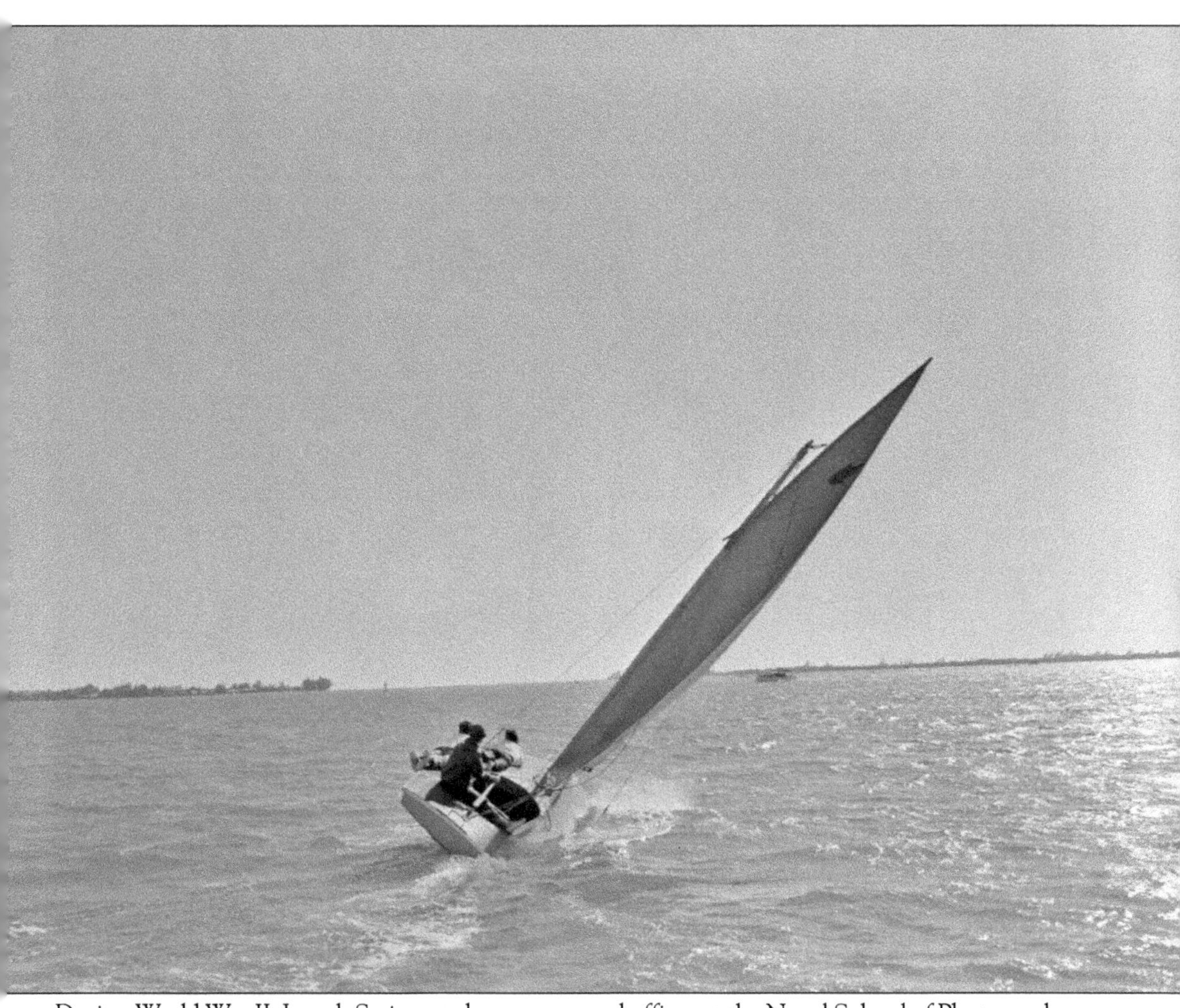

During World War II, Joseph Steinmetz became a naval officer at the Naval School of Photography in Pensacola, Florida. He wrote two naval photography textbooks. According to Steinmetz, "Ninety percent of the information we got from the enemy was obtained through aerial photographs." This picture shows a sailboat heeling in the wind on the Sarasota waters. (Courtesy of SCHR, Joseph Steinmetz Collection.)

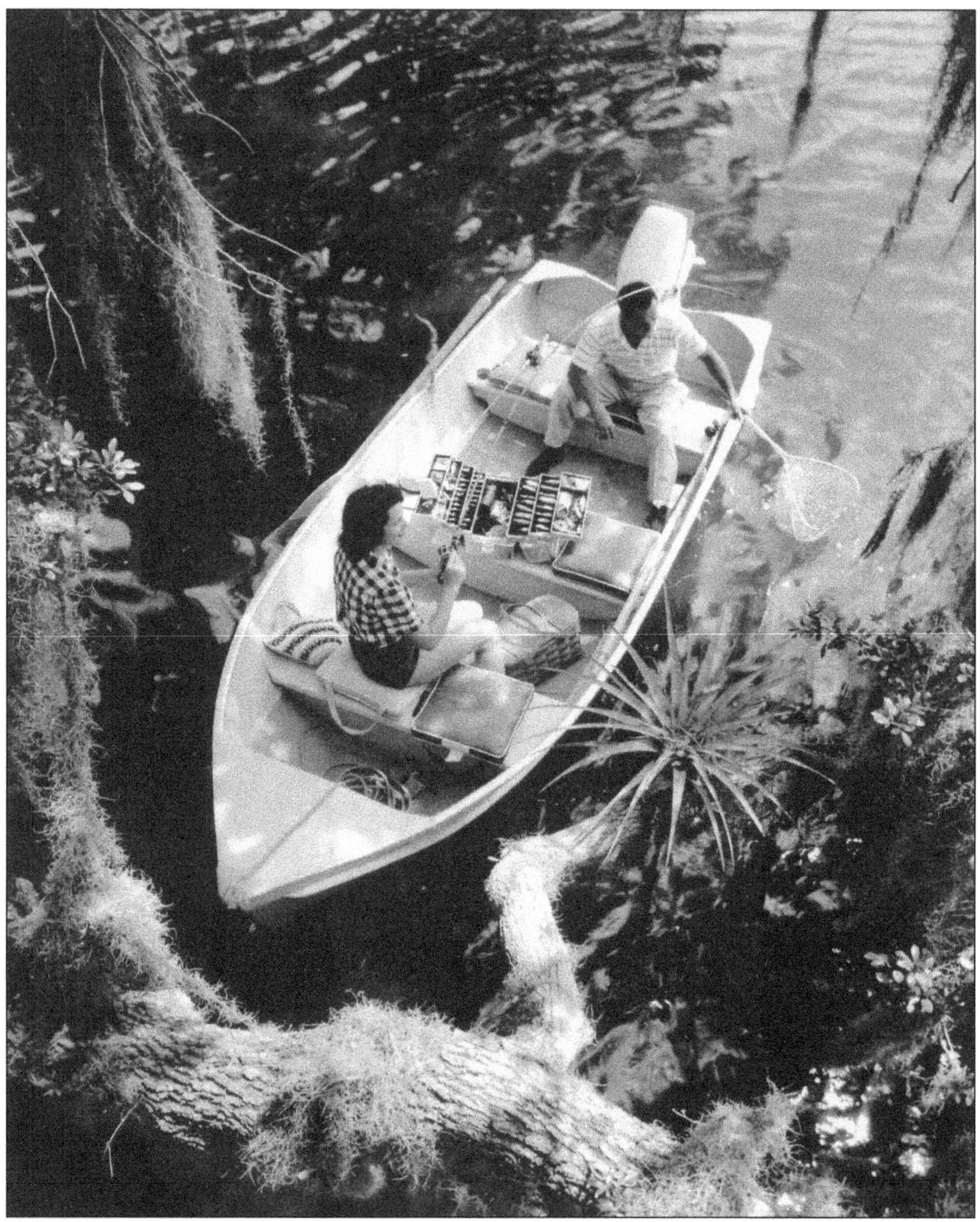

In this Steinmetz photograph of a couple fishing, epiphytes are visible on the tree overhead. Epiphytes are air plants that can grow on trees. A few different types of epiphytes are bromeliads, orchids, and Spanish moss, as seen hanging on this tree. (Courtesy of SCHR, Joseph Steinmetz Collection.)

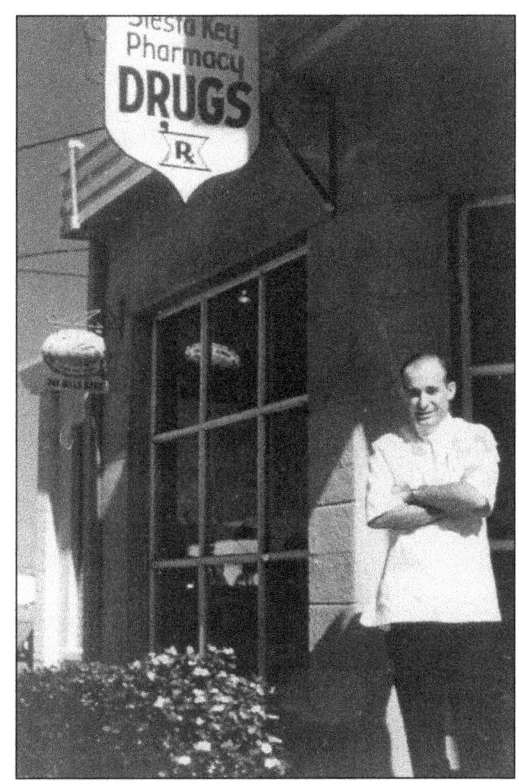


John B. Davidson first opened a drugstore on Siesta Key in 1958. He worked 12 hours a day. He swept the sidewalk in front of his pharmacy at 8:30 a.m. and closed up shop at 9:00 p.m. He had a soda fountain in the store that he operated along with filling prescriptions. Davidson Drugs is the oldest established drugstore under the same continuous ownership in Sarasota. Davidson's sons Richard and Robert help run the three thriving stores, which employ 100 employees. They provide mail service in their Sarasota store. Tourists and residents like shopping for gifts and local books at Davidson's. (Courtesy of Davidson Drugs.)

Pictured here is the Sensitive Women's Writing Salon (SWWS) writers group. These published writers and artists, who have lived all over the world and now choose Sarasota to live and create, meet weekly to critique each other's work. From left to right are Brenda "Bree" Hill, Emma Weisseneder, Louise Mathewson, Marcia Lang, the author, and Marguerite "Jill" Dye. (Author's collection.)

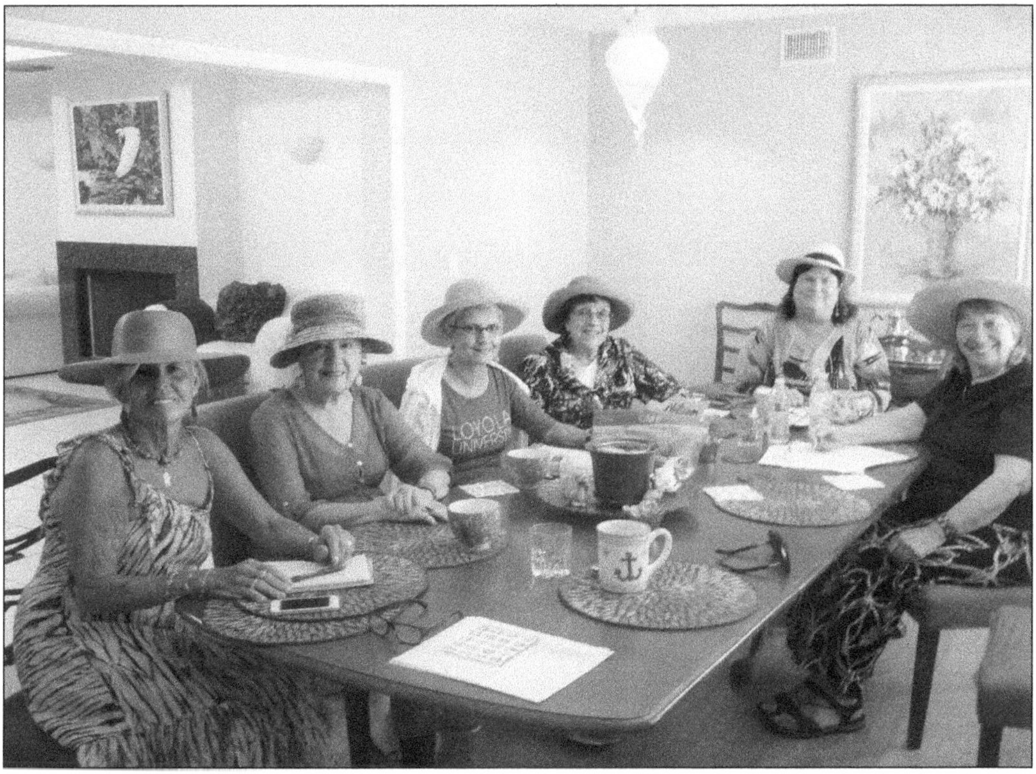

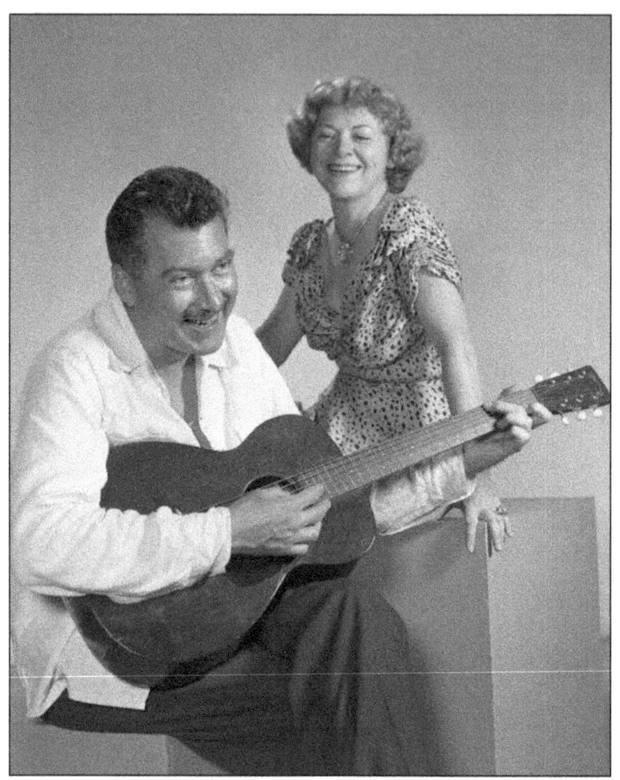

Joseph Steinmetz took this picture of his friend MacKinlay Kantor and his wife, Florence Kantor. Kantor was known as a colorful fixture in Sarasota. He started writing seriously when he was a teenager working with his mother at the local newspaper in his hometown of Webster City, Iowa. His first book was published at age 24. Moving to Siesta Key with his wife in 1937, Kantor found the wild and private surroundings on Siesta Key to be a good place to write. His novel *Glory for Me* was made into a movie called *The Best Years of Our Lives*, which won eight Academy Awards in 1947. Kantor is probably known best for his novel *Andersonville*, based on his great-uncle's experience in a Civil War prisoner-of-war camp. *Andersonville* won the Pulitzer Prize for Fiction in 1956. (Courtesy of Lois Duncan.)

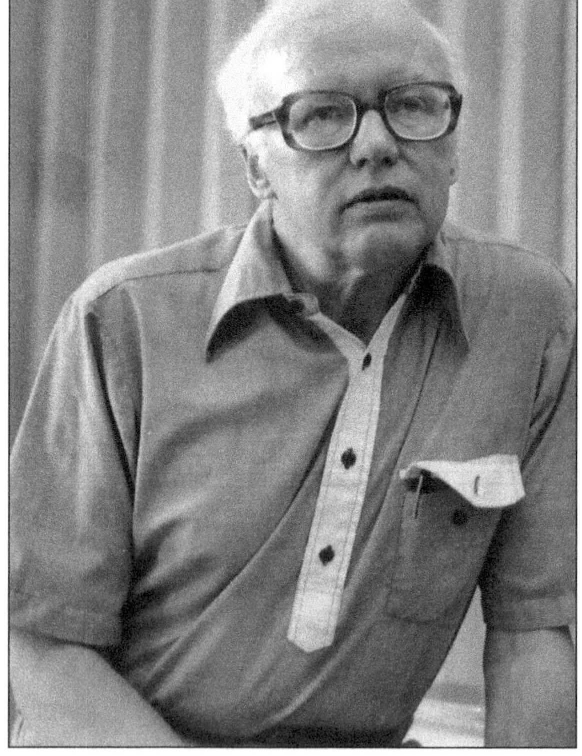

Author J.D. McDonald moved to Sarasota in 1951 and began using the Florida culture in his mystery books. He was a prolific author who managed to write 200 short stories and 70 novels while living here. McDonald was an environmentalist who cared about the growth of Sarasota, where he lived for 35 years. He donated his written work to the University of Florida. (Courtesy of SCHR.)

# *Four*

# Casey Key

## Lat 27.1501 N, Long 82.4807 W

Tourists often drive slowly down Casey Key to admire the architecture of the large homes. In addition to fishing at the jetty, people flock to the public beaches on the south end of the island. Casey Key is located south of Siesta Key and was once detached, until Midnight Pass was filled in. The island is named after John Casey, a surveyor who worked in the area in the late 1880s. Isaac Shuman and his family from Missouri were the first nonnative residents of Casey Key in the early 1900s.

Those accessing Casey Key can use two bridges. The north bridge, located in Osprey, is called the Blackburn Point Bridge. The southern bridge, located in Nokomis, is called the Albee Road Bridge. Both bridges were named after local families and are opened on demand for boaters. Before the south bridge was built, there was a pontoon barge to get across.

On the north end of the island is a quaint library called the Casey Key Library, which is open to residents of the island and sponsored members. Sarasota Scullers, a youth rowing program, is located near the library. Also nearby is an old Florida-style restaurant called the Casey Key Fish House. On the south end of the island are two public beaches with pavilions, a few small motels, and the North Jetty Fish Camp and bait shop, which is now owned by Sarasota County.

In the mid-1920s, Sarasota County leaders wanted to open the barrier islands, including Casey Key. A bond was issued in 1924 to help develop the new county of Sarasota, and as a result, five bridges and 15 roads were built. In 1927, a bridge opened to traffic and attached Casey Key to the mainland. The earliest remaining houses on Casey Key, dating back to the early 1900s, reflect the Mediterranean Revival style typical of architecture in Sarasota.

Thanks to the Army Corps of Engineers, some residents of Casey Key acquired reclaimed land due to the dredging of the Intracoastal Waterway.

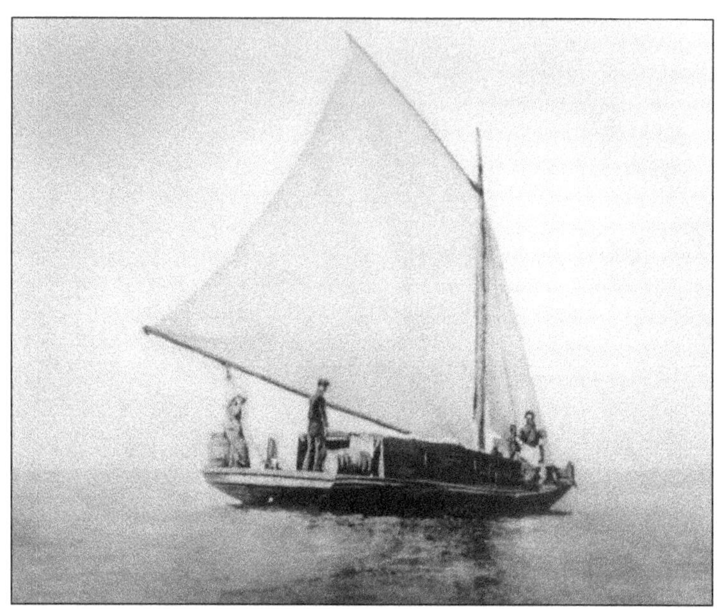

Blackburn Point Bridge is named after the Blackburn family, who moved to Osprey from Iowa. They came to take advantage of the Homestead Act of 1862 and claimed land running from South Creek to Blackburn Point Road. John and Belinda Blackburn arrived with two of their five children, and later, their son Benjamin Franklin Blackburn relocated to the area in 1884. Pictured here is a painting of John sailing on his schooner. (Courtesy of SCHR.)

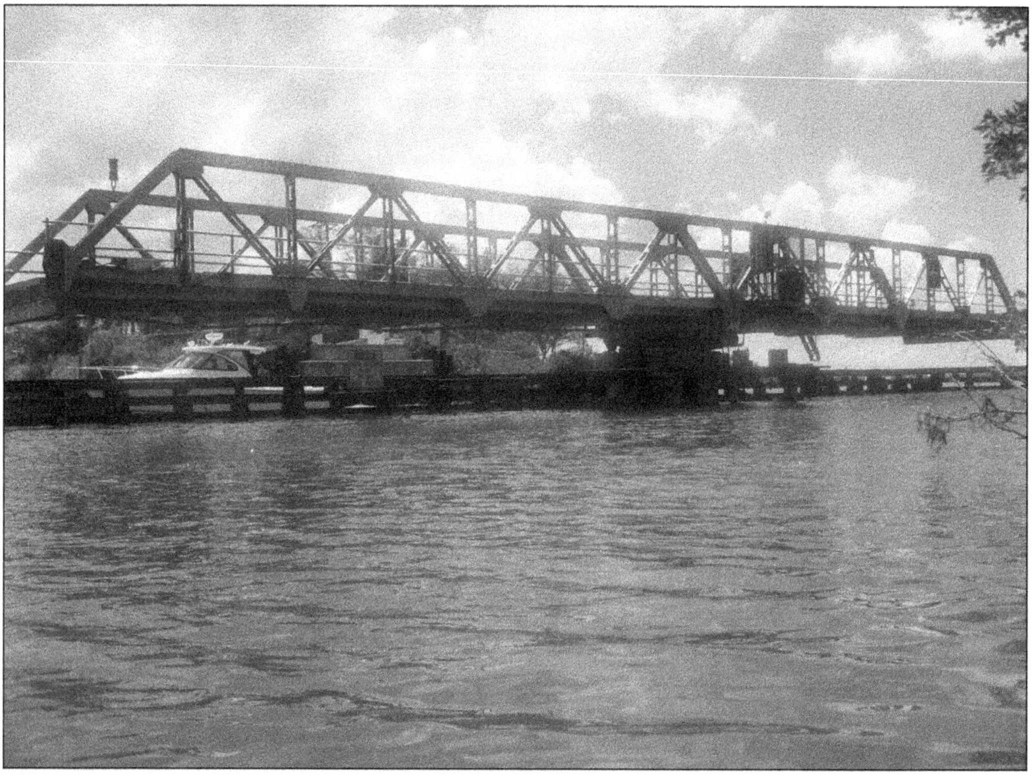

Blackburn Point Bridge was the first one built on Casey Key by the Champion Bridge Company of Wilmington, Ohio. Large fenders protect the narrow bridge from the wide working barges that have to navigate on the Intracoastal Waterway. The bridge rotates at its center, dividing the waterway in half and making a narrow path for vessels to pass through it. In 1926, H.T. Campbell was hired as the first bridge tender for $50 a month. The job was 24 hours a day, and the bridge tender had to provide the oil for the lamps and bridge. (Courtesy of Connor Keane.)

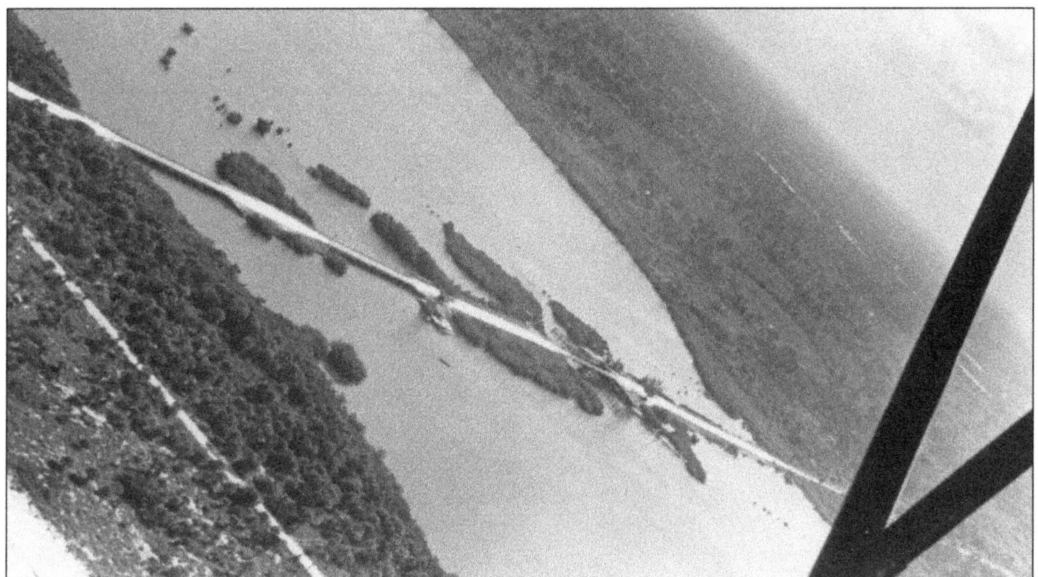

Blackburn Point Bridge, also known as "the Flying Bridge," is one of the last single-lane swing bridges that exists in Florida today. The bridge is used for commercial and recreational boating and provides access to Casey Key by car and boat. The bridge is considered a landmark, so when it became unsafe for travel in early 2000, it was closed for repairs rather than being torn down. At the time, 350 residents were forced to use the Albee Road Bridge for access. Many residents wanted to keep the historic bridge. The Coast Guard and Florida Department of Transportation (FDOT) were interested in building a larger, wider bridge that would allow two boats to pass. However, in the end, the original bridge was fixed. (Courtesy of SCHR.)

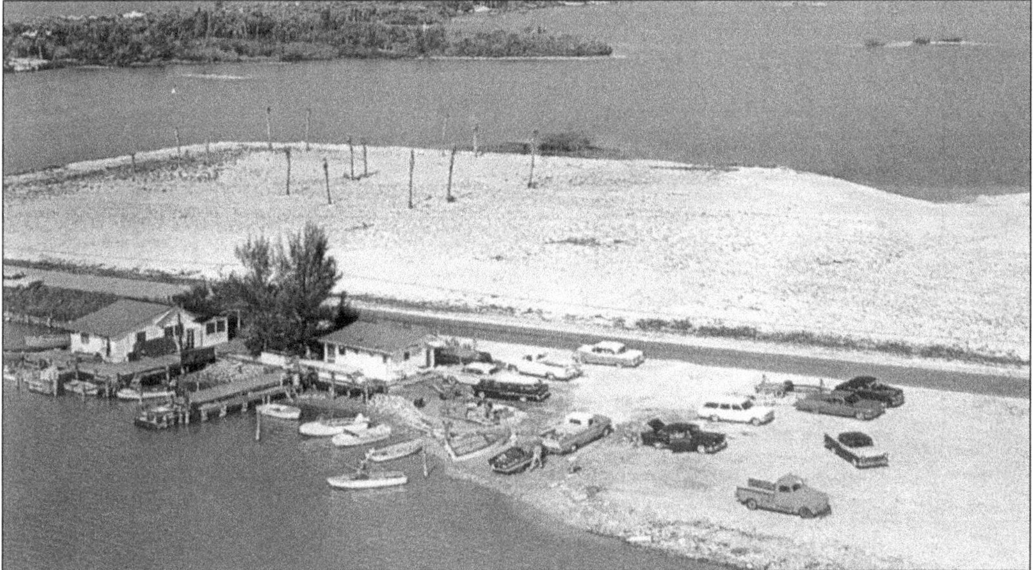

Meeks Landing was owned by the Meeks family and has been used for many businesses over the years, including bait and sandwich shops; a few restaurants, including the Salty Dog, Captain's Cove, and Walt's Fish Market; and a marina that sold boats and rented slips. Today, it is home to the Casey Key Fish House restaurant, owned by James Von Hubertz, who purchased it in 1999. (Courtesy of James Von Hubertz.)

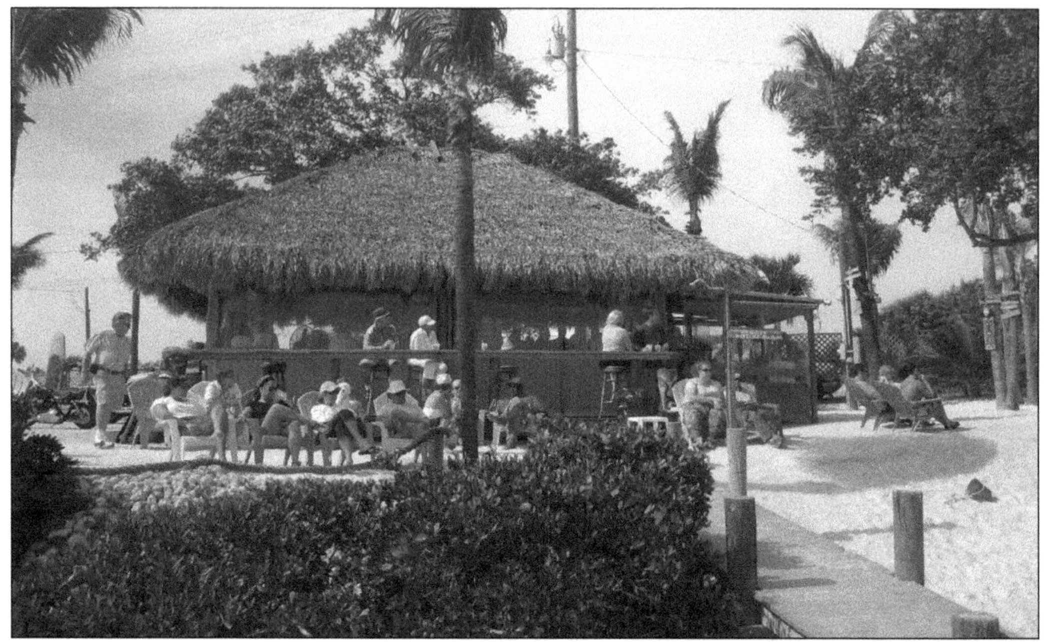

The Casey Key Fish House went through trying times when lightning struck the restaurant and started a kitchen fire. Months passed before permits were granted to rebuild. Food and drinks were served from a portable food truck at the old tiki bar. Wearing green "Save the Tiki Bar" T-shirts, 200 local residents gathered at Sarasota Town Hall on a rainy Monday night to rally support for the restaurant, after which the business was able to reopen and a new tiki bar was built, as seen here. This establishment is still one of the few remaining fun places in the area where patrons can arrive by water or land to eat and listen to live entertainment. (Author's collection.)

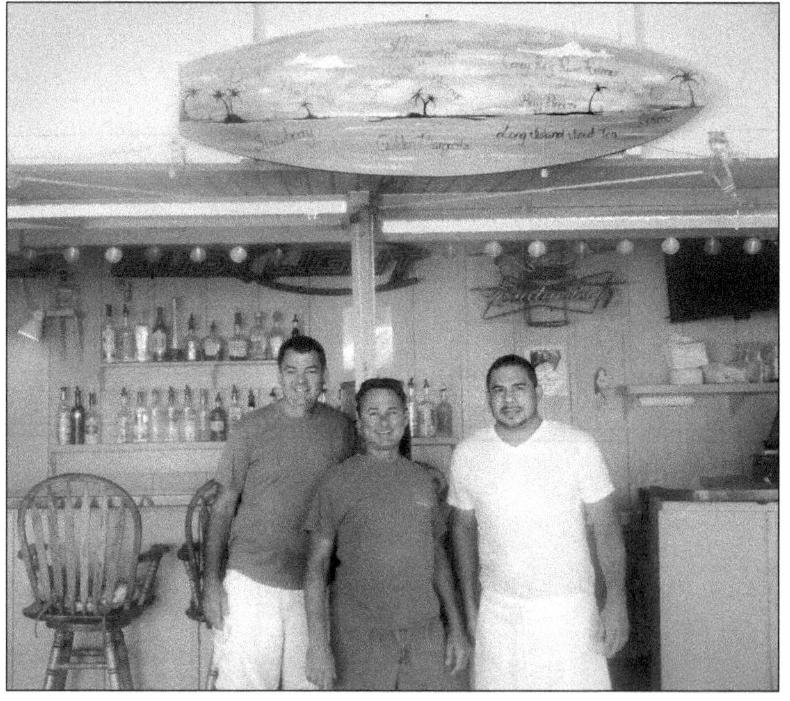

Here are chef Cesar Vega (right), owner Jimmy Von Hubertz (center), and server Joe Zax in the bar area. Many of the Casey Key employees work here long term and join the eclectic group of patrons. Local residents from Casey Key, Osprey, and surrounding areas are often seen mingling here. Not shown here, bartender Skeeter and Chef Willie have also been here from the start. (Author's collection.)

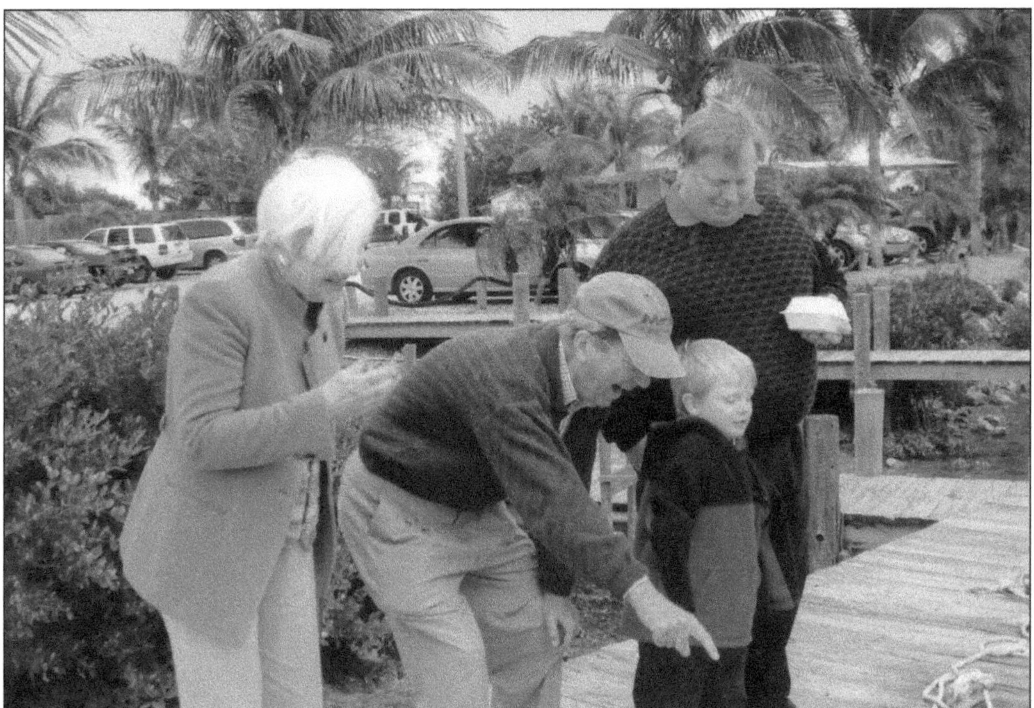

After dining at the fish house, families often walk the docks at the marina next door to observe fish in the water and birds in their natural environment. Here, from left to right, are Elizabeth Elder, Douglas Elder, Connor Keane, and David Keane. (Author's collection.)

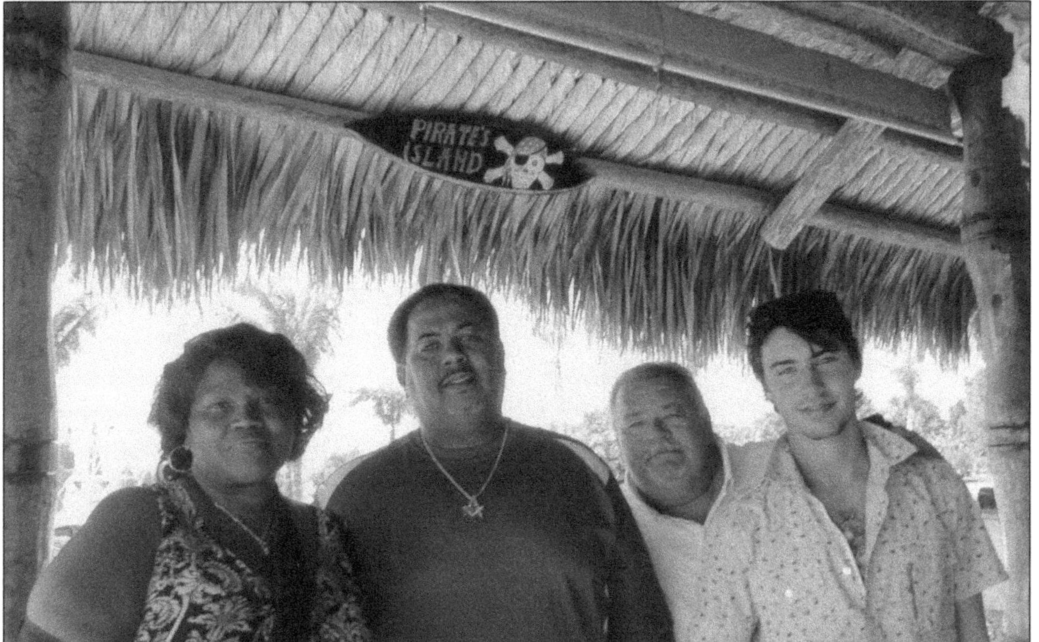


Visitors and locals like meeting at the Casey Key Fish House. The couple on the left are snowbirds from Harrisburg, Pennsylvania. When asked how they heard about the place, they said it was by word of mouth. (Author's collection.)

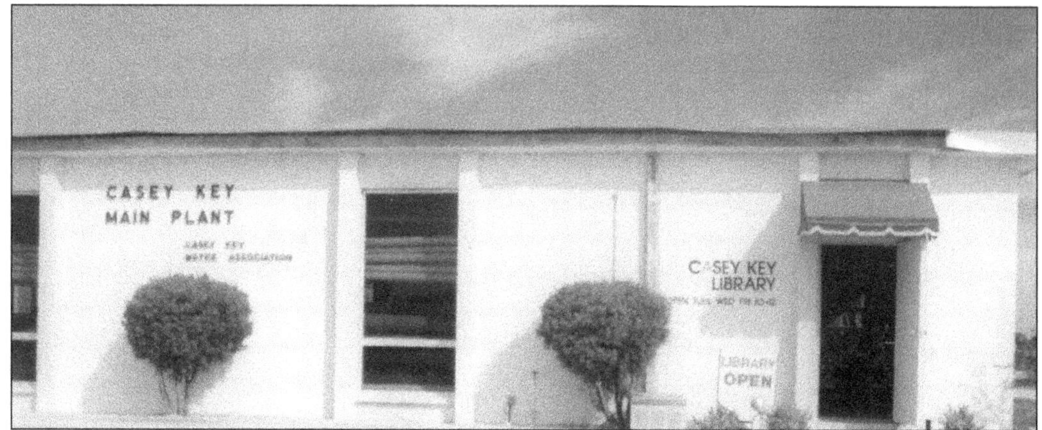


The Casey Key Library is located at 800 Casey Key Road. Residents Marian Shaw, Fran Howard, and Jane Vulte started the library back in 1986. When the library needed a home, Bill Shaw, president of the Casey Key Water Company and owner of the building, provided the space where it is still located today. When the building was sold, the library was asked to continue paying rent. An endowment was given in early 2000 to support the library and local community. (Courtesy of the Casey Key Library.)

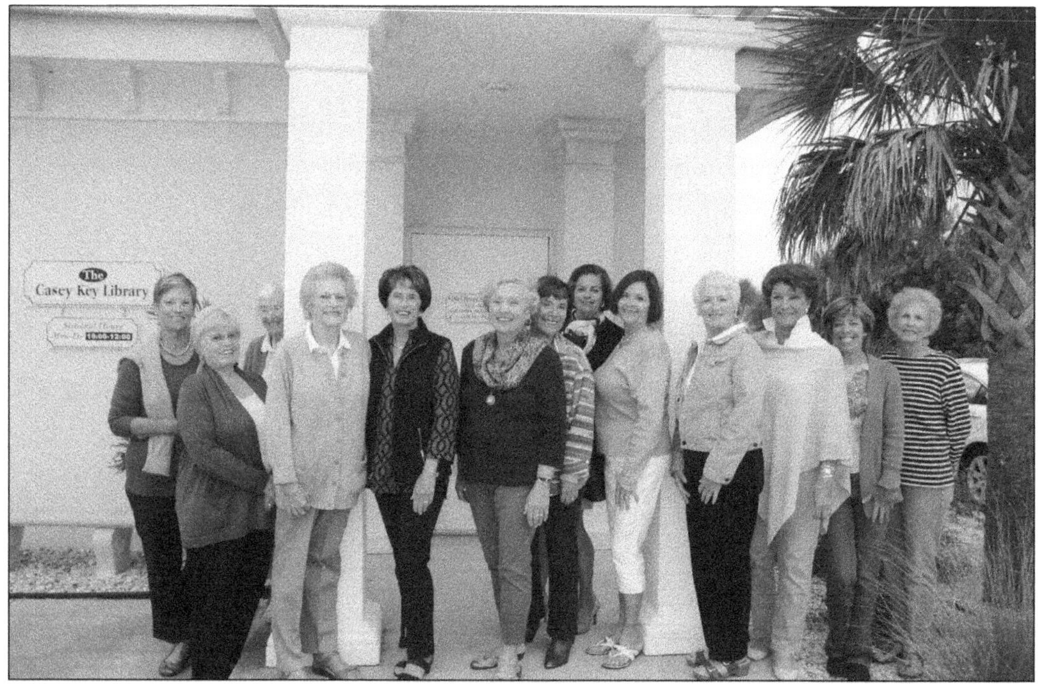


The Casey Key Library, which is private, is available only to residents of Casey Key. It has grown from a small library and book exchange to a nonprofit organization that supports the children's literacy programs in the community. With no public funding, the library relies on income from an endowment and gifts from its members. From left to right are Grace Schulz, Barbara Tafaro, Ann Carruthers, Fraya Cole, Betsy Dale, Connie Davis, Sandy Warner, Nancy Arbuckle, Jill Montgomery, Zoe Moore, Maggie Urciuoli, Polly Giuffrida, and Marianne Dent. Missing from the photograph are Fluff Thayer and Chuck Snyder. (Courtesy of Douglas Elder.)

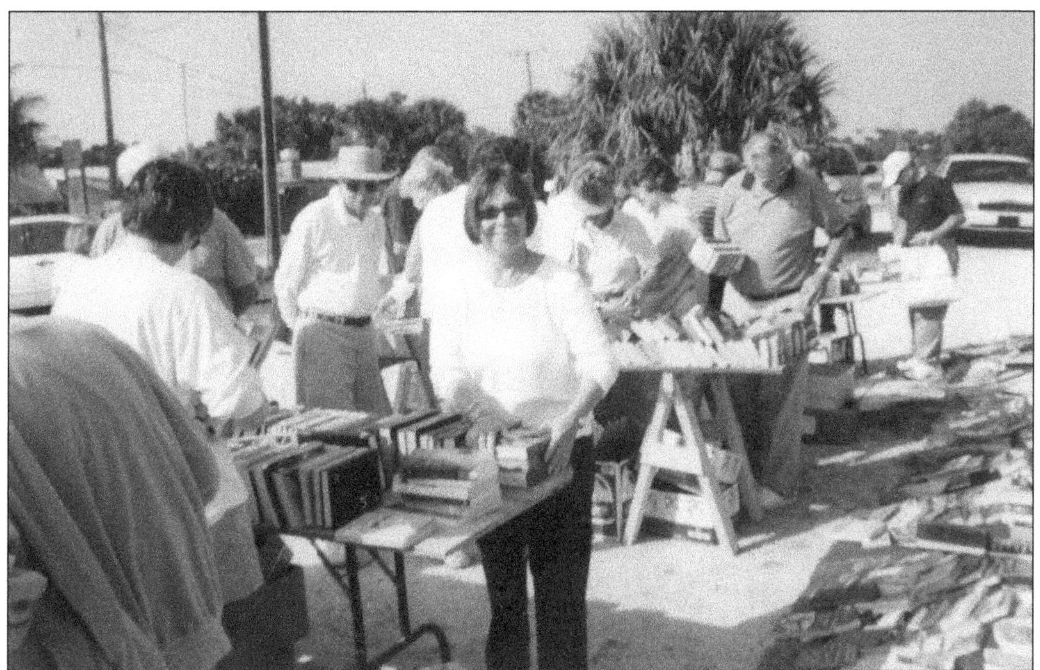

Pictured here is Sandy Warner, who works hard to raise money for the library at the community book sale. (Courtesy of the Casey Key Library.)

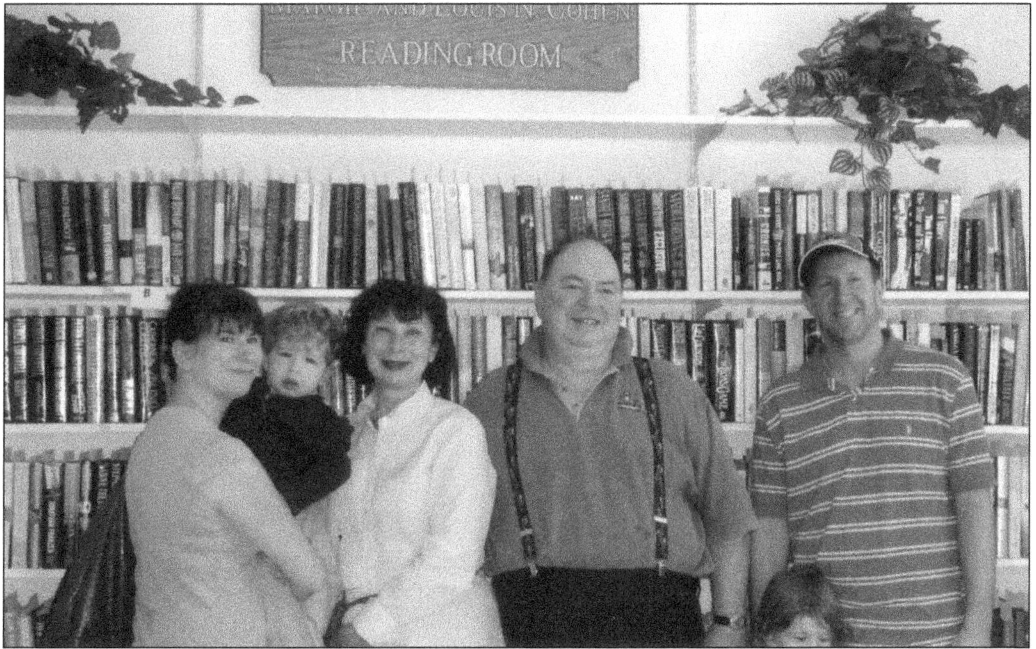


The Casey Key Library raises money through author appearances, as well as an annual public book sale in February. Bobette Cohen (center) and family honored her parents by donating a reading room in their name. Three generations are photographed in front of the sign in remembrance of their parents and grandparents, Margie and Louis N. Cohen. (Courtesy of the Casey Key Library.)

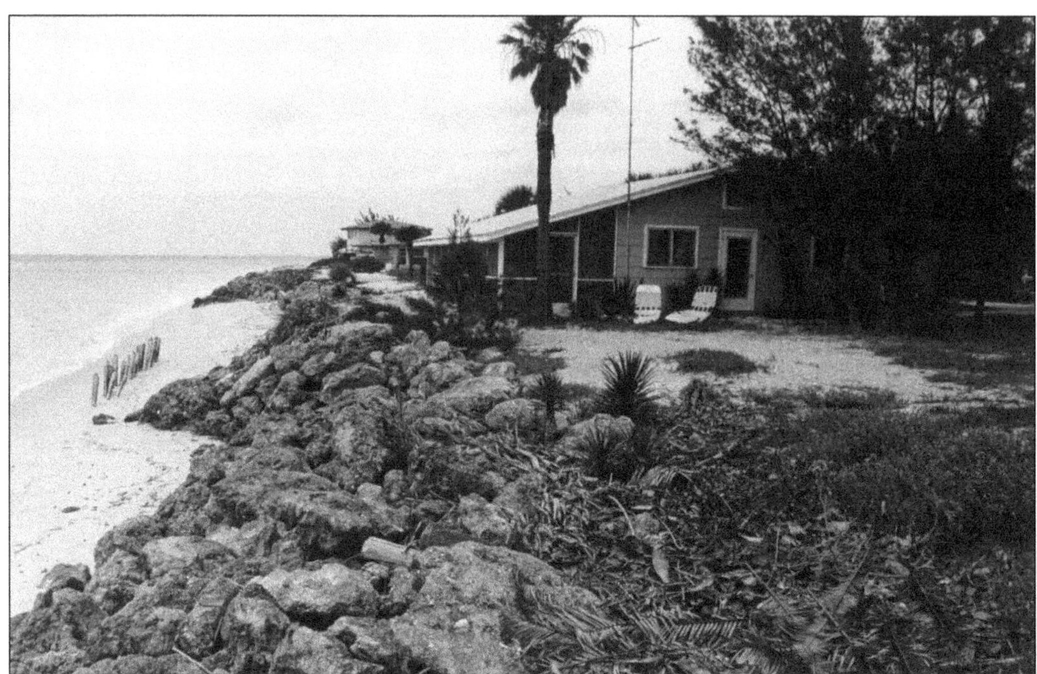

This simple cottage was built with a beautiful view of the Gulf of Mexico on the north end of the island. There is no public beach or place to turn a car around on this end of the island, but the sunsets are beautiful here. The house is no longer standing and has been replaced with a larger home. (Courtesy of SCHR.)

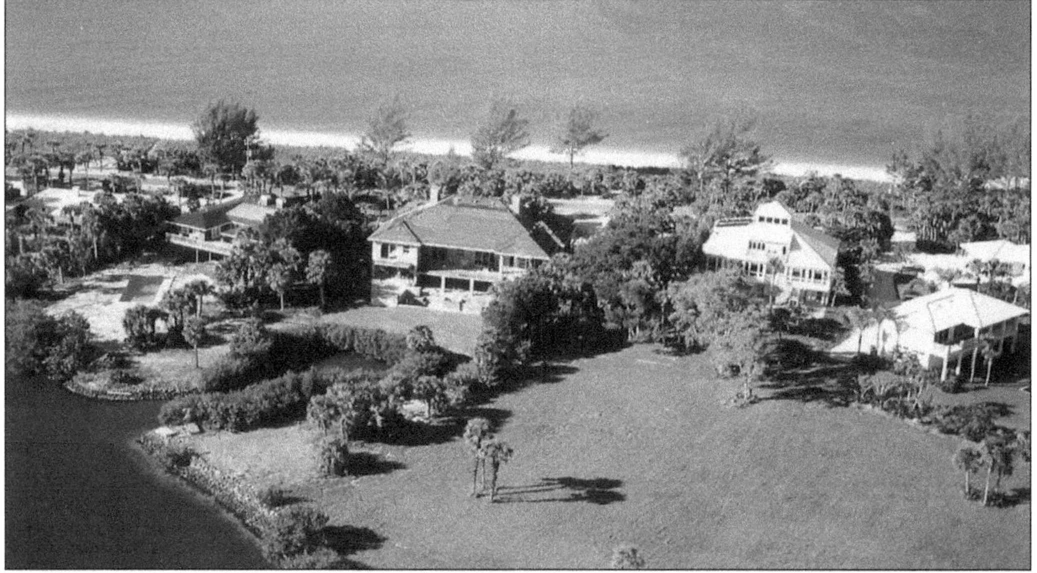

Casey Key is an exclusive island offering beautiful beaches. Today, the island is full of elaborate homes designed in many different styles of architecture. Some residents of Casey Key acquired land due to the dredging of the Intracoastal Waterway. Over the years, nicknames have been established for various parts of the island. "Connecticut Row" was adopted by some neighbors in the 1600 block. "Cutlers Bayou Yacht Club" was also used to identify a particular area. (Courtesy of Fluff Thayer.)

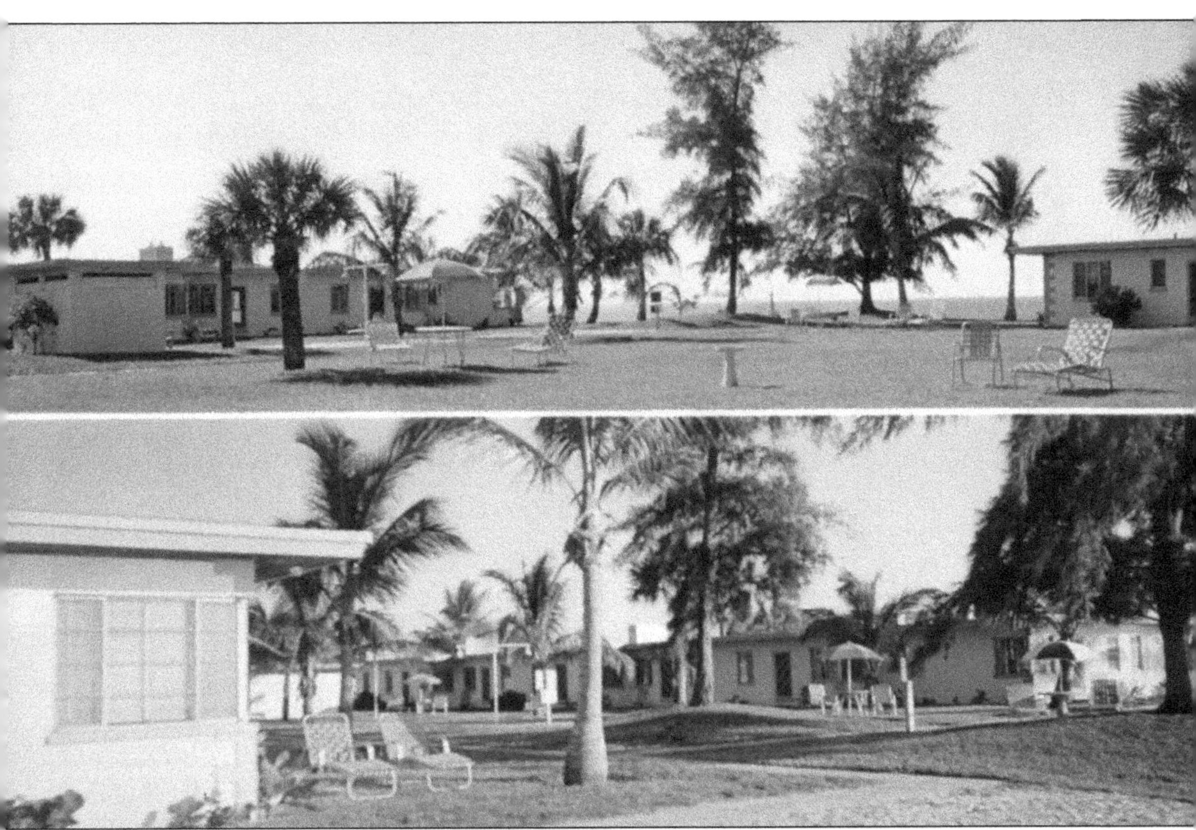

The Gulf Surf Resort is one of the few motels located on the island. This exclusive island has only a few places for visitors to stay. Among the motels that existed over the years were the Island House and On the Beach, which offered beach and/or bay access. If a storm demolishes a commercial property, the remaining land becomes strictly residential. (Courtesy of SCHR.)

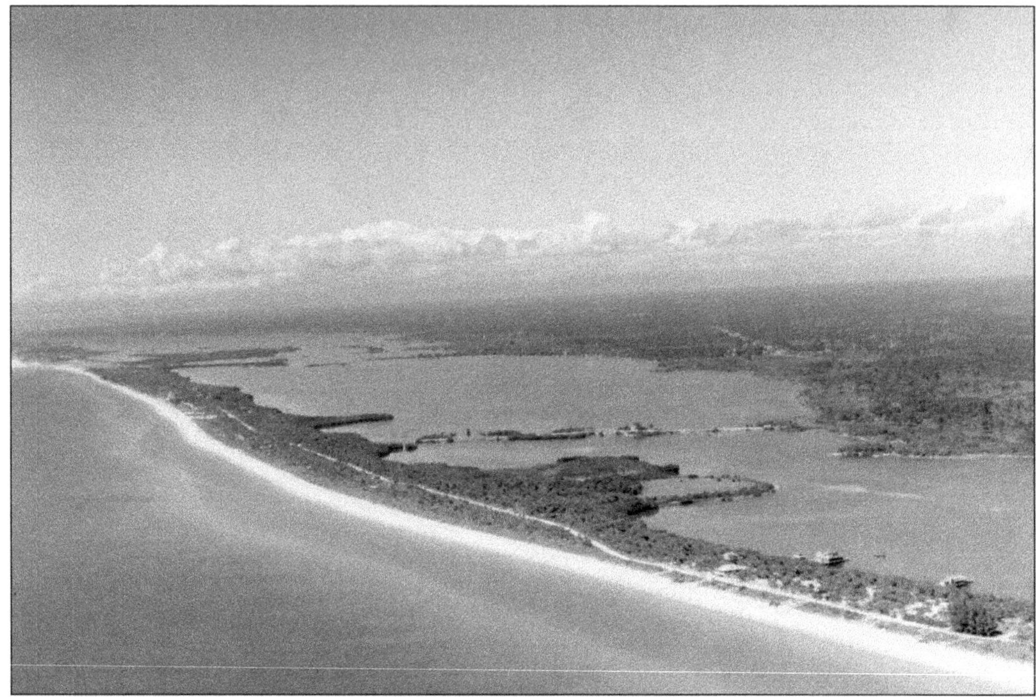

The Intracoastal Waterway runs from Virginia to Texas. It was built after World War II so that cargo could travel inland, safe from naval attacks. In the late 1800s, the US Corps of Engineers surveyed and identified waterways in the southwest portions of Florida. Dredging began in 1895 and was finally completed in 1967. The resulting channel is 9 feet deep and 100 feet wide. (Courtesy of SCHR.)

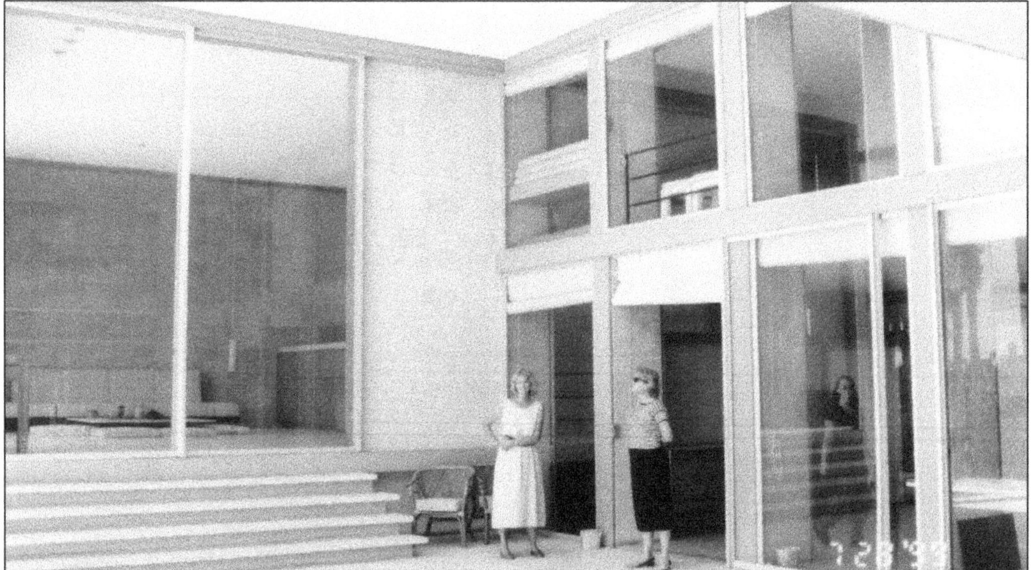

The Deering House, built in 1958, is located at 3013 Casey Key Road. It was designed by Paul Rudolph, who was an architect for the Sarasota School of Architecture. The Deering House was designed with native materials to merge indoor and outdoor spaces. (Courtesy of SCHR, Ed Holt Collection.)

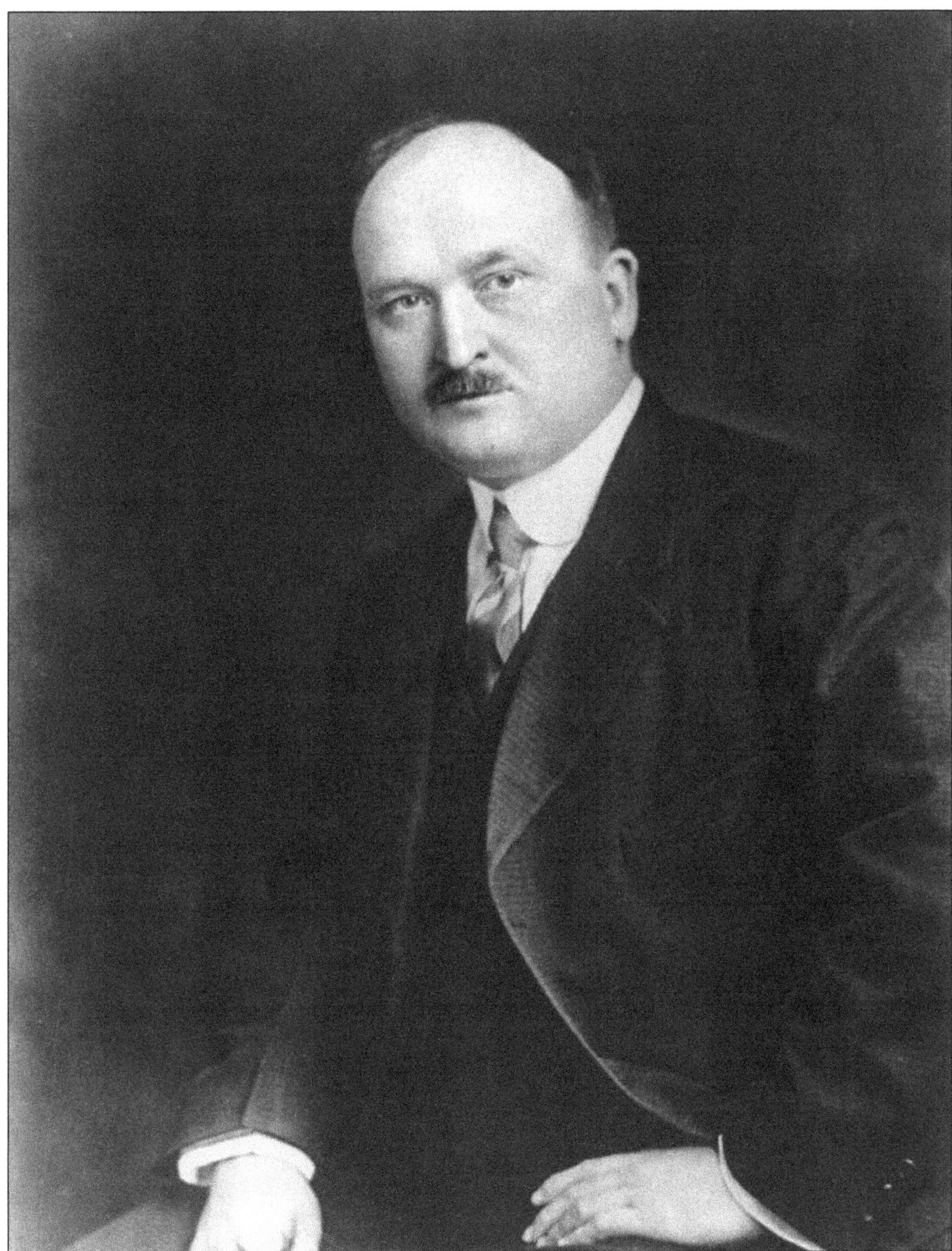

The southern bascule bridge, which opens on demand, was named after Dr. Fred Albee, a Harvard graduate, world-renowned orthopedic surgeon, inventor, and author. He came to Florida to visit some friends from Maine and decided to purchase land. Over the years, he acquired several parcels from the Palmer family. In 1917, he purchased 112 acres in what would become Nokomis and Dona Bay. (Courtesy of VMA.)

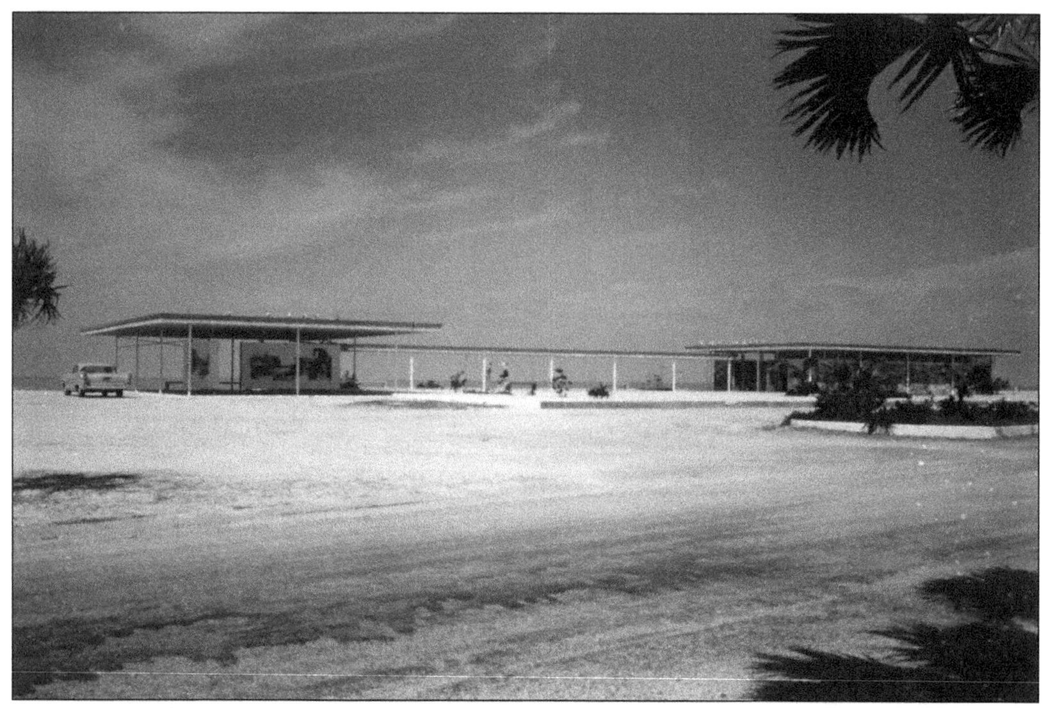

Built in 1954, the Nokomis Beach Pavilion was the first of its kind in Sarasota County. Designed by architect Jack West, a member of the Sarasota County School of Architecture, the pavilion and plaza provide, according to a *Sarasota Herald-Tribune* article, a classic example of the "minimalist forms associated with mid-century modern architecture." The pavilion has flat, thin rooflines on multiple planes, ribbon windows, and a design that creates a "strong interplay between interior and exterior spaces." (Courtesy of SCHR.)

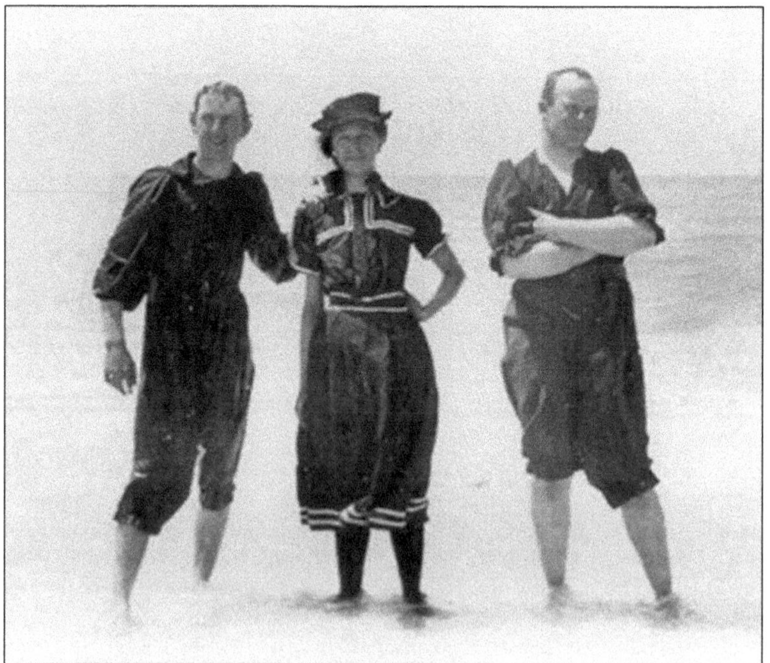

Pictured here is a group modeling the bathing attire of the 1920s. The Nokomis Beach is located on the south end of the island, directly across from the Albee Road Bridge. The beach is used for many recreational activities, including a drum circle that meets twice a week at sunset. The public beach is south of the Albee Road Bridge and near the jetties at the south end of the island. (Courtesy of SCHR.)

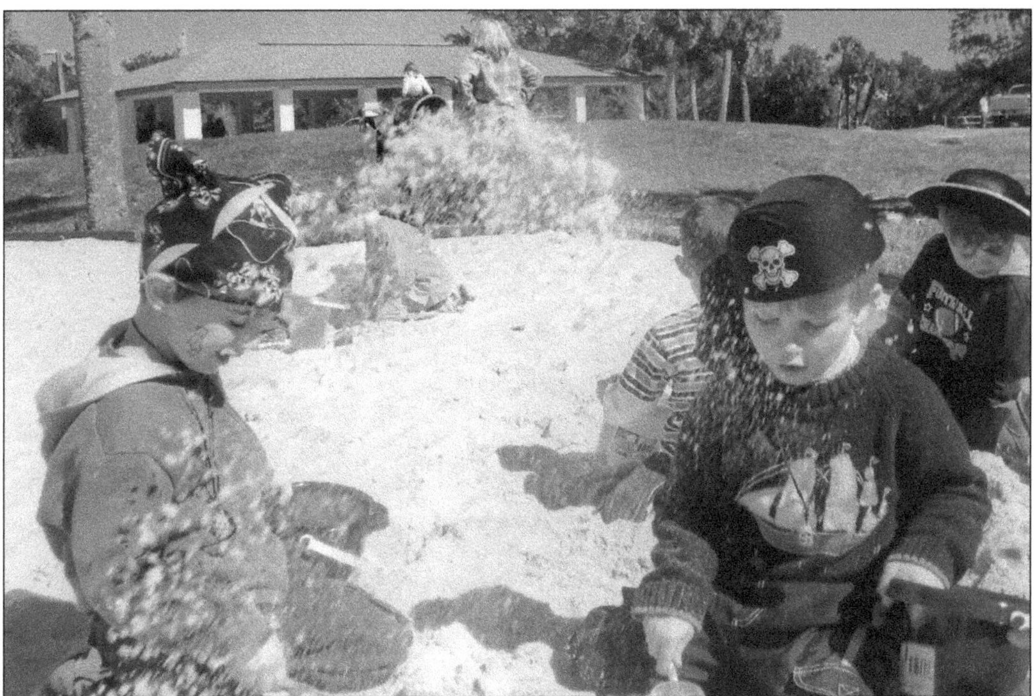

The North Jetty Park is located on the south end of the island, close to the jetty. A sheltered picnic area is available for party rentals through the Sarasota Parks and Recreation Department. There is also a pirate ship playground. Pictured here is a pirate-themed birthday party in 2006. (Author's collection.)

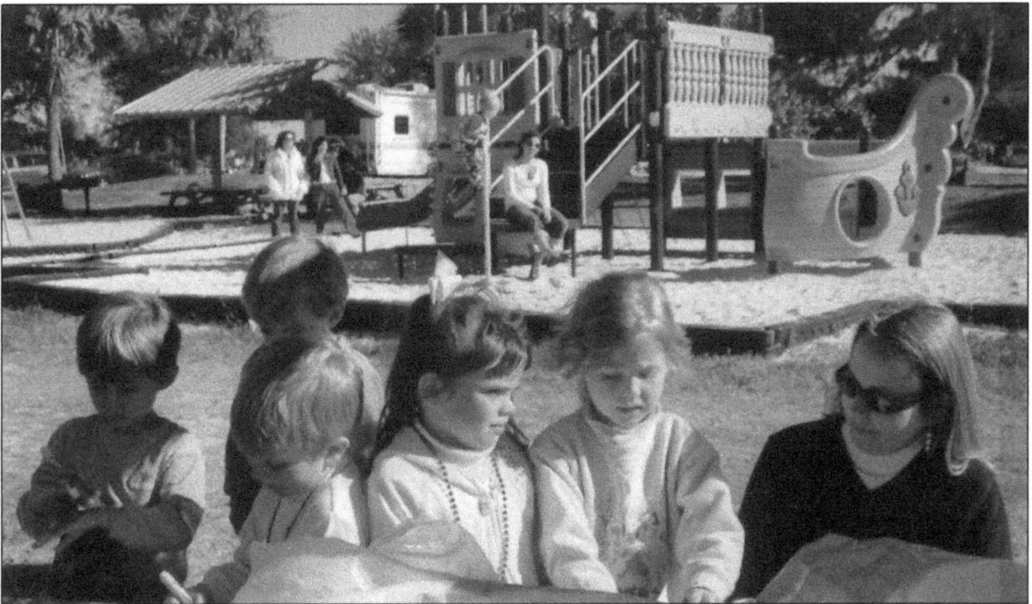

Both girls and boys enjoy having birthday parties at the North Jetty Park's pirate ship playground, which offers a low-cost party venue. Partygoers need only bring a few shovels and their imaginations. These children are waiting to have their faces painted by Jill Griffin from Wellesley, Massachusetts. (Author's collection.)

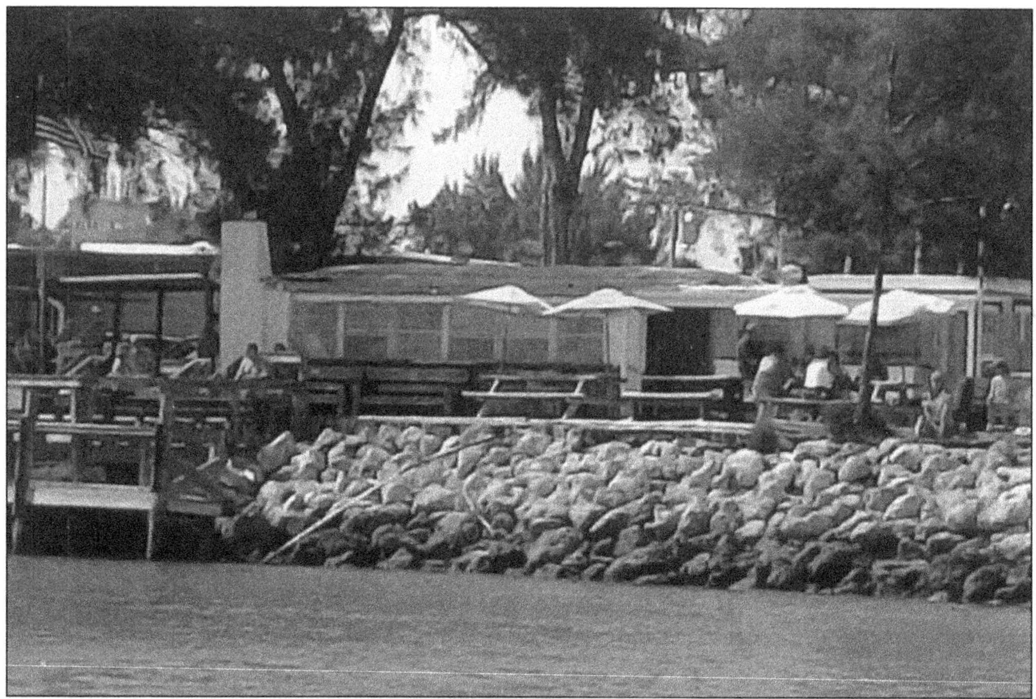

The North Jetty Fish Camp is located on the North Jetty in Nokomis. It has been a fish camp for many years. Marilyn Sawyer purchased a trolley car from Tampa and transformed it into a restaurant, which she owned for 31 years. When she decided to retire from the business, Sarasota County purchased the property and continues to offer a basic menu and sell live shrimp for bait. Many come for the coffee and to socialize. (Author's collection.)

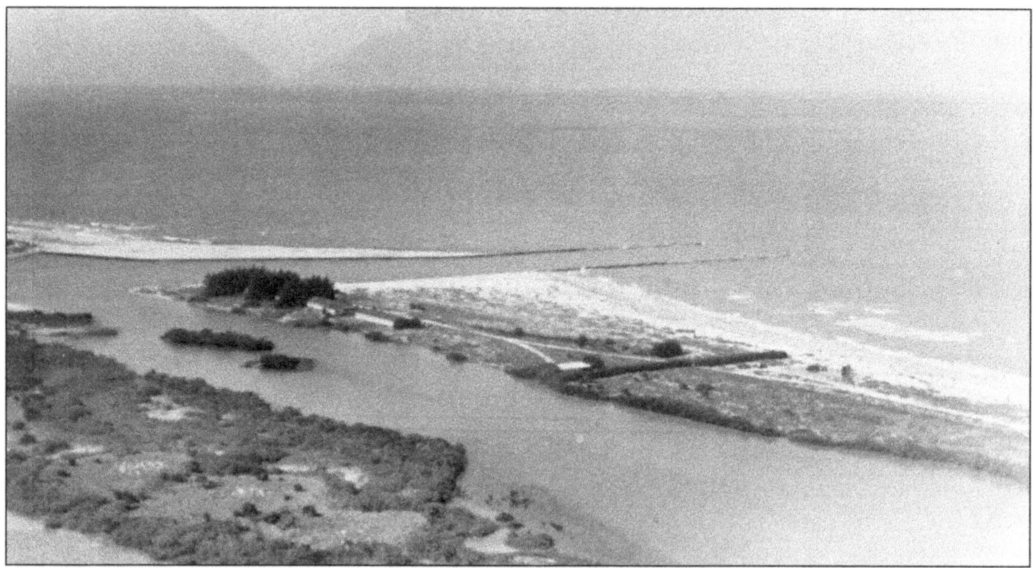

The Intracoastal Waterway leads out to the Gulf of Mexico from the North Jetty, located in Nokomis. When Casey's Pass was reinforced with jetties in 1937, it was 3 feet deep and 75 feet long, though not as wide as it is today. The major dredging took place from 1960 to 1967. The jetty has large rock boulders that fishermen use daily. (Courtesy of SCHR.)

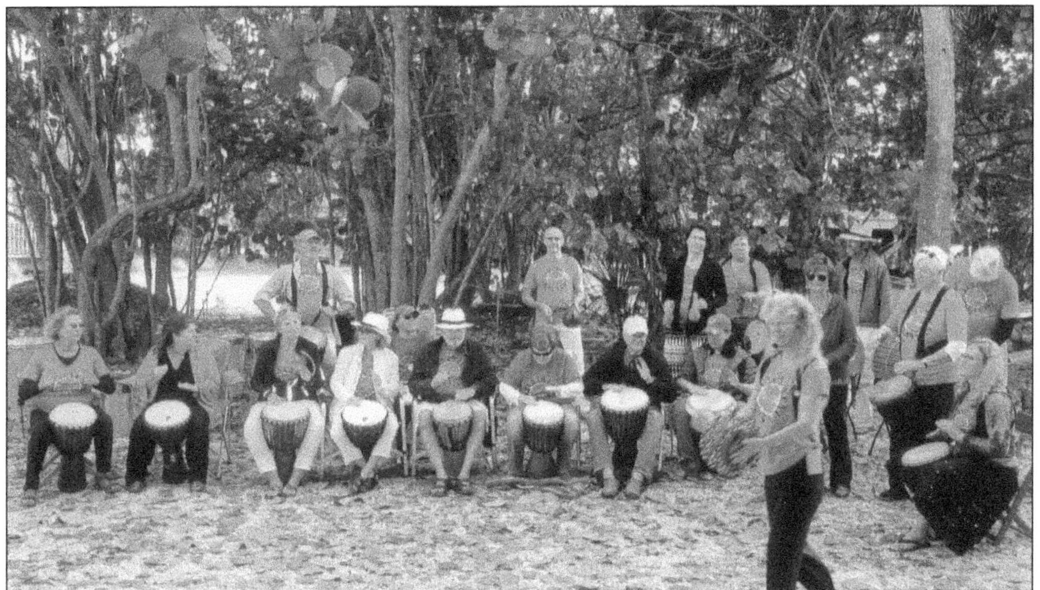

The Rhythm Inlet provides music classes to local residents, ranging in ages from prekindergarten to the elderly. Owners Jeff Henna, trained in classical and world drumming, and Barbara Gail (in front on right), trained in drumming, dance, and teaching, first came to the area from Maine to camp at Oscar Scherer Park in 2001. The rangers soon discovered their musical talent and asked them to perform for the campers. Their success allowed them to branch out into the community. (Courtesy of David A. Keane.)

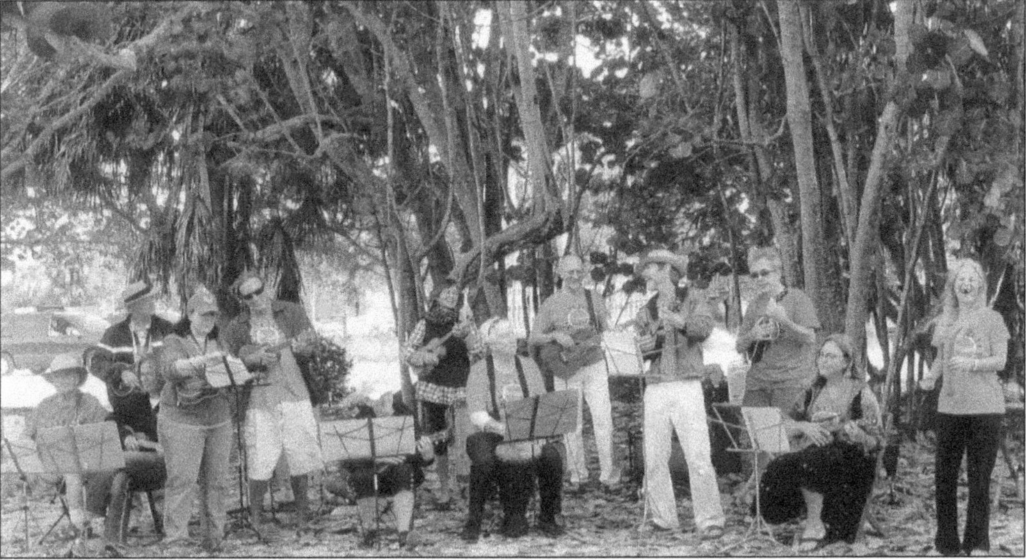

Here, Rhythm Inlet students perform a concert on Casey Key. Jeff Henna (fourth from right) and Barbara Gail (far right) opened the Rhythm Inlet in Nokomis in 2005. This was a good location for them to teach drums and percussion from around the world, such as West African djembe, Afro-Cuban congas, Brazilian samba (used in parades), and flat, Irish, and Middle Eastern frame drums. Their goal is to give people from the community "joy from making music together." They provide educational programs, including workshops at New College, Island Village Montessori School, and Warm Mineral Springs. (Courtesy of David A. Keane.)

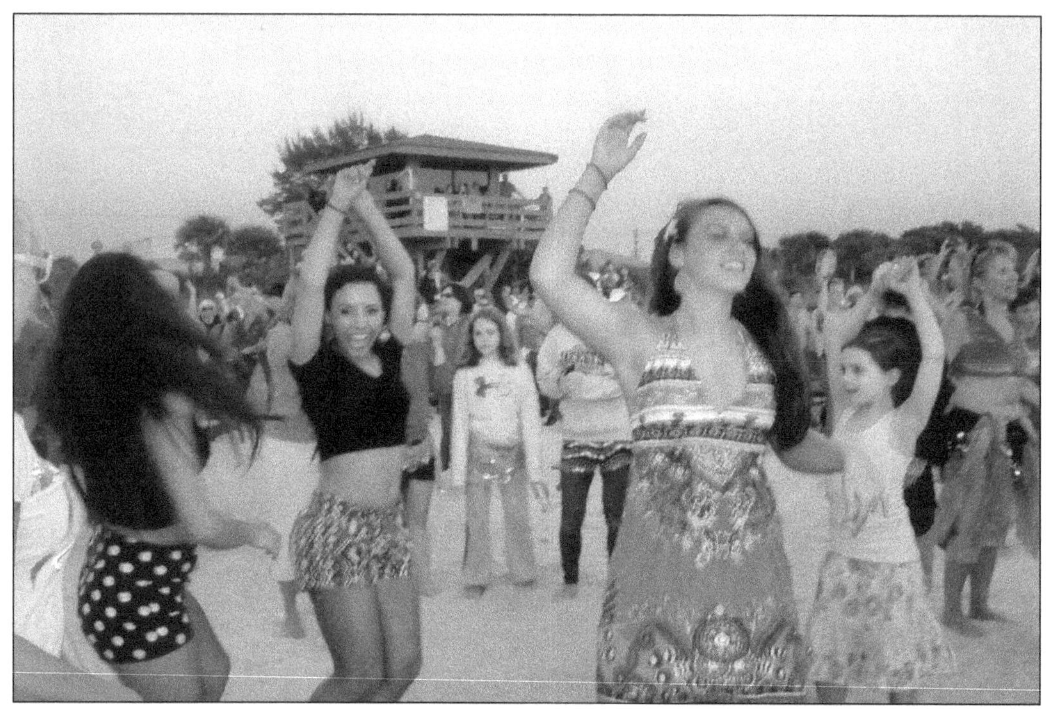

People young and old dance to the drums on Nokomis Beach. In the background is a lifeguard station. At sunset, someone in the group will play a conch shell. (Author's collection.)

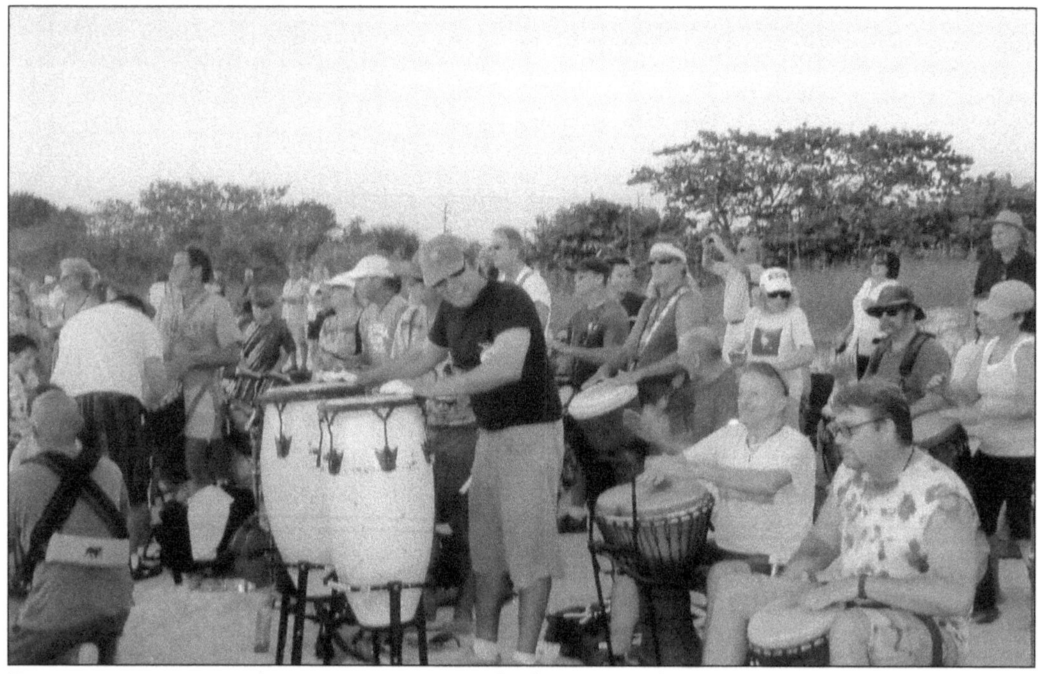

Drummers come together at sunset to watch the sun go down. It was originally a ritual to give thanks. Today, people come from all over to play on Nokomis Beach. Once a rhythm is established, drummers will follow the lead. There is also a biweekly drum circle on Siesta Key. (Author's collection.)

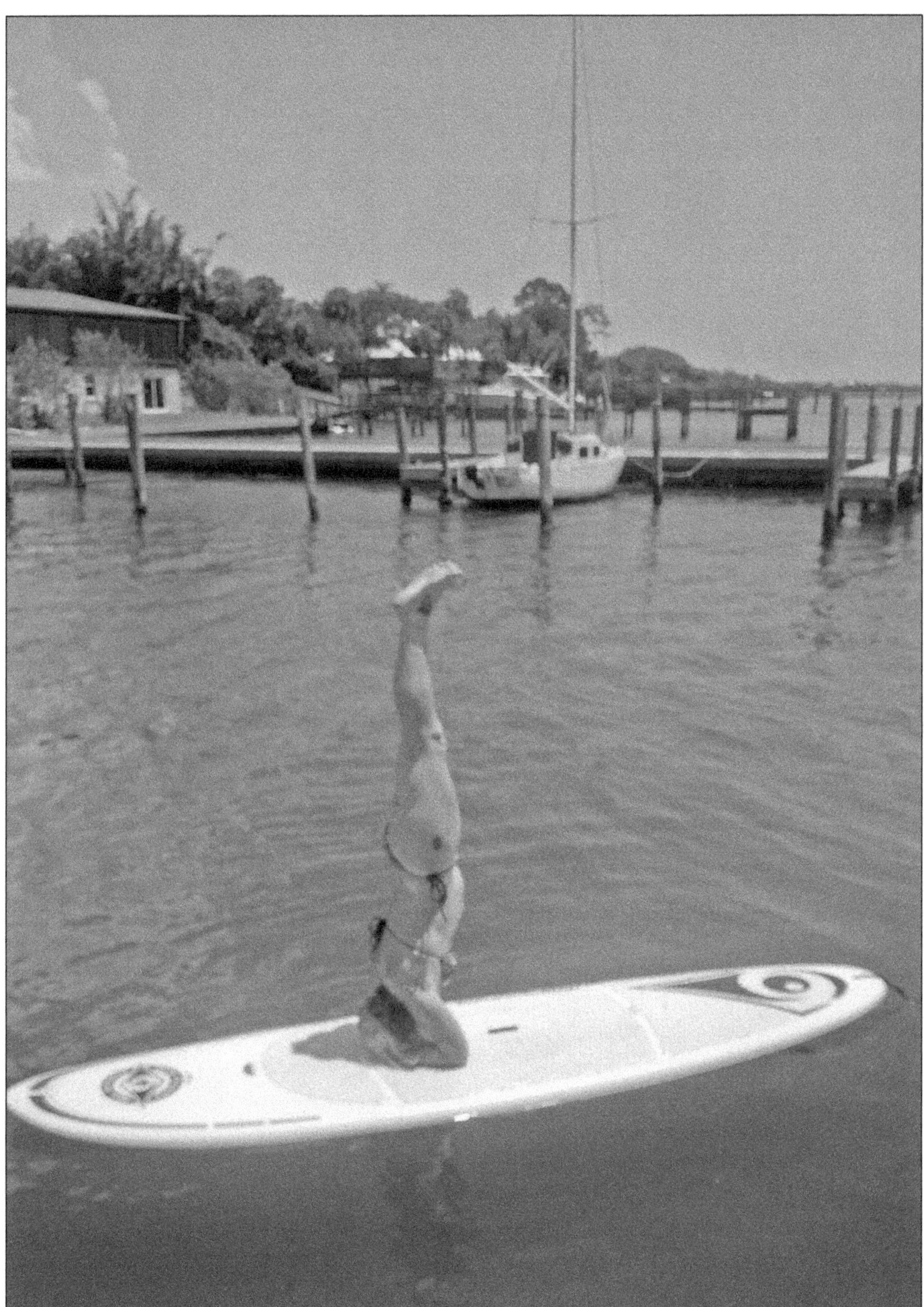

Carolyn Garcia teaches yoga and Pilates at her Yoga Plus studio in Nokomis. She also enjoys teaching paddleboard yoga, as seen here. Through exercise and meditation, she believes in achieving balance of the mind, body, and soul. (Courtesy of Carolyn Garcia.)

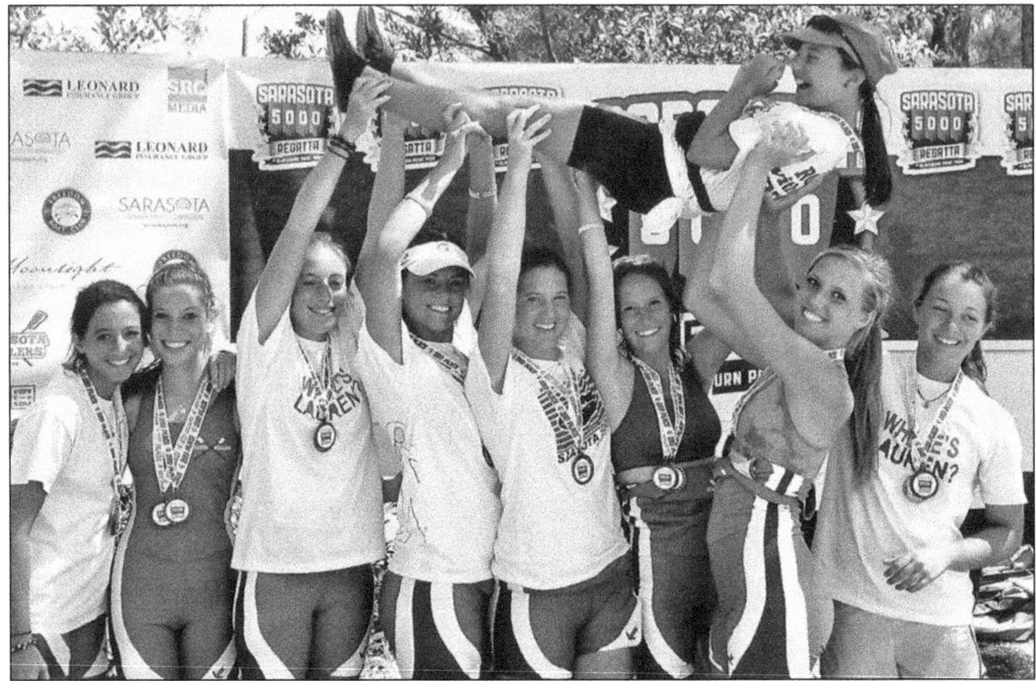


The Sarasota Scullers started with the help of Betsy and Peter de Manio, residents of Siesta Key who introduced adults to the sport of sculling. Their friend Mary Ann Garcia asked if the local high schools would be interested in sculling and donated money for a boat. Glenn Darling, a youth rowing instructor with the Sarasota Scullers, held a meeting at Riverview High School. Over 100 students attended, and the program began in 1991. (Courtesy of Penny Allen.)

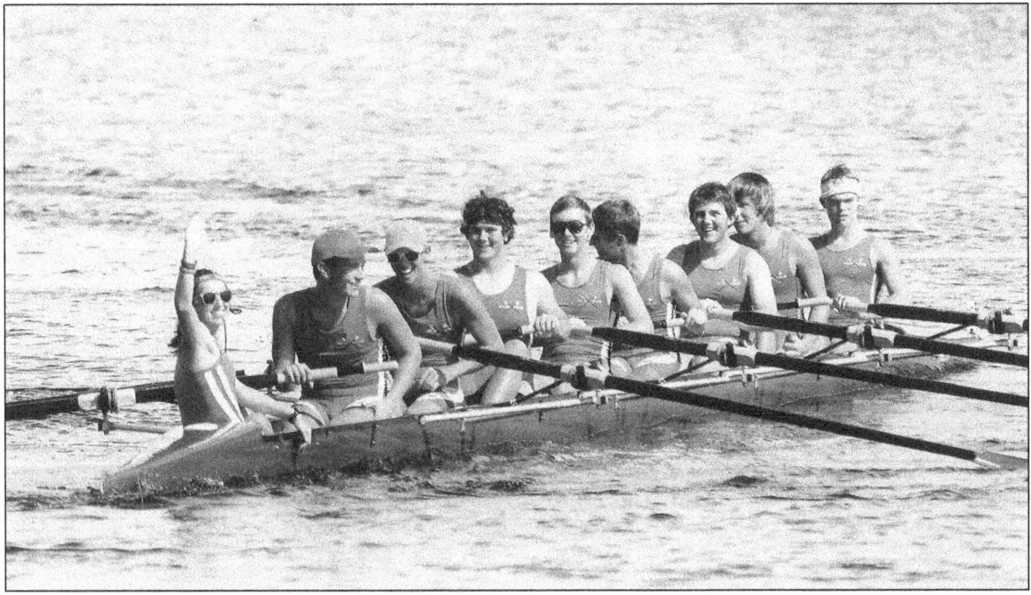

Under the guidance of head coach Dragos Alexandru, or "Coach Alex," the Sarasota Scullers Youth Rowing Program has grown to be one of the most successful rowing teams in the Southeast. The program is available for grades six through twelve. Middle school students practice twice weekly, and high school practice is six days a week. (Courtesy of Penny Allen.)

The Sarasota Scullers practice hard. The mission of the team is "to evolve teens into competitive athletes with a spirit of honor, self-respect, good sportsmanship, teamwork, high moral standards, good health and strong character." Pictured here are Kalyanna Thompson (left) and Katie Allen, who won first place at the state championship girls lightweight double. (Courtesy of Penny Allen.)

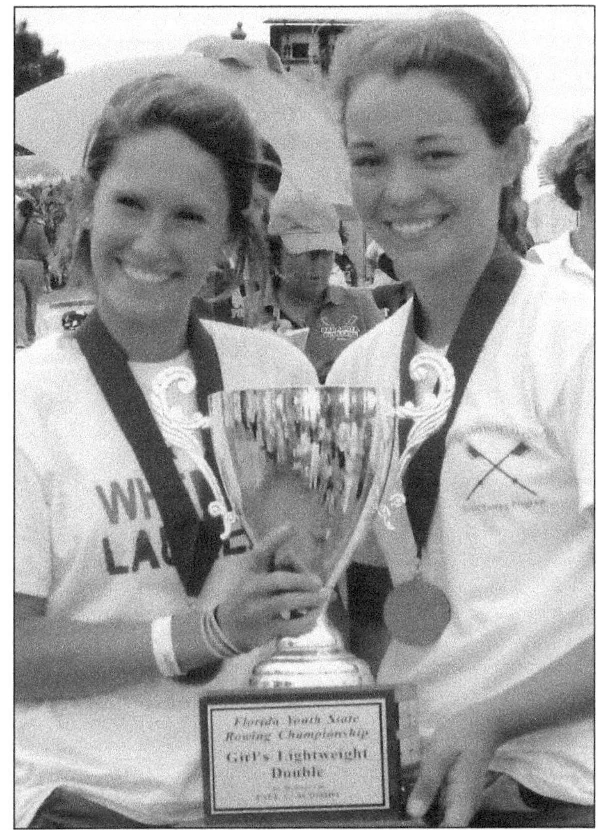


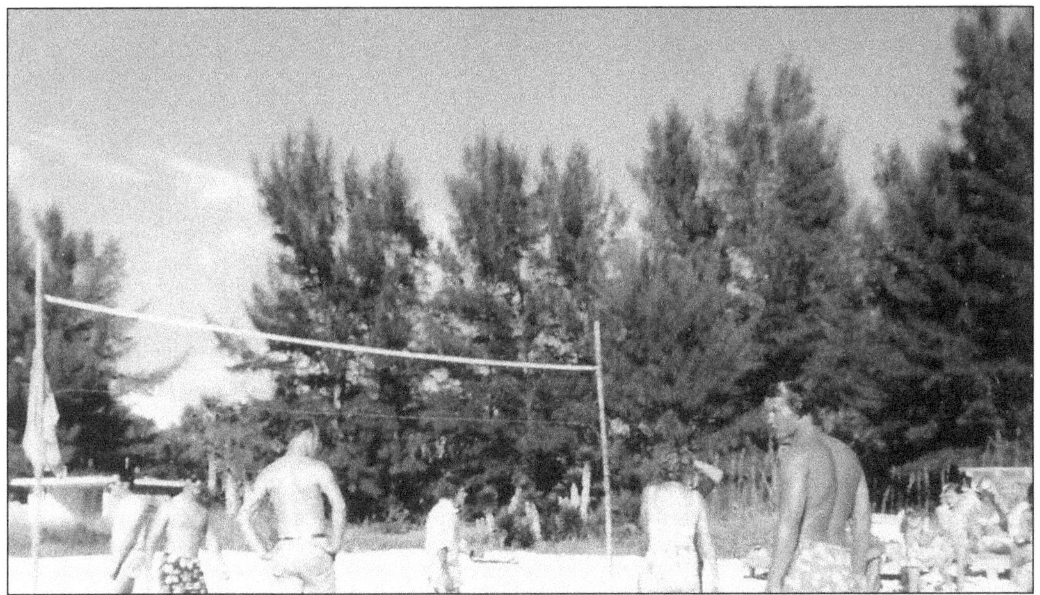

As seen in this 1970s photograph, the beach area on the Carruthers' property was much larger than it is today. During this time, residents were encouraged to remove the tall Australian pines and replace them with sea oats, which helped fight beach erosion. Daily games of volleyball were usually started by Tim York from the mainland. (Courtesy of Ann Carruthers.)

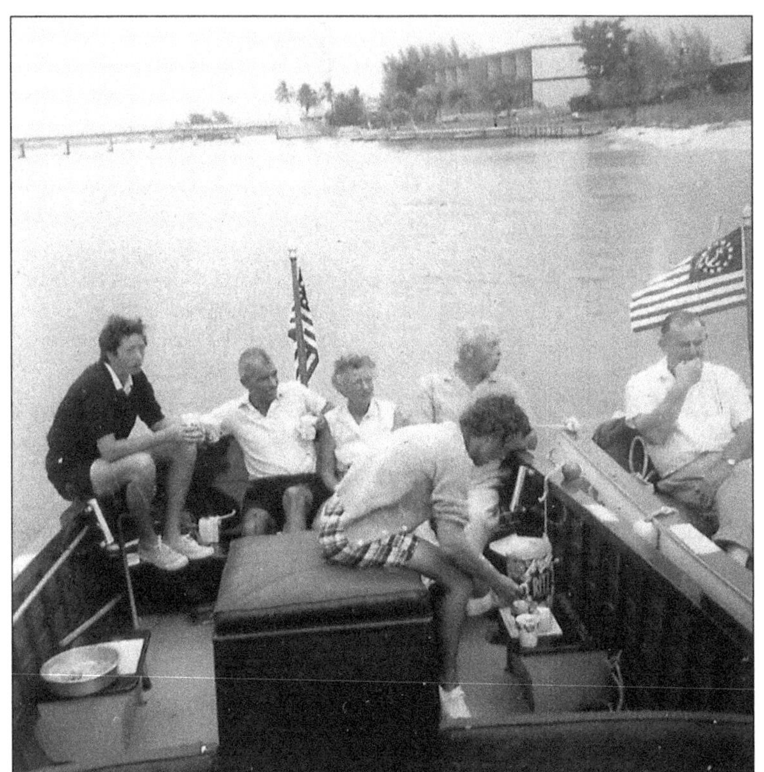

Neighbors on Casey Key enjoy watching the sunset during happy hour. Shown here are two boats rafted together in Midnight Pass. From left to right are Ann Carruthers, Welles Murphy, Ann Murphy, Grant McKeough, Marty Mason, and Herman Myers on the rafting boat. (Courtesy of Ann Carruthers.)

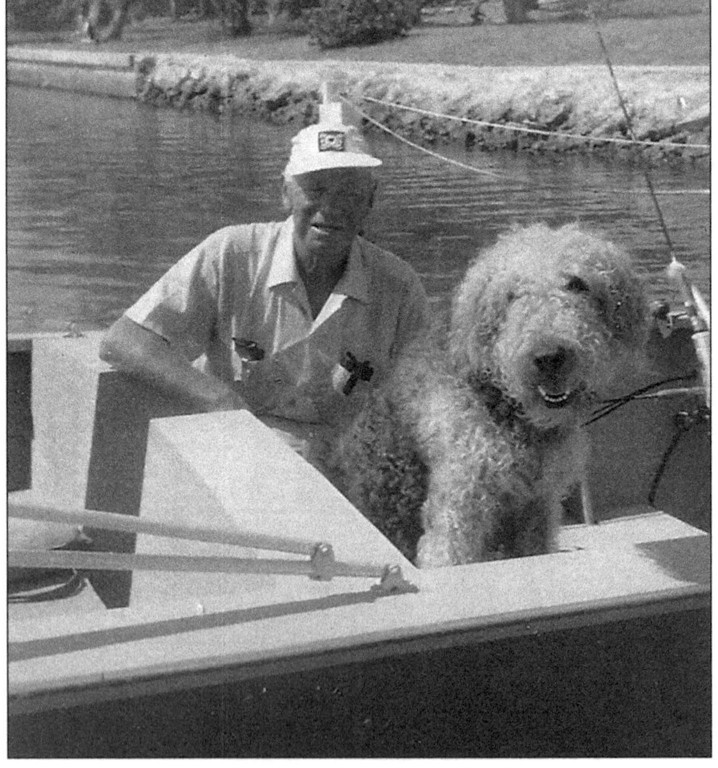

Casey, a large fluffy dog, enjoys fishing with Grant McKeough on the Intracoastal Waterway. In 1962, the bay and inland waterways were dredged. Piping the shell from the bay to the Gulf shore changed the appearance of the beach from fine coral to dirty shell. During this time, areas were in essence rebuilt due to the sand and shell being redistributed. Allegedly, the land known as Casey Key Estates is rebuilt land. (Courtesy of Ann Carruthers.)

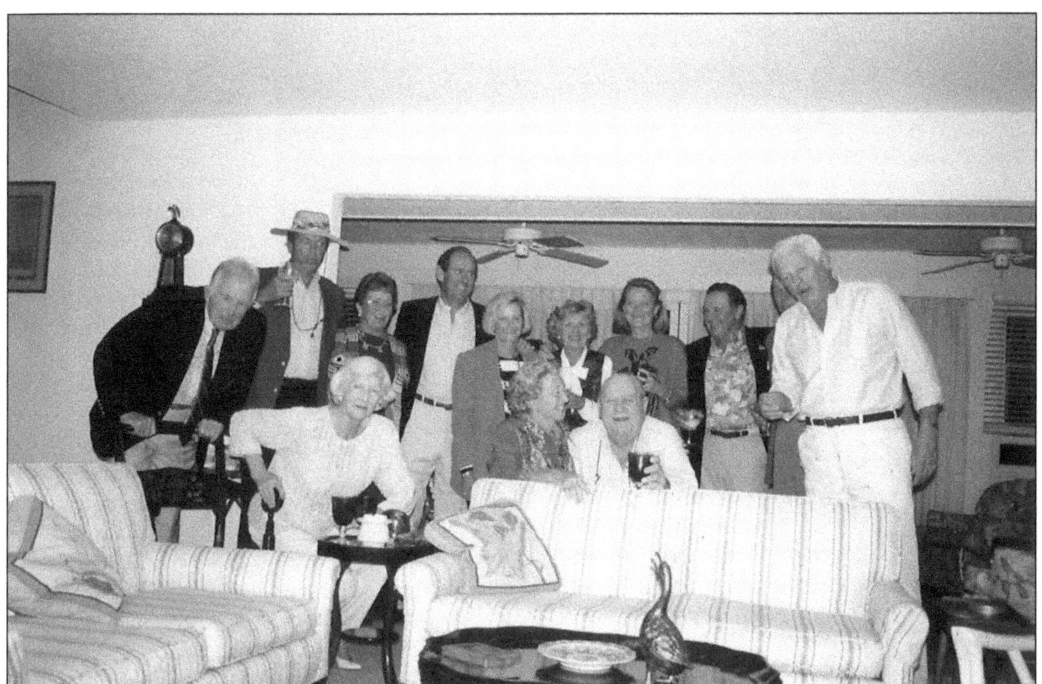

Over the years, some residents have adopted nicknames for specific sections of Casey Key. Pictured here are neighbors from Connecticut who refer to their strip of the island as "Connecticut Row" (indicated with asterisks below)—except for the Thayers, who are from Long Island, and the McKeoughs, who are from Canada. Pictured are, from left to right, (first row) Connie Watson, Ann Carruthers*, and Willy Abels; (second row) Bill Watson, Ralph Heath, Martha Thomas, Art deCordova*, Jeri deCordova*, Sarah Leigh*, Anita Heath, Bud Thomas (not hidden), George Carruthers*, and Alec Thayer*. The Thomases and Abels are not Casey Key residents. (Courtesy of Fluff Thayer*.)

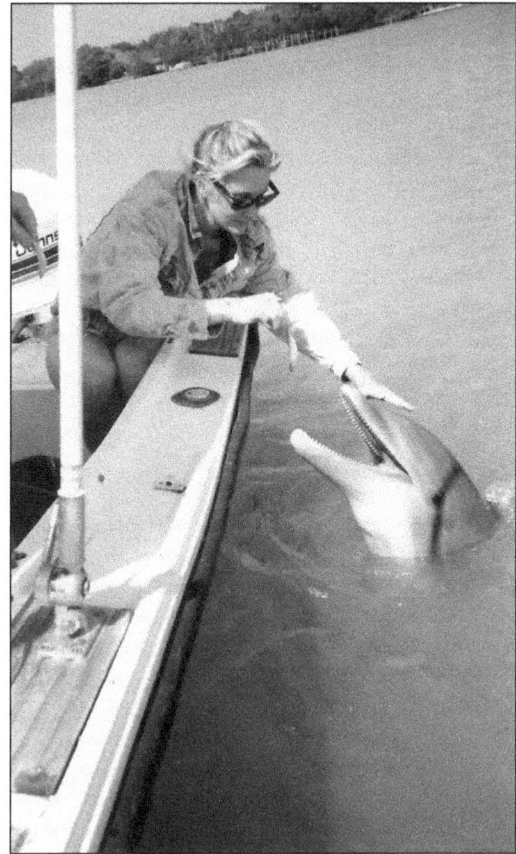

Many dolphins inhabit the Gulf of Mexico, and one in particular liked to hang out in the Intracoastal Waterway, just north of the Albee Road Bridge. He was nicknamed "Beggar" because he loved to get treats from boats waiting to pass through the bridge every half hour. Although he looks adorable, a closer look shows that he has a nice row of teeth. Today, people are asked not to feed the wildlife so the creatures will learn to obtain food in the wild. (Courtesy of Fluff Thayer.)

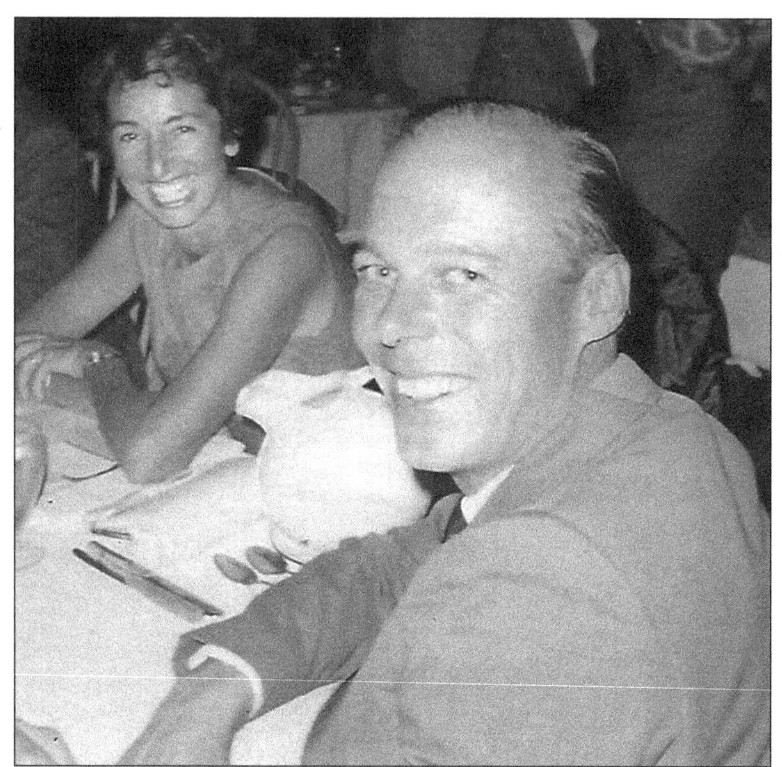

Neighbors on Casey Key enjoy getting together and celebrating life. Two places that the Carruthers chose to socialize were the Admiral's Wardroom (Pelican Alley), just over the Albee Road Bridge, and the Cardinal Hotel. Pictured here in 1966 are Ann and George Carruthers at their engagement party, which was held at the Cardinal Hotel in Nokomis. (Courtesy of Ann Carruthers.)

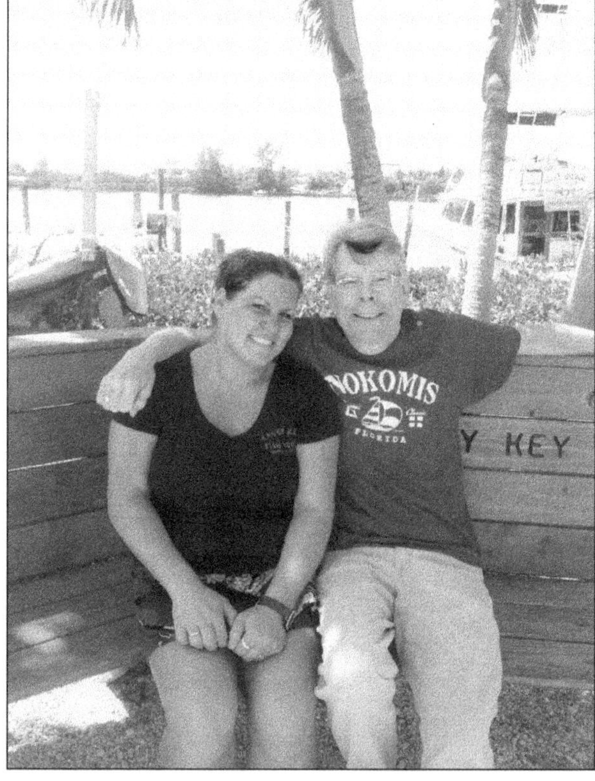


Stephen King wrote *Duma Key*, set in Sarasota County on a fictional Casey Key. In 2007, he was inducted as a grand master of the Mystery Writers of America. The author enjoys vacationing on Casey Key and eating at the Casey Key Fish House, where he is pictured with his favorite server, Gabrielle "Gabby" Groeschel. (Courtesy of Gabrielle Groeschel.)

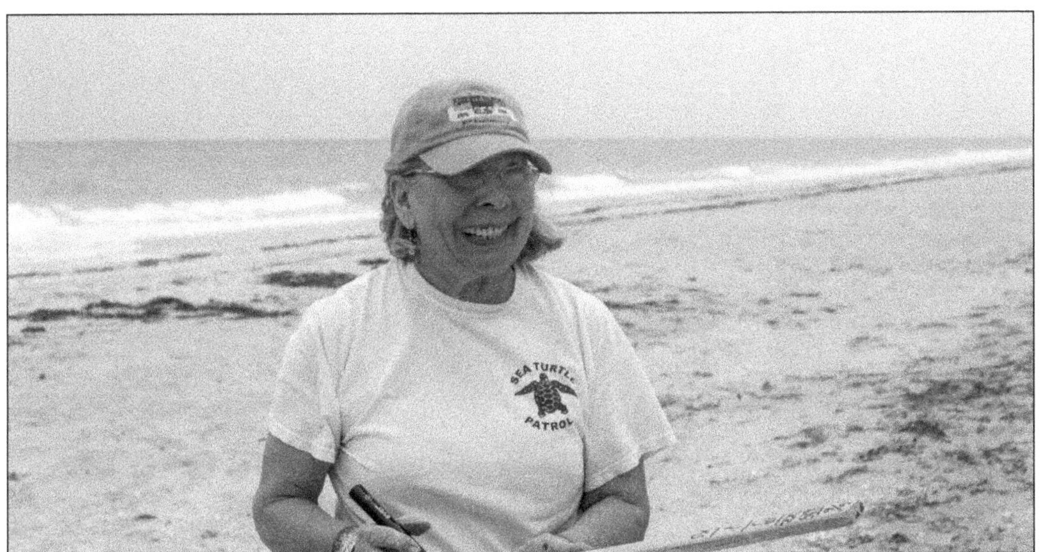


Mary Jo Perkins is a talented artist who takes photographs, then re-creates the scenes with watercolors. She and other artists who practice this medium call themselves "phartists." Mary Jo is also involved with Mote Marine's turtle-assistance program on the south end of the island. Loggerhead turtles lay eggs on Casey Key Beaches. Like tourists, loggerhead turtles only stay a short time. Volunteers are responsible for locating, staking, marking, and protecting the turtles, then checking the nest 72 hours after hatching. Florida has an ordinance that requires oceanfront homes and businesses to dim lights at night from May to June during the nesting season. (Courtesy of Jack Perkins.)

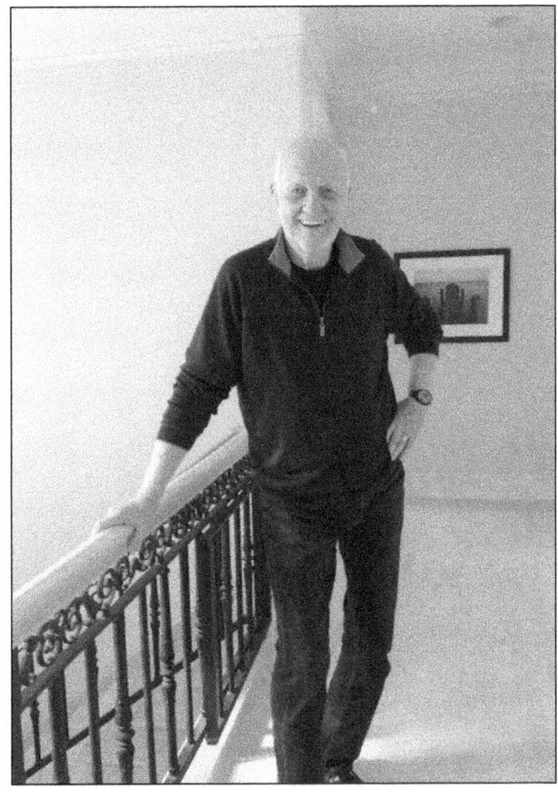

Casey Key resident Jack Perkins is an Emmy-winning television correspondent for NBC and was later a host for the acclaimed A&E series *Biography* for a total of 35 years. He retired with his wife, Mary Jo, to an uninhabited island off the coast of Maine called Moosewood, where he started writing poetry and taking photography lessons. His two poetry books, *Island Prayers* and *Marveling*, are a combination of breathtaking photographs and thought-provoking poetry, which he calls "poetography." (Courtesy of Jack Perkins.)

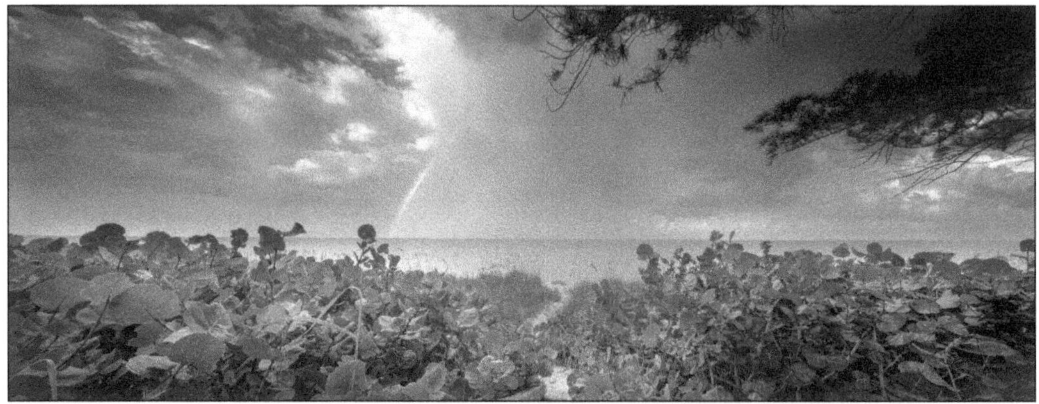

This beautiful black-and-white photograph was taken by Clyde Butcher, who captures the natural beauty of the beach. The sea grape plants help hold the sand from erosion caused by storms. A rainbow is captured off in the distance. (Courtesy of Clyde Butcher.)

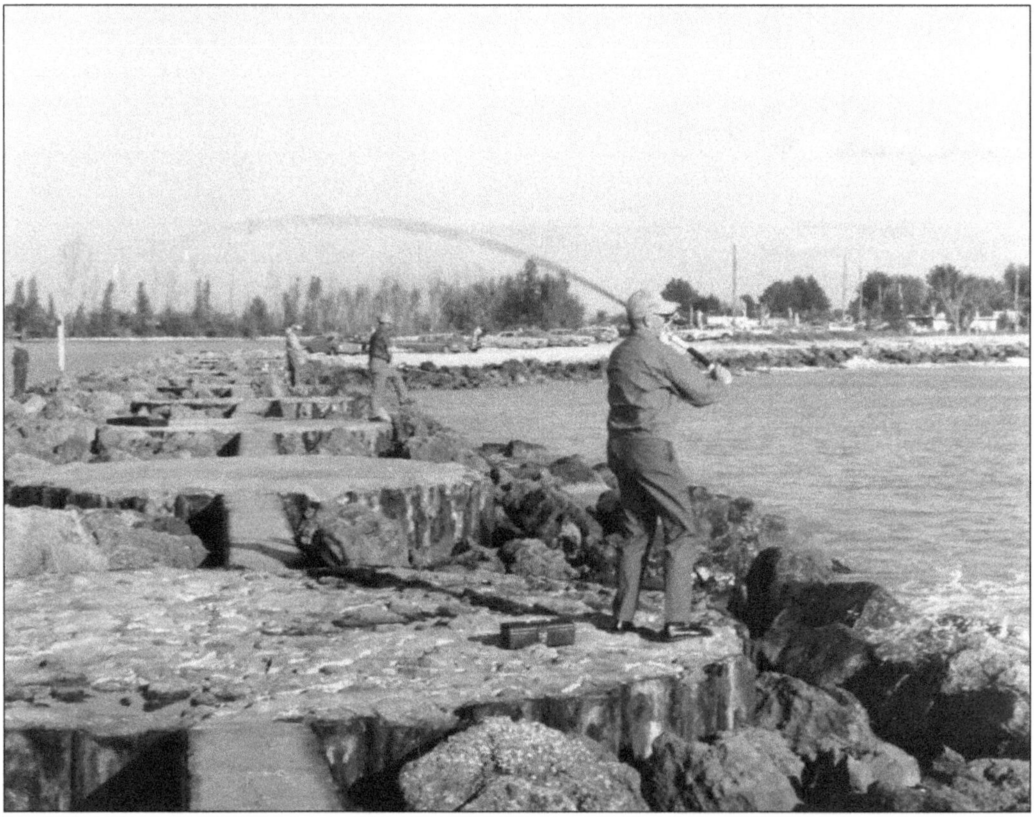

This man is standing on the North Jetty, where the large boulders provide a perch for local fishermen, who often take advantage of the incoming or outgoing tides. Throughout the year, fishing contests are held. Farther south, near Boca Grande Pass, there are large tarpon tournaments. (Courtesy of SCHR.)

# *Five*

# Venice Island

## Lat 27.0994 N, Long 82.4500 W

Surveyor John Casey and Rev. Jessie Knight were some of the first individuals to come to Venice. In the 1870s, Robert Rickford Roberts homesteaded on the south side of what is now called Roberts Bay. He sold a portion of his land to citrus farmer Frank Higel. The Venice area was originally known as Horse and Chaise because of a clump of trees that was shaped in this manner; local fishermen thought the clump of trees resembled a horse and carriage. In 1888, the post office was established under the name of Venice. Mrs. Potter Palmer promoted the area by extending the Seaboard Air Line Railway to Venice from Nokomis in 1911.

Venice was incorporated as a city in 1927. During the great Florida land boom of the 1920s, city planner John Nolen was hired to design a city for land owned by Dr. Fred Albee. When Albee sold his property to investors from the Brotherhood of Locomotive Engineers (BLE), Nolen's plan was expanded to include industrial and agricultural land east of the city.

The BLE cleared the land, paved roads, prepared construction sites, invested millions (1925–1927), and hired the New York architectural firm of Walker & Gillette to build "the city of Northern Italian Renaissance architecture."

During the early part of the 20th century, Venice was a small fishing and farming community. The BLE encouraged prospective buyers to purchase farmland and agreed to clear and level the land so that it would be ready to plant right away. In the early 1930s, Venice was hit hard by the Great Depression. City employees went unpaid, and electric streetlights were turned off due to lack of funding. The BLE went into receivership, and its holdings were liquidated.

Before the 1950s, the small population could not afford a hospital. Residents of Venice would have to travel to Sarasota until O.W. Caspersen, a wealthy businessman from Venice, donated $10,000 and started a hospital. He started a committee run by Mrs. Charles McGee Roberts and Brazil E. Bowen. In December 1951, South Sarasota County Memorial Hospital was opened.

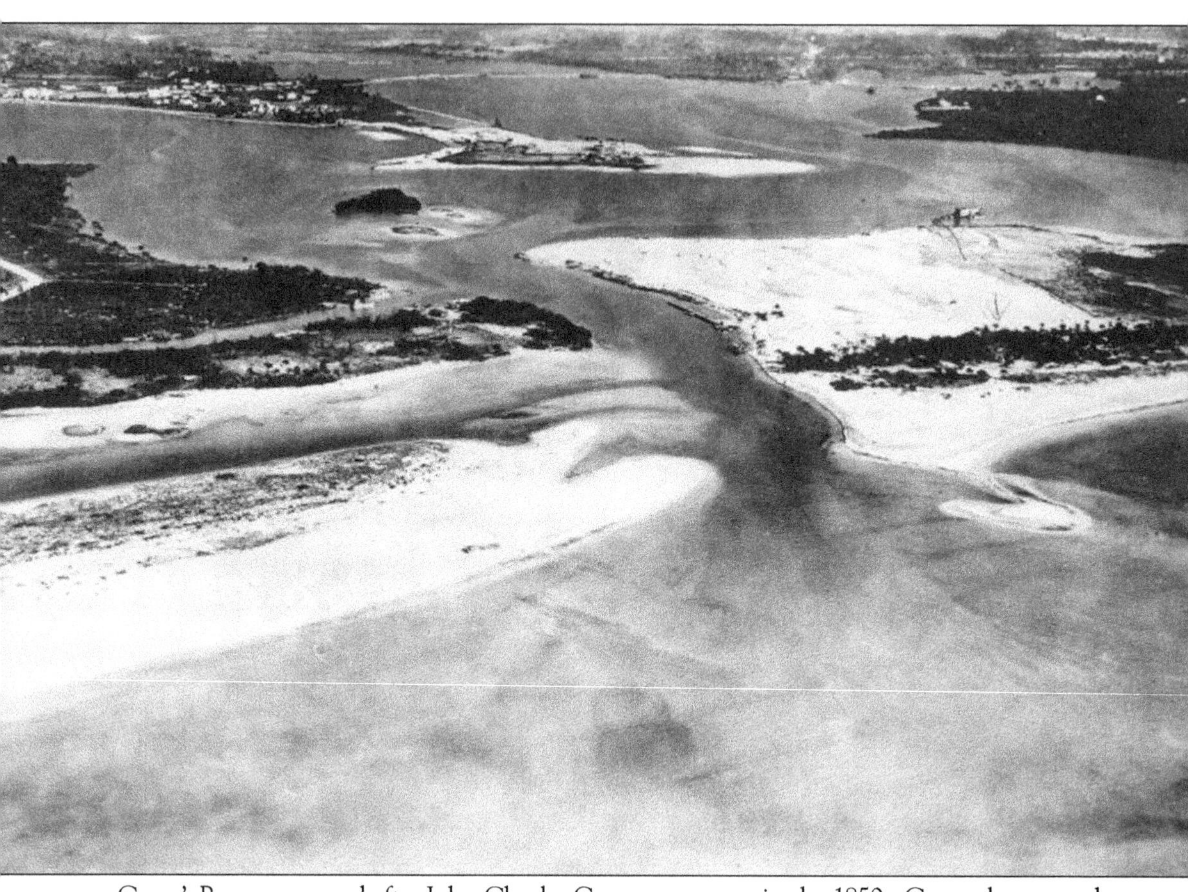

Casey's Pass was named after John Charles Casey, a surveyor in the 1850s. Casey also spent three years working for the US Coast Guard and Geodetic Survey, which was completed in 1851. The pass later became a jetties project thanks to the River and Harbor Act of 1935. (Courtesy of VMA.)

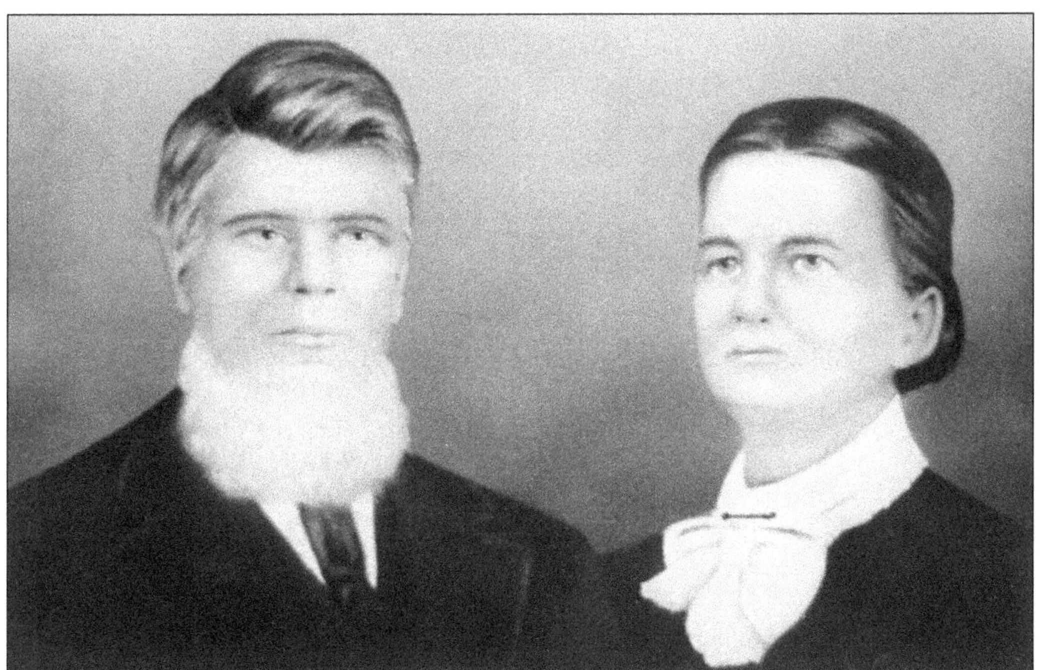

In 1868, Rev. Jesse Knight, his wife, Caroline Rebecca Varn Knight, and their family came to Venice. He acquired land grants of 160 acres through the Armed Occupation Act of 1842 and the Script Warren Act of 1850, awarded to veterans who had served in the military. In 1903, Reverend Knight deeded property for the first church, called Knights Chapel. The Methodist Episcopal church was demolished during a hurricane in 1926. (Courtesy of VMA.)

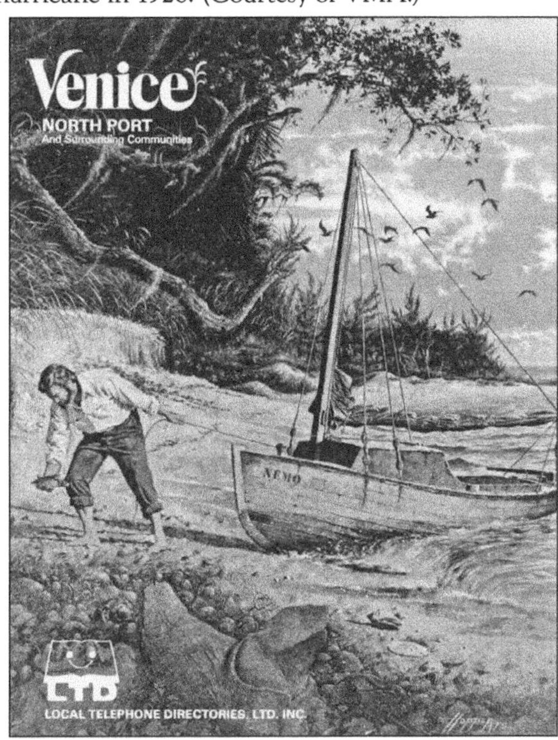


Frank Higel, from Philadelphia, was a Union officer who purchased land from Robert Roberts. In 1881, he acquired the land in Horse and Chaise (now Venice). Higel built an attractive two-story wooden house with outdoor balconies to catch the sea breeze. He was one of the pioneers who suggested the Venice name for the first post office. The Higel family worked as fishermen, boatbuilders, and contractors. They also canned and sold citrus goods, including jam, lemon juice, and orange wine. This painting of Frank Higel was used for the cover of a telephone book. (Courtesy of VMA.)

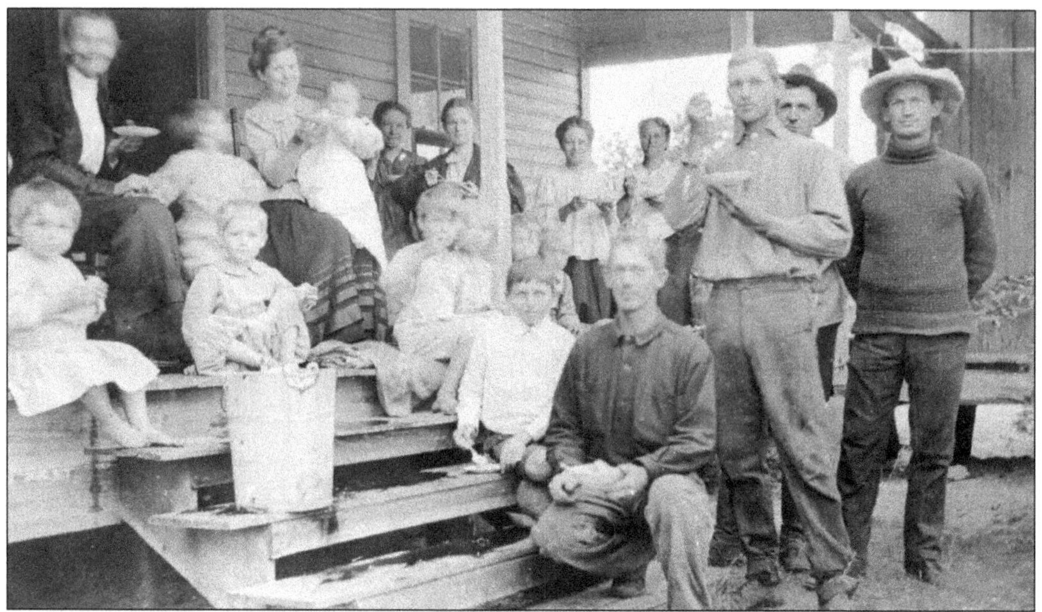

This is a photograph of the Curry family. Darwin Curry was the first postmaster in 1888. The Currys and Higels decided on the name Venice for the post office, which was located south of Shakett Creek (now Portia Street) in Nokomis. Shakett Creek gets its name from having to shake something to get the livestock to cross through the creek. A historical marker identifies the post office on the corner of Portia Street and Hillcrest Avenue. (Courtesy of VMA.)

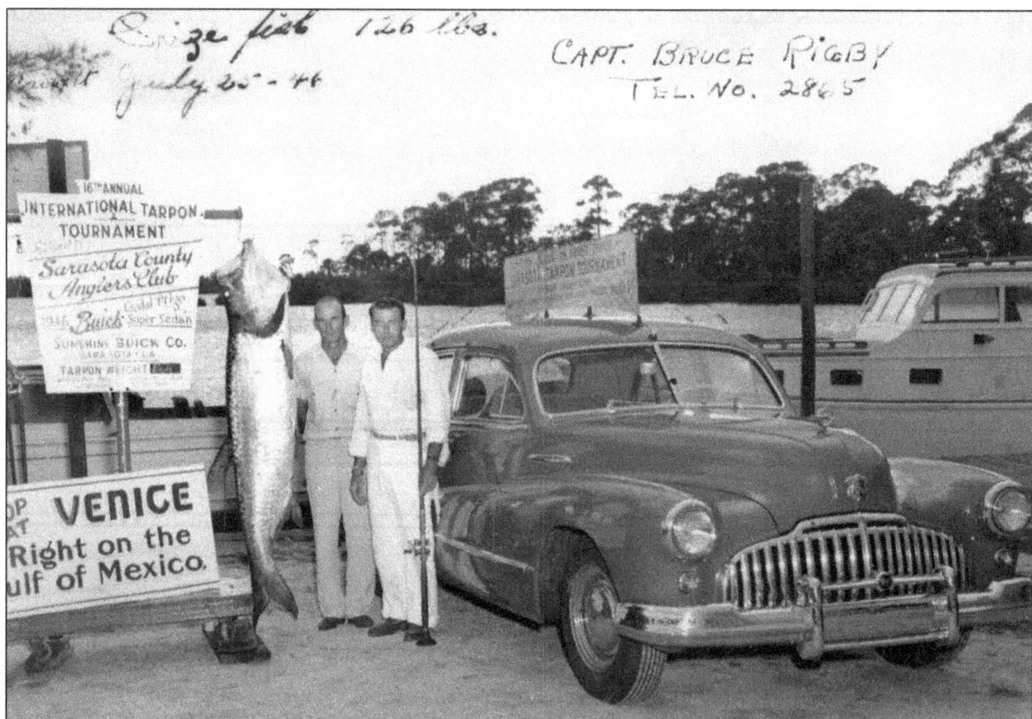


The 16th Annual Tarpon Tournament took place in Shakett Creek in 1946. Pictured are Capt. Bruce Rigby (left) and Roger Townsend with their catch, a 126-pound fish. (Courtesy of SCHR.)

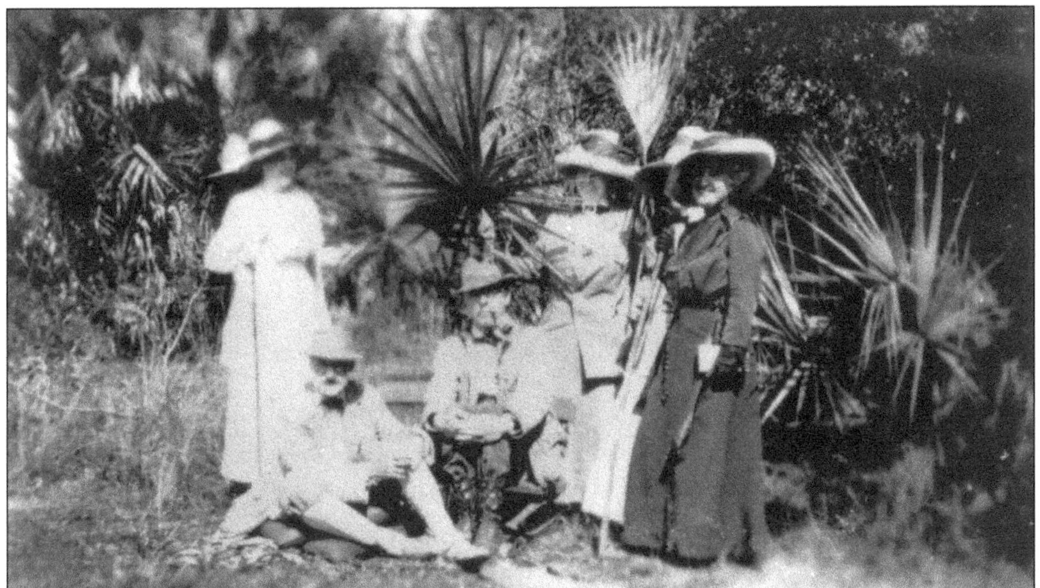

In 1910, Bertha Honore Palmer acquired many acres in Sarasota County, including Venice, from Joseph Lord of Manatee County. A wealthy widow and businesswoman from Chicago, Palmer came to the area with her two sons, Honore and Potter. She became one of the largest landowners in the area, acquiring about 25 percent of Manatee County. Palmer (far right) is pictured here on her land in Osprey. She provided running water for her guests who stayed in the Frank Guptill House. (Courtesy of Historic Spanish Point.)

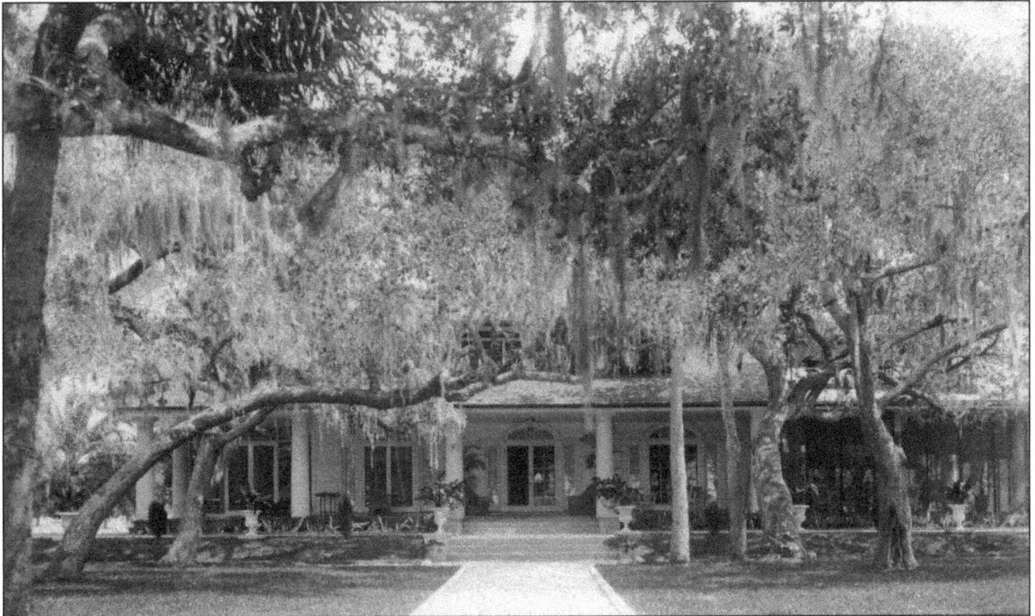

Bertha Honore Palmer started the Sarasota-Venice Company to market and develop her land, hiring Joseph Lord as an officer. She made plans to develop Venice but felt the cost was too high, and during World War I, manpower was scarce. She did plat a small area of six streets and sold the land for homes. Palmer bought an old hunting lodge for herself in Osprey, called the Oaks. (Courtesy of Historic Spanish Point.)

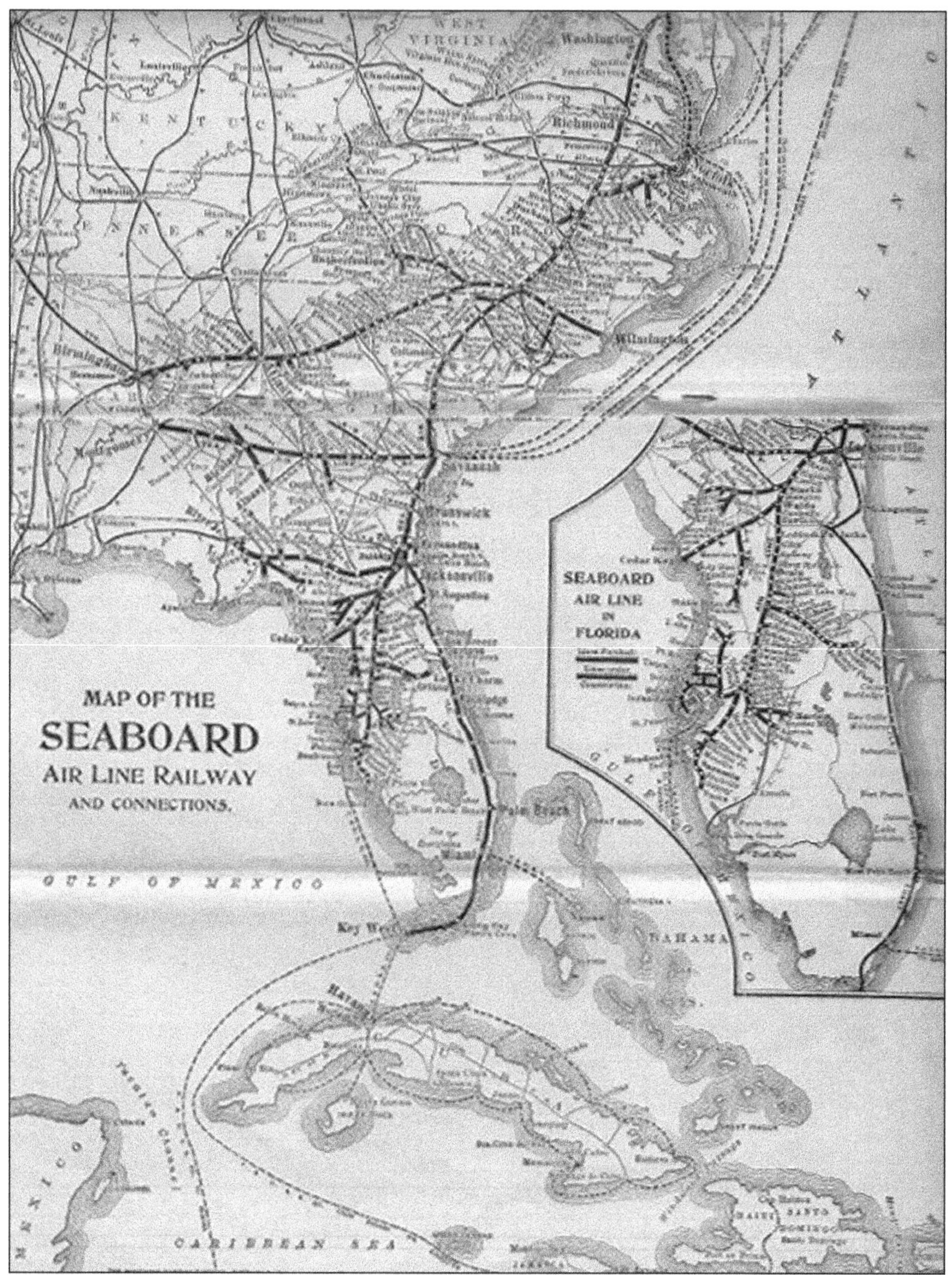


Bertha Honore Palmer convinced the Seaboard Air Line Railway to extend its tracks 16 miles from Fruitville Junction in Sarasota down to Venice in 1911. The new rail stop was called the Venice Train Station, which helped the community to grow and gave farmers another way to transport and sell their goods. It was not until the Florida land boom that the railway extended farther south. In 1915, Palmer's Sarasota-Venice Company platted, surveyed, and filed with the Town of Venice. At that time, it consisted of only four blocks and six streets. Palmer hired Charles Wellford Leavitt to design a resort town. He did as requested, but the Palmers felt the cost was excessive and dropped the idea of developing all of Venice. (Courtesy of VMA.)

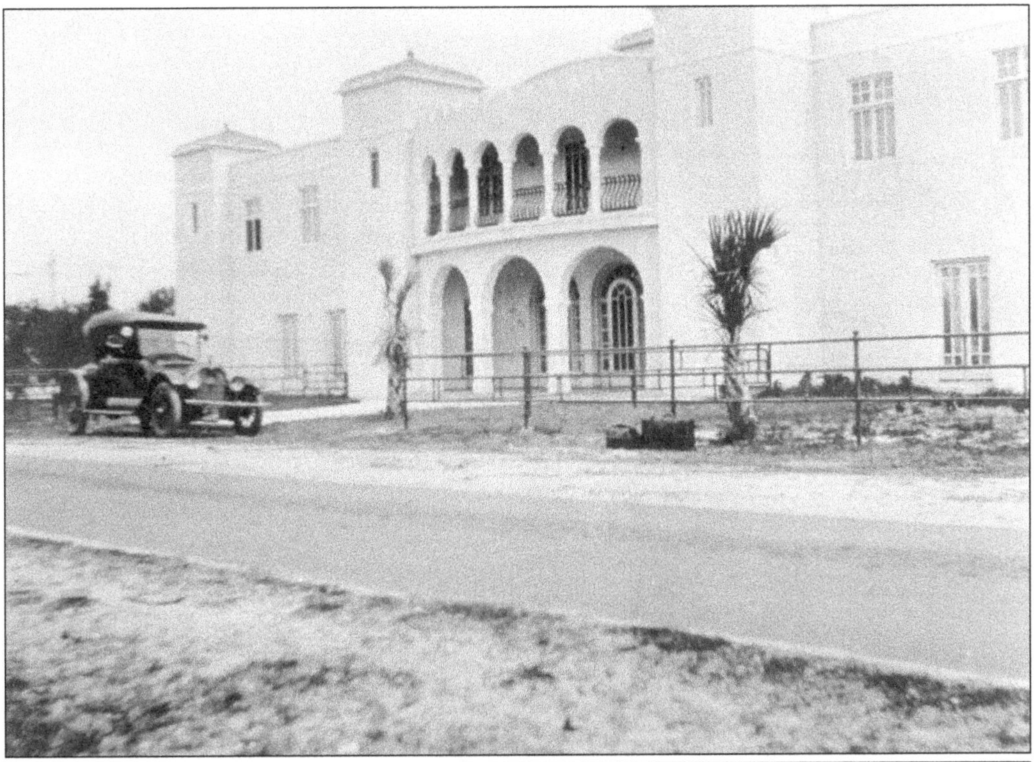

Over the years, Dr. Fred Albee acquired several parcels from the Palmer family. In 1917, he purchased 112 acres in what would become Nokomis and Dona Bay. He built a home and the Pollyanna Inn Resort (pictured). In 1925, Albee was able to buy a prime piece of property, 2,916 acres, which eventually would become the city of Venice. He hired city planner John Nolen to develop Venice. Nolen staffer Hale Walker designed a resort that would include canals for gondoliers, houseboats, and luxurious hotels. (Courtesy of VMA.)

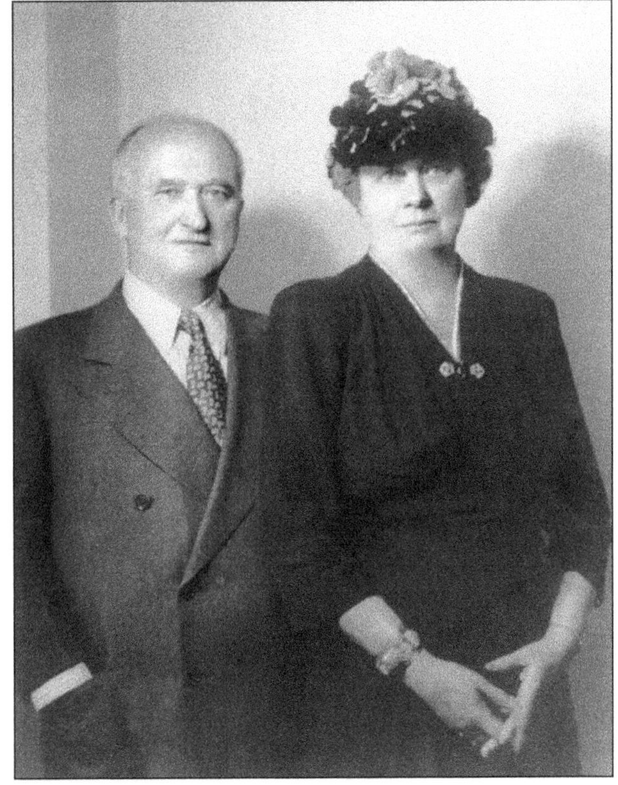

Based on the advice of his wife, Louella, Dr. Albee decided the timing was not right and the cost was not feasible, thus he did not develop Venice. In 1925, he sold the land to the Brotherhood of Locomotive Engineers, which finally was able to develop the wonderful and beautiful island of today. (Courtesy of VMA.)

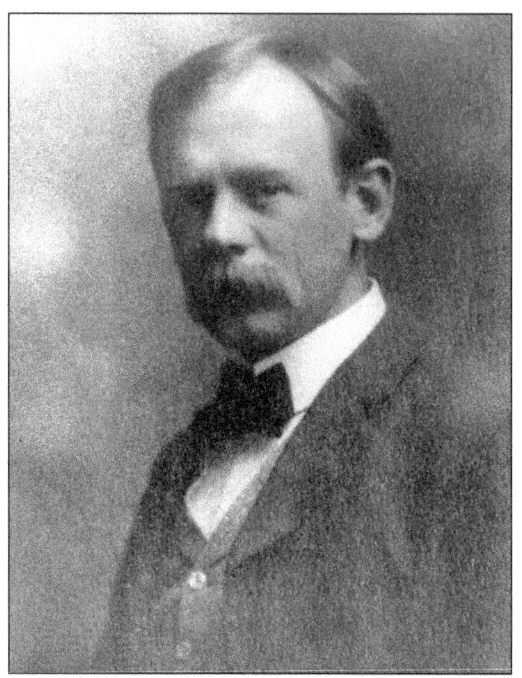

World-renowned city planner John Nolen was first retained by Dr. Fred Albee. After purchasing and developing part of Nokomis, Dr. Albee obtained land in Venice from the Sarasota-Venice Land Company and wanted Nolen to develop a city. In 1926, when the Brotherhood of Locomotive Engineers offered to purchase the land, Nolen was able to complete plans for the city for the new owners. (Courtesy of VMA.)

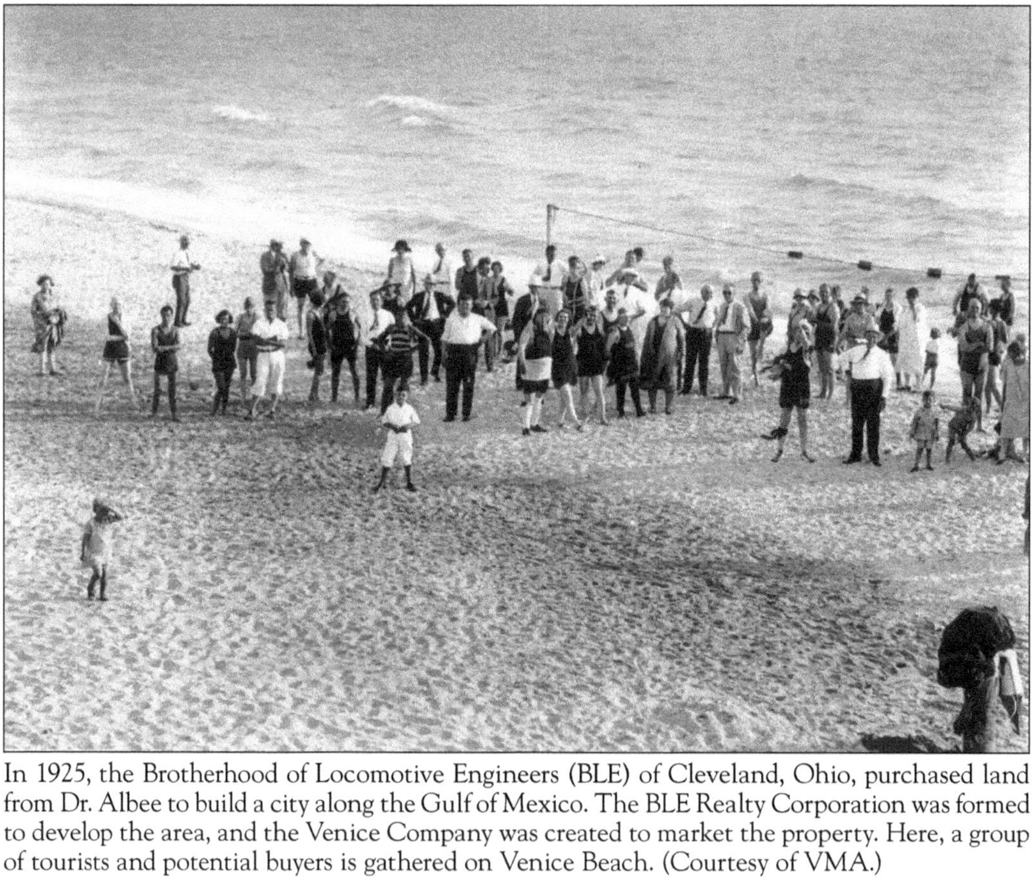

In 1925, the Brotherhood of Locomotive Engineers (BLE) of Cleveland, Ohio, purchased land from Dr. Albee to build a city along the Gulf of Mexico. The BLE Realty Corporation was formed to develop the area, and the Venice Company was created to market the property. Here, a group of tourists and potential buyers is gathered on Venice Beach. (Courtesy of VMA.)

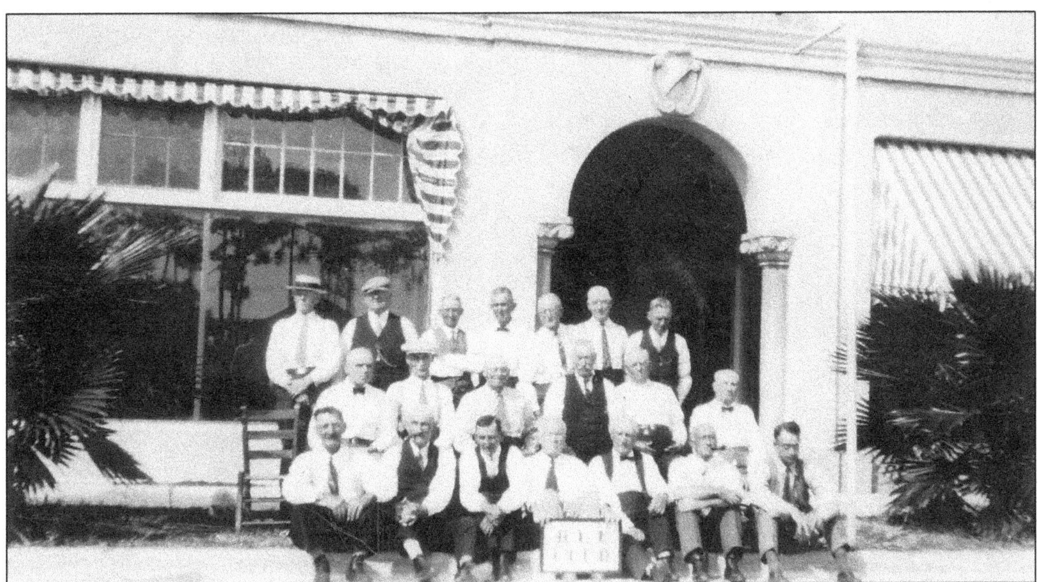

Here, the BLE group poses in front of the San Marco Hotel in 1927. For entertainment, the BLE built a beach casino, civic center, playground, and band pavilion. The less than 1,000 residents who lived in Venice enjoyed wrestling, boxing, croquet, clock golf, and archery. (Courtesy of VMA.)

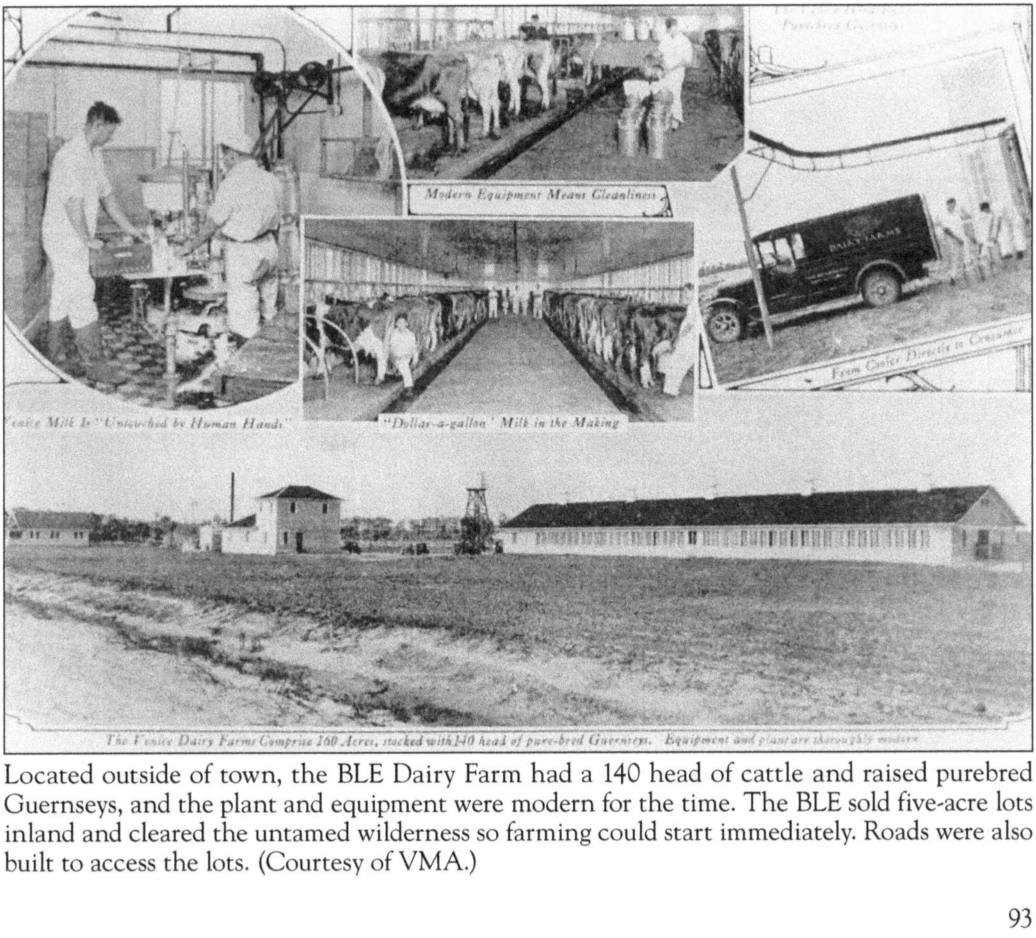

Located outside of town, the BLE Dairy Farm had a 140 head of cattle and raised purebred Guernseys, and the plant and equipment were modern for the time. The BLE sold five-acre lots inland and cleared the untamed wilderness so farming could start immediately. Roads were also built to access the lots. (Courtesy of VMA.)

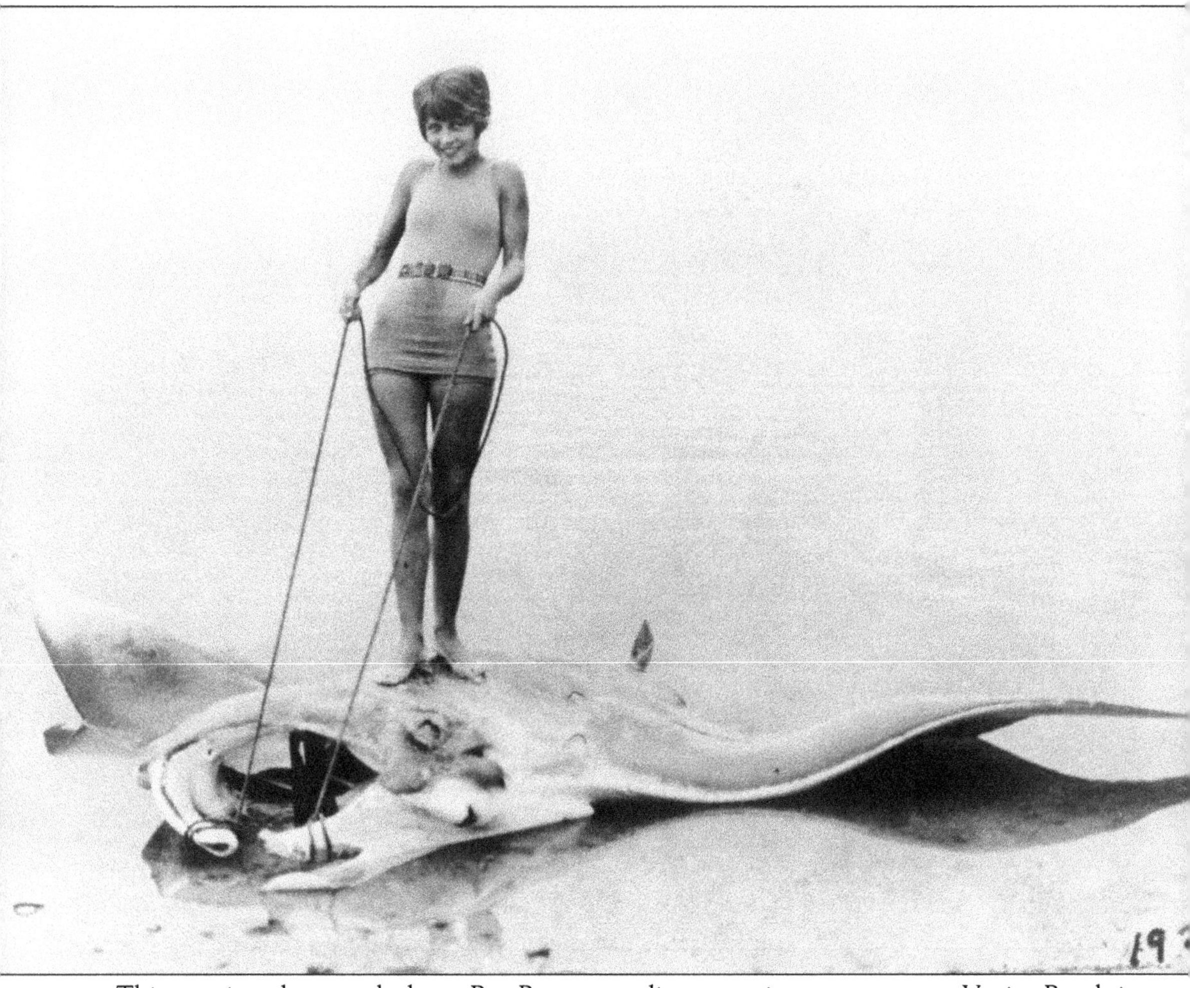

This amazing photograph shows Bea Brown standing on a giant manta ray at Venice Beach in 1927. Brown was a daughter of Jay E. Brown, an official from the BLE. Venice Beach has always been a place for young people to gather and have fun swimming, collecting shells, or just hanging out at the beach. (Courtesy of VMA.)

In the 1920s, the BLE hired architects from the New York firm of Walker & Gilbert, contractor George A. Fuller, and landscape architect Prentiss French. They envisioned a uniquely attractive community that would conform to a Northern Italian Renaissance architectural style. (Courtesy of VMA.)

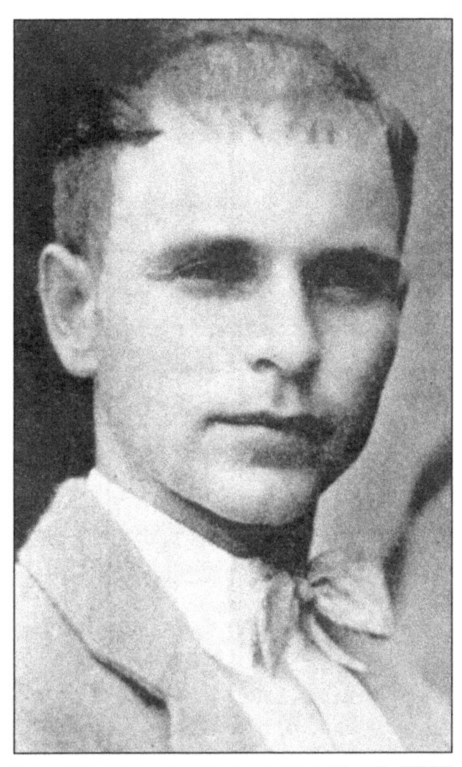

Built in 1927, the Venice Train Station was home to the Seaboard Air Line Railway. The train was used by many people, including prospective buyers and cadets from the Kentucky Military Institute (KMI). Ringling Bros. and Barnum & Bailey Circus wintered in Venice from 1960 to 1992. The last train to use the tracks belonged to the circus when it left Venice. The station fell into disuse and was abandoned for many years, until Sarasota County purchased it from the railway. The county restored it, and in 2005, it became available to the public for tours. (Courtesy of VMA.)

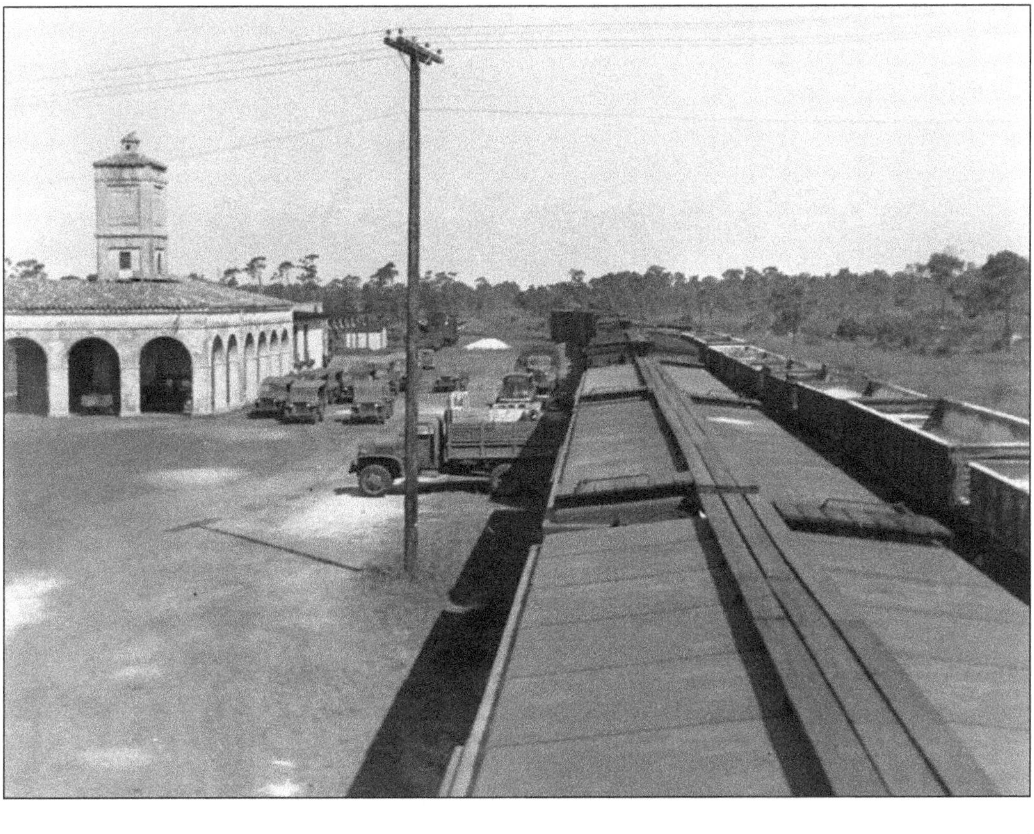

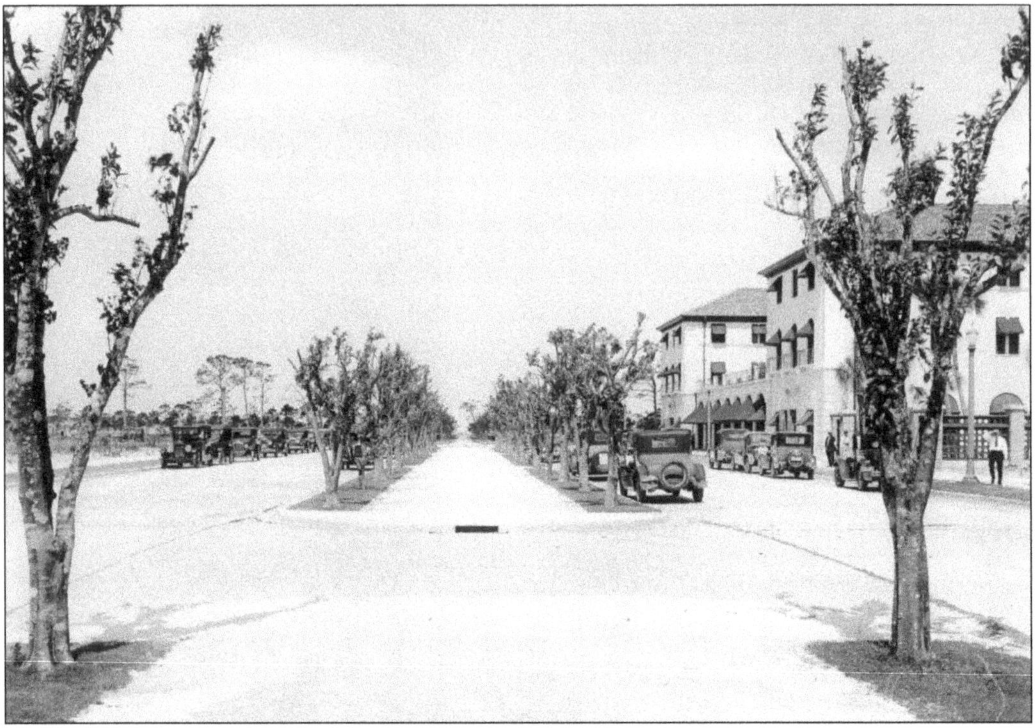

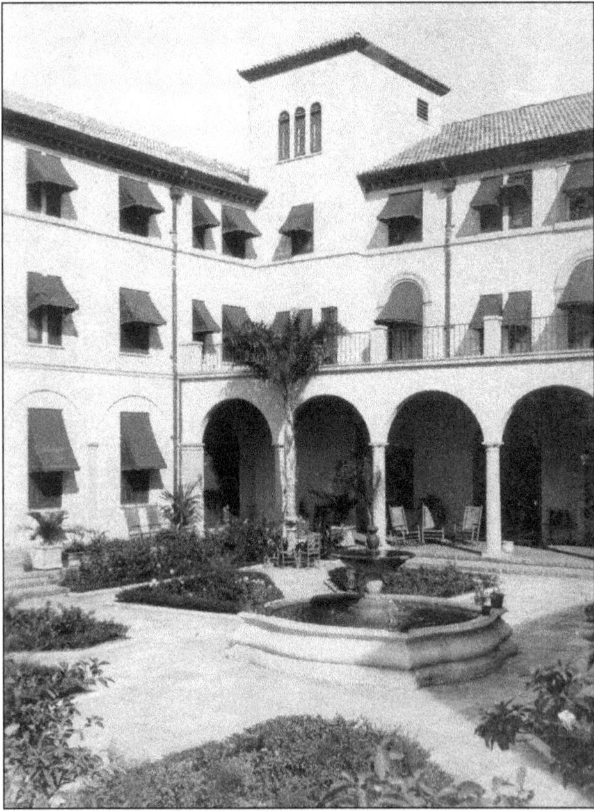

In 1926, Venice celebrated the opening of Venice Avenue. That same year, the Hotel Venice, residential housing, and three large residences in the Gulf View subdivision were built, along with sidewalks and six miles of graded streets. Once Venice Avenue was paved, it became the gateway to Venice Beach. This was a 200-foot-wide boulevard with a 100-foot-wide parkway in the center. (Courtesy of VMA.)

Hotel Venice opened on June 21, 1926. The attractive 100-room lodging boasted ceiling fans, large windows, and ventilating doors, along with amenities such as ice machines, a bakery, a barbershop, and laundry facilities. A sprinkler system was also in place for safety. Guests enjoyed eating in the spacious dining room decorated with large cypress beams and a plaster ceiling. Two other early hotels were the San Marco and the Park View. (Courtesy of VMA.)

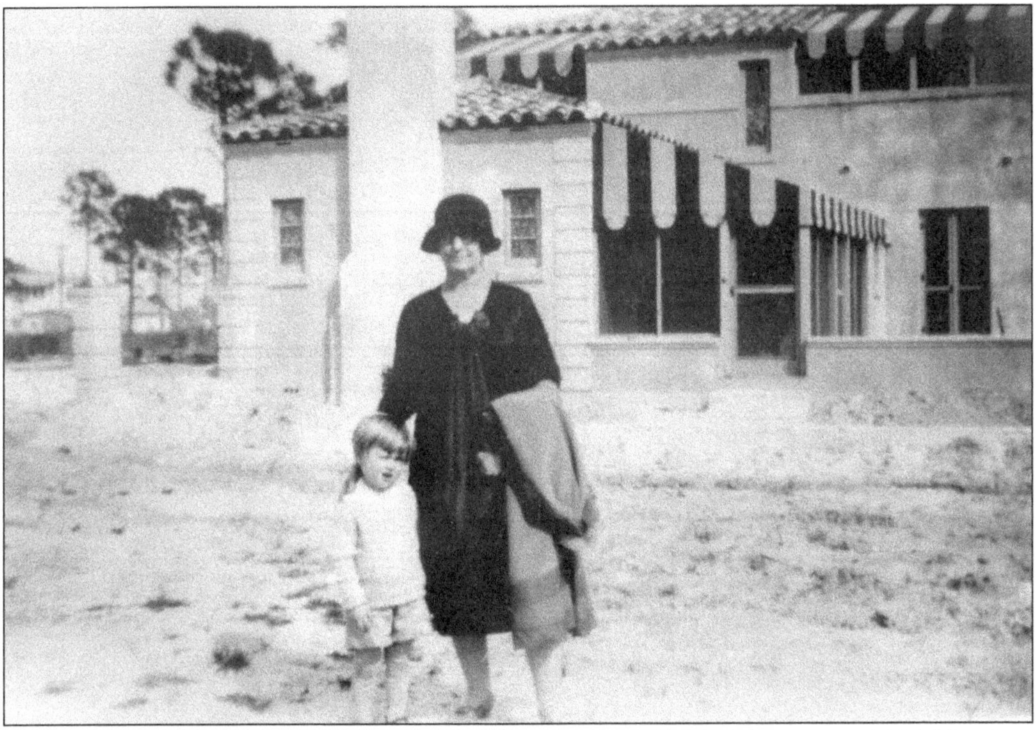

Residential construction started with large homes along Venice Avenue in 1926. The first subdivision was the Gulf View, which was the most expensive. Architectural firm Walker & Gillette approved all design work prior to building. The firm wanted to create a community with character by setting architectural standards, including sloping roofs with colored tiles. White or light-colored houses set off the tiled roofs and awnings. Even the placement of the building—its setback and its relationship to other structures—was considered. M.M. Gleichman of Tampa designed the moderately priced homes in the Edgewood subdivision. (Courtesy of VMA.)

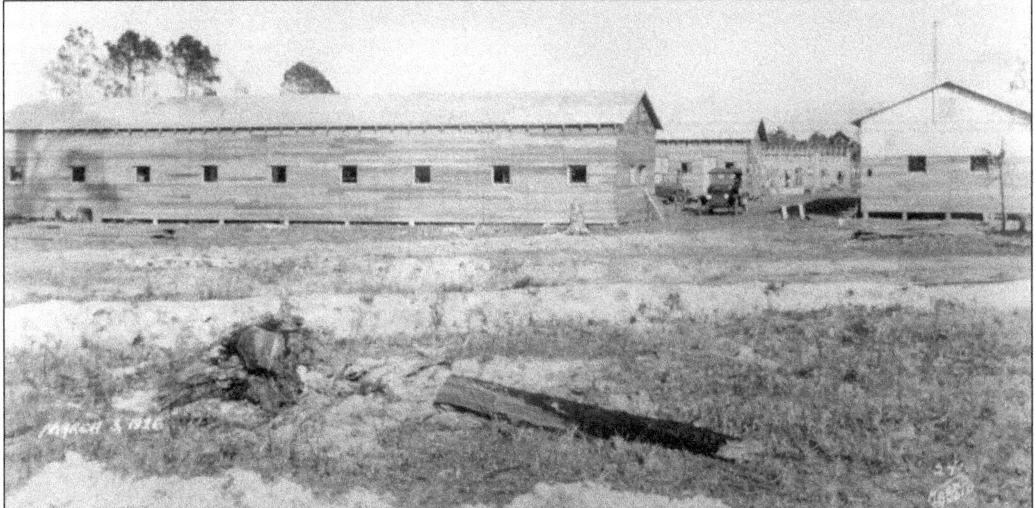


Fuller Construction came to the area to build a city in the mid-1920s. Barracks were constructed outside of town to house the workers, who were referred to as "Fuller's Army." Local men were hired in addition to the union men to help build the city. (Courtesy of VMA.)

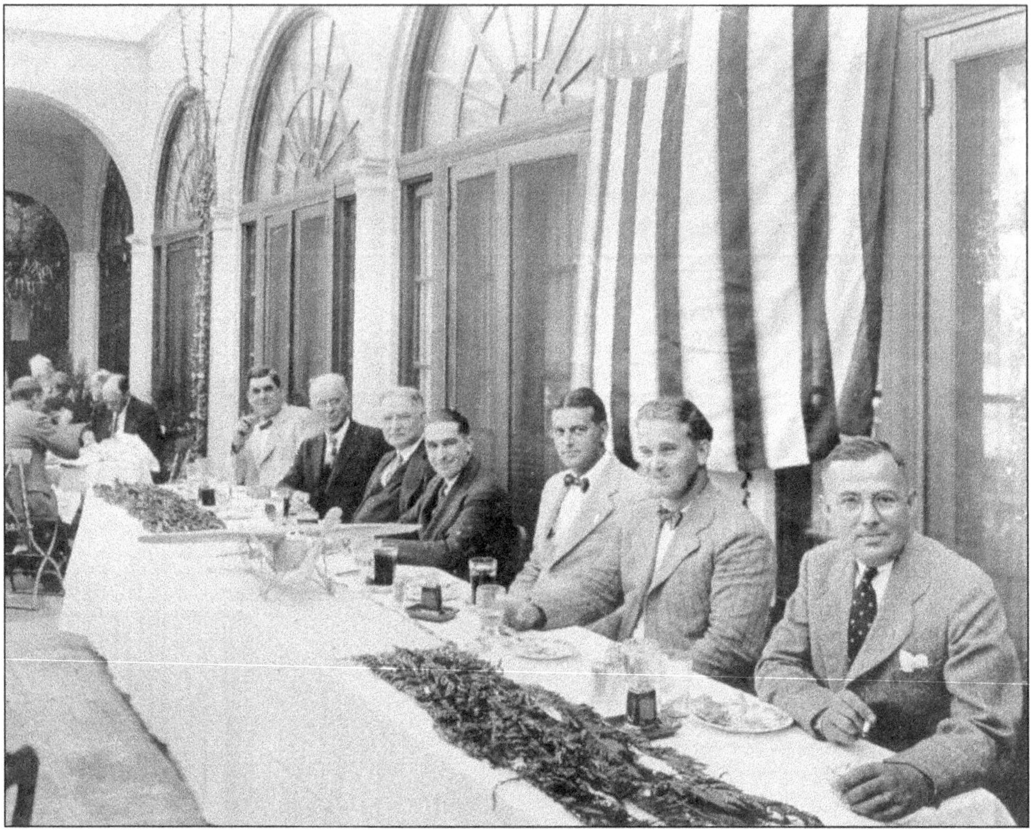

In December 1926, Venice had its first council meeting, and Florida governor John W. Martin appointed Edgar L. Worthington as the first mayor of Venice. At this first meeting, fire and police departments were assigned. In 1927, the Florida Legislature designated Venice, formerly a town, as a city after annexations of the surrounding areas. In 1948, a group of BLE men gathered at the Hotel Parkview. They are, from left to right, Leon Prine, Col. George D. Lindsay (editor of the *Sarasota Herald-Tribune*), Stanton Ennes, Capt. George W. Haldeman, Mayor E.L. Worthington, J.D. Summers, and C.M. McLennan. (Courtesy of VMA.)

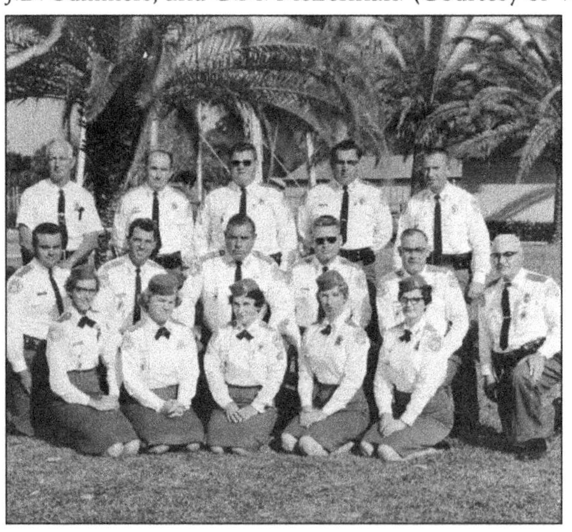

The Venice Police Department was older than the city. Allen "Pete" Edge was one of the first lawmen in Venice. Along with the fire department, the police department was voted to go into effect in 1926. The department could afford only one police officer and patrol car until 1931, when it was suspended. Fortunately, the Kentucky Military Institute came to town, and its taxes helped to reemploy the Venice police force. The job was difficult, and the police were on call 24 hours a day. Officers had to use their own guns and sit outside a phone box to wait for an emergency call. It was not until 1946 that a police radio was used in the patrol car. (Courtesy of VMA.)

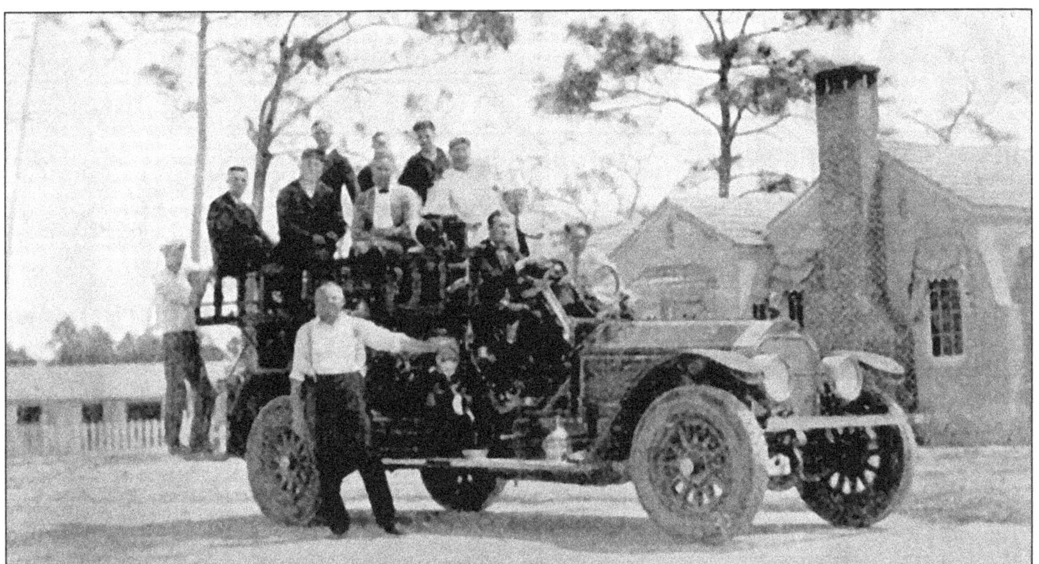

In 1926, J.M. Keys bought the American LaFrance fire engine from Moore Haven. The fire company called it "Old Betsy." At the time, there were 32 volunteers to man the truck. Old Betsy could hold 750 gallons of water and 40 gallons of chemicals to use in putting out a fire. The BLE provided the fire company with a building on St. Augustine Avenue to use as a fire station, and Venice mayor Edgar L. Worthington appointed J.C. Haladay as fire chief. Times were tough after the Great Depression, and in 1931, the new mayor had to suspend all city departments. (Courtesy of VMA.)

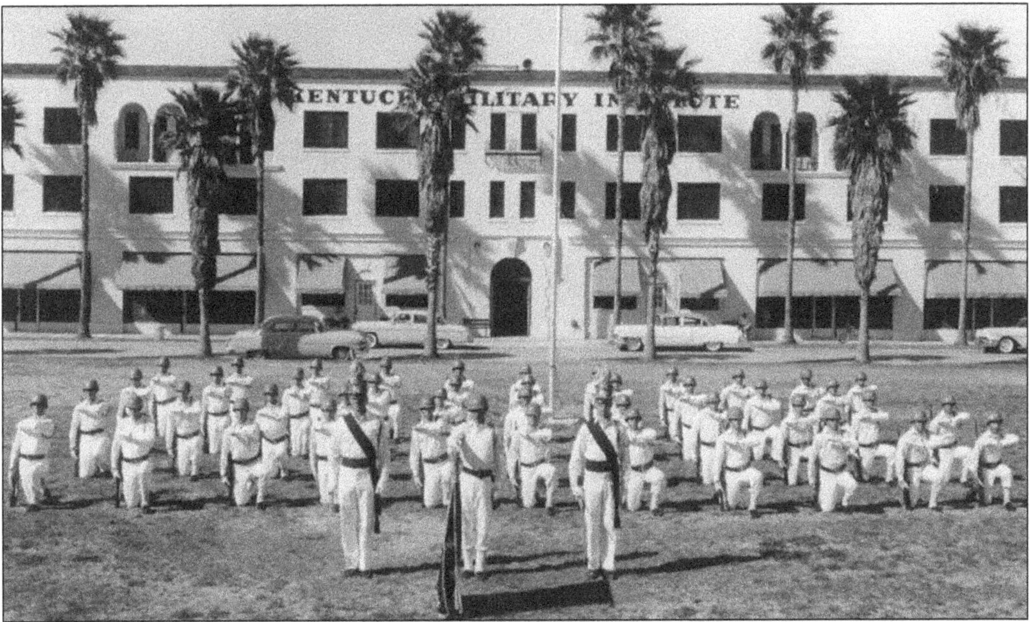

In 1932, the Kentucky Military Institute of Lyndon, Kentucky, moved its winter quarters to Venice. It rented both the San Marco Hotel and Hotel Venice and set up a school for cadets. For 40 years, the students, teachers, and even some parents would come to Venice to study and live. They would arrive by train after the New Year and stay until Easter. In some ways, they were considered early snowbirds. (Courtesy of VMA.)

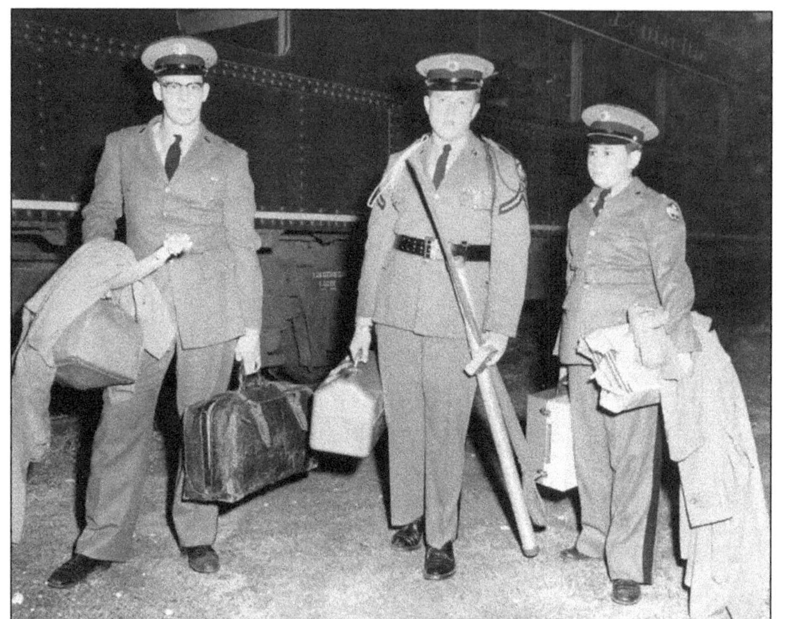

Here, Kentucky Military Institute cadets are waiting to catch a train. Thanks to Mrs. Potter Palmer, extending the line to Venice made it easy for the cadets to depart from the local station. With the growing antiwar protests, the school closed in 1971. (Courtesy of VMA.)

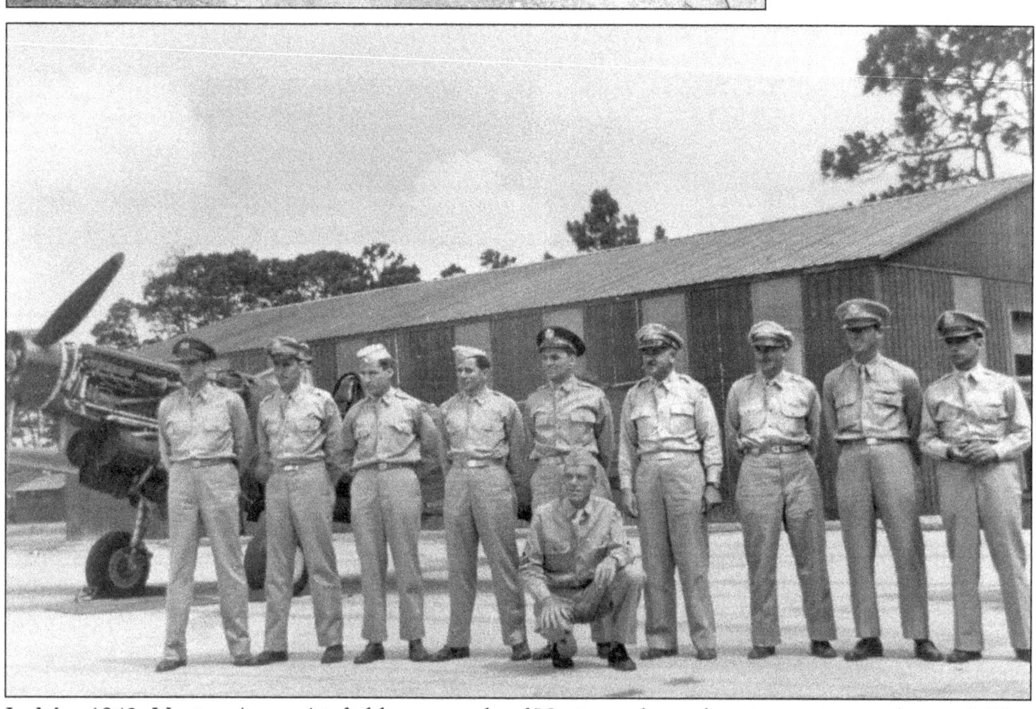

In May 1942, Venice Army Airfield was south of Venice, where the airport is now located. The 27th Service Group was relocated from McDill Field in Tampa. It was to provide training for pilots and crews for the US Army Air Forces. Three other air forces groups came to Venice—the 13th Fighter Squadron in 1943, the 53rd Fighter Group (transferred from Fort Myers), and, later, the 14th Fighter Squadron. These groups trained for service as pilots and ground crew. After World War II, the city acquired the air base in a quitclaim deed from the federal government, with the stipulation that the county would always use it for an airport. (Courtesy of VMA and US Army.)

To help raise money for World War II, the country sold war bonds. Note Uncle Sam with a boxing glove and Hitler's face at the top. (Courtesy of VMA and US Army.)

Students of the pioneer families attended school only three months a year, if and when a teacher was available. Many schools of that time were one-room schoolhouses, equipped with few supplies. Transport was by boat or on foot. (Courtesy of VMA.)

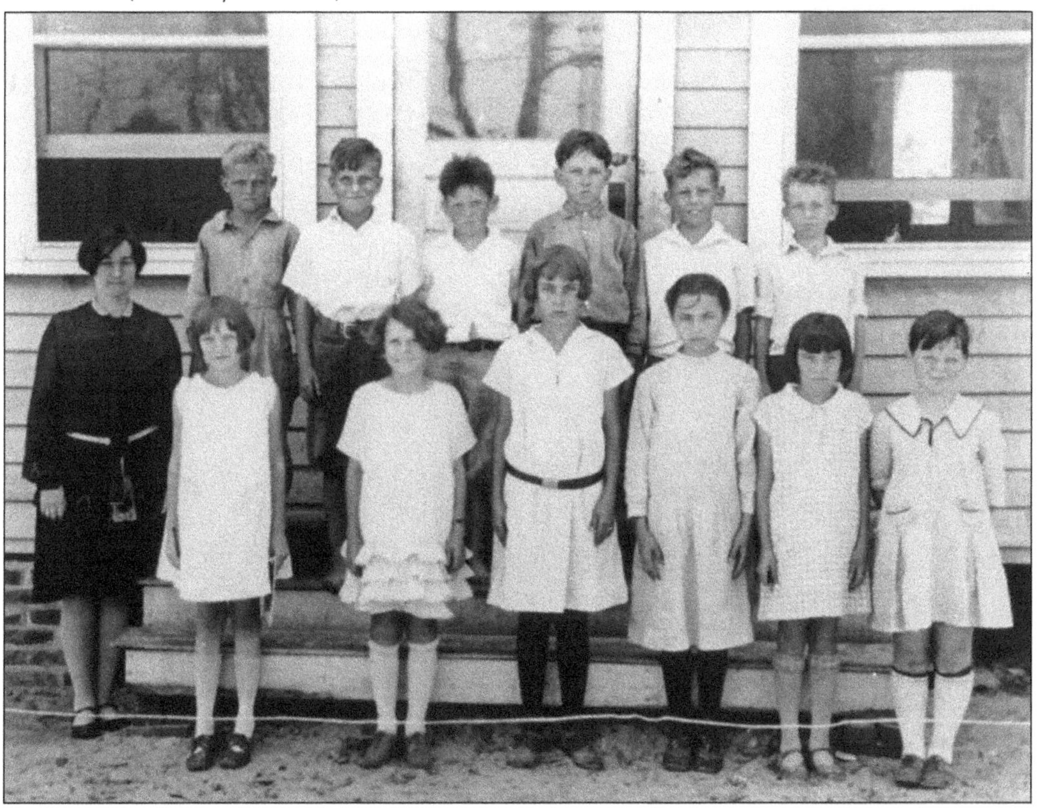

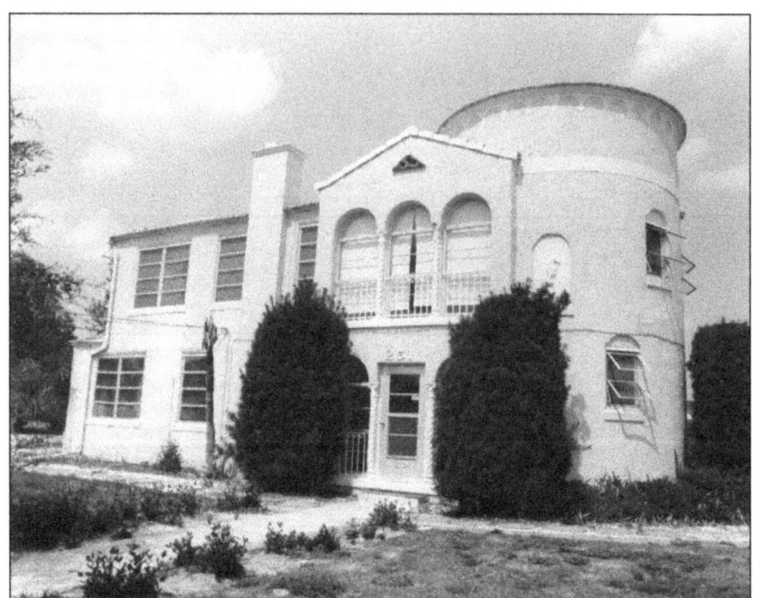

As part of the development in the mid-1920s, the BLE built the Triangle Inn in a residential section of town. The Mediterranean Revival–style inn was the only bed-and-breakfast available at that time. In 1996, it was listed in the National Register of Historic Places and the City of Venice's local registry of historic places. It is home to the Venice Museum and Archives. (Courtesy of VMA.)

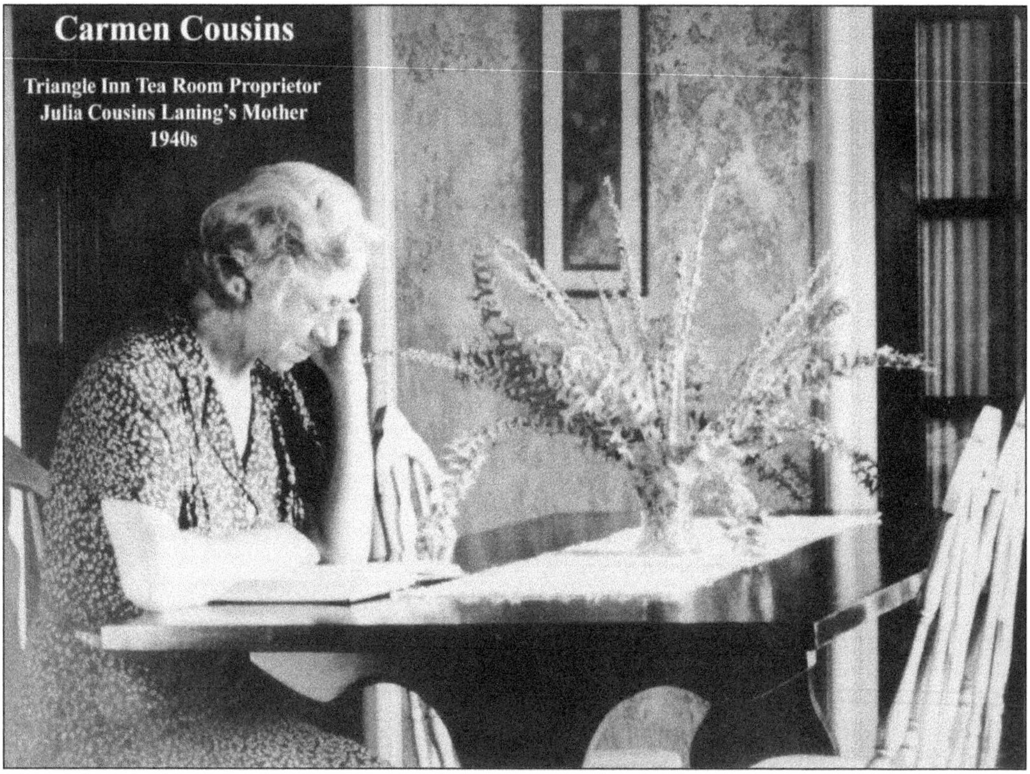

Carmen Cousins

Triangle Inn Tea Room Proprietor
Julia Cousins Laning's Mother
1940s

Carmen Cousins and her husband, Mitt, were hardworking people. They owned a farm on Jackson Road and a tearoom on Venice Avenue and bought the Triangle Inn. In 1933, money was tight. They rented out their farm and moved into small rooms on the first floor of the inn for a few years. They served breakfast and dinner. The dinner was available to residents of Venice. If they had a large group, they would borrow tables and chairs from neighbors. In an interview, Julia said that things were not very grand at the time but they got by. (Courtesy of VMA.)

Carmen Cousins's children Julia and James enjoyed their rural farm, where they played with the local wildlife. When times got tough, they moved into the Triangle Inn. Julia was a shy girl, and she was forced to help in the family business. She begged to go home, and when they returned to their farm, they lived above the garage and continued to rent out the house. Julia was able to attend college and eventually married, her name becoming Julia Cousins Landing. Pictured here are Julia and Jim with a wild alligator at their Jackson Road farm. (Courtesy of VMA.)

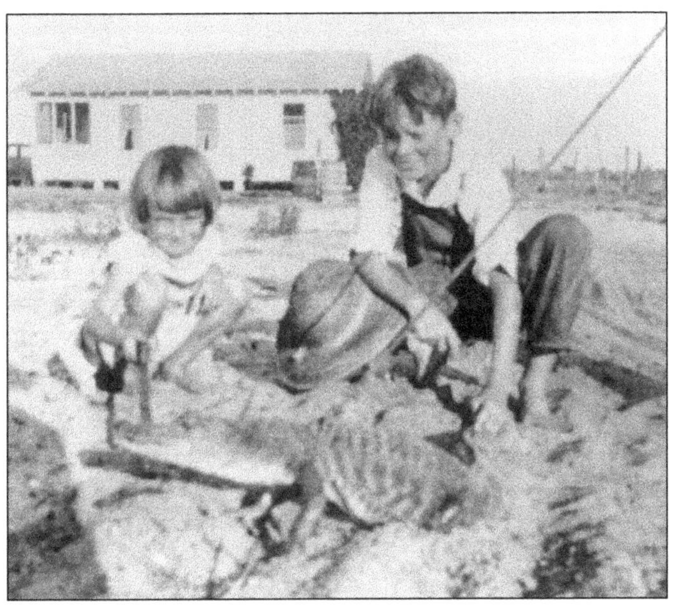

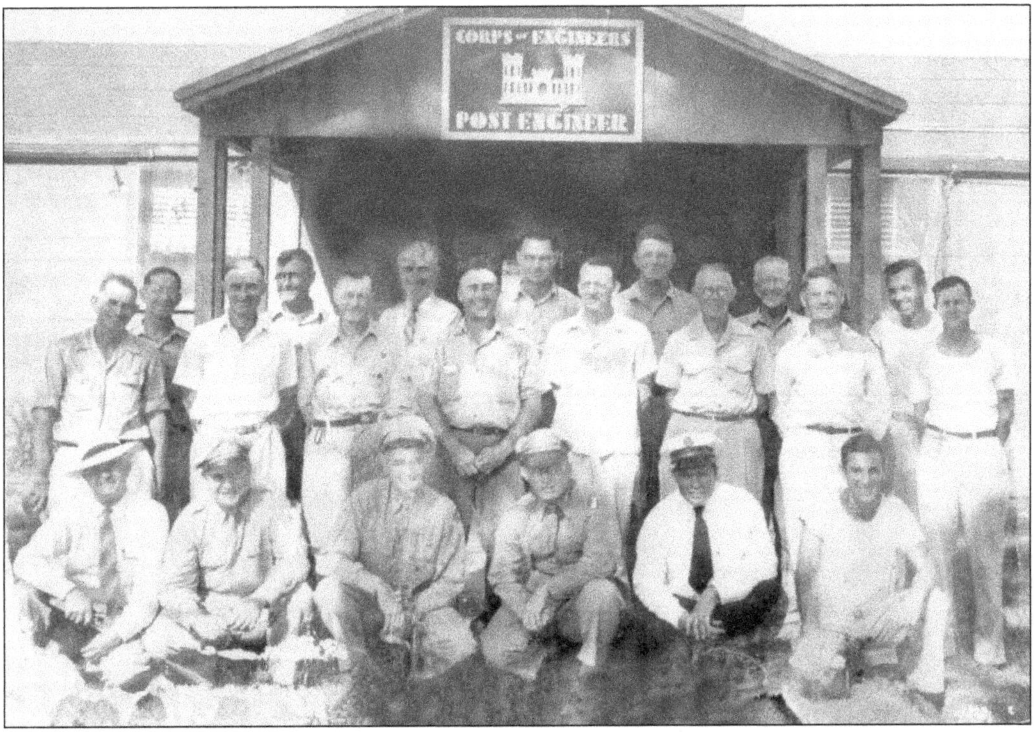

The Venice Jetties, also known as Casey's Pass for surveyor John Casey, were dredged in 1937–1939. Built by the Army Corps of Engineers and locals, the pass was a structured inlet running into Roberts Bay and Dona Bay. By 1937, a 100-foot-wide and 8-foot-deep channel had been dredged. (Courtesy of VMA.)

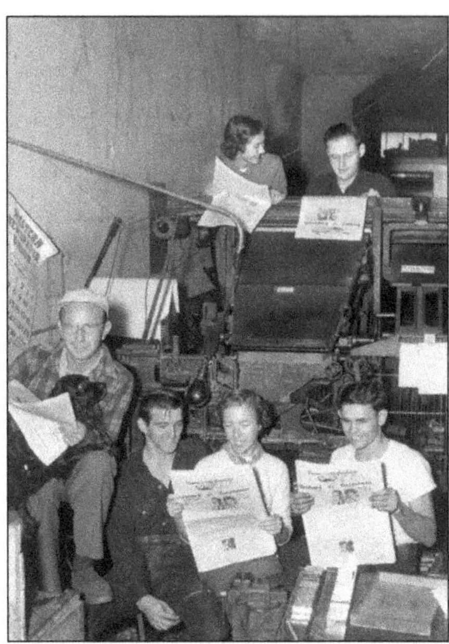

Carol H. Williams opened the *Gondolier* newspaper in 1946. The paper was then sold to Pete and Janie Conover in 1948. This picture shows the 1950 staff. From left to right are (first row) Frank Berger, Mickey Gibo, Libby Brook, and Don Hall; (second row) Janie and Pete. (Courtesy of VMA.)

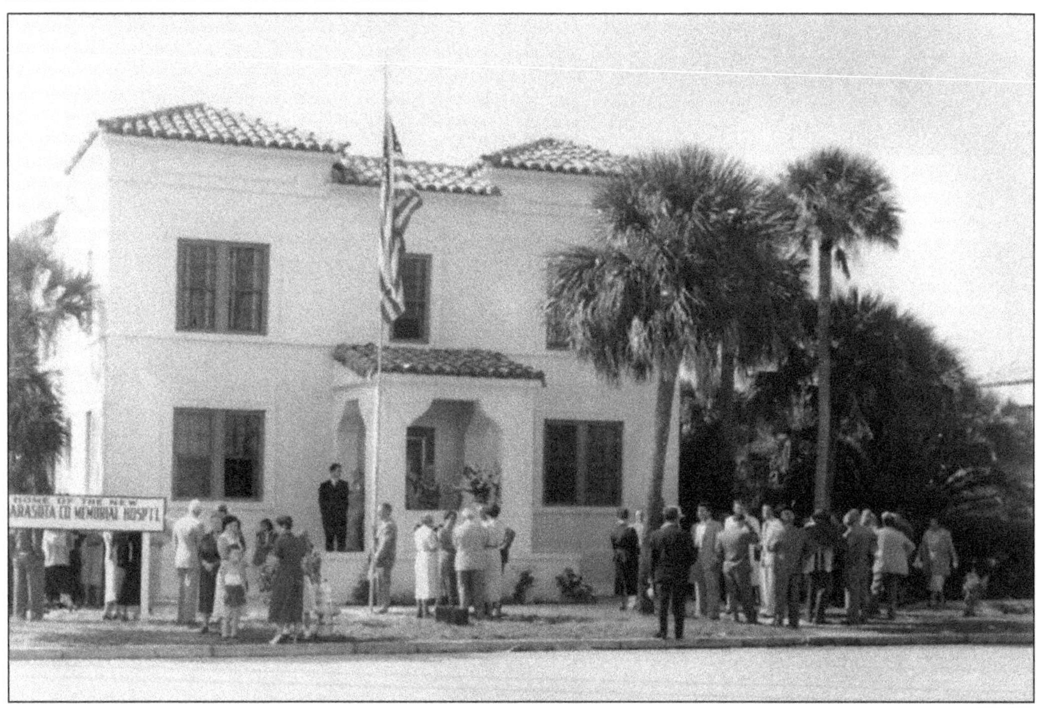

In 1951, Venice Hospital opened to the public. This project was a long time coming and would not have been possible without the help and dedication of businessman O.W. Caspersen and Mrs. Charles McGee Roberts. Caspersen's young niece became ill, and they had to drive 20 minutes to bring her to the closest hospital in Sarasota. Caspersen donated a large amount as seed money to build the hospital in Venice. Mrs. Roberts wanted to help people and supported his plan by raising money. Memberships to the hospital association were sold for $5 a year or $100 for a lifetime. The first month, 30 patients were admitted. Private rooms with bath cost $20 daily, and a bed in the ward was $10 a day. The operating room was completed in 1952. (Courtesy of VMA.)

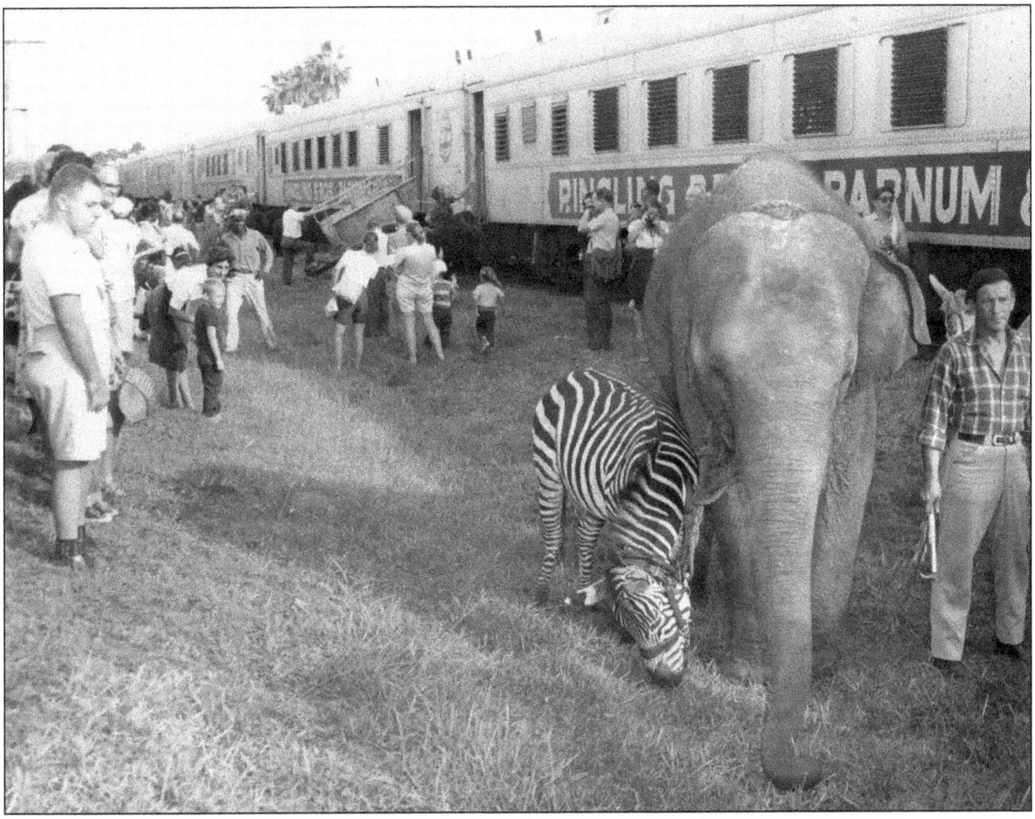

In 1960, the Ringling Bros. and Barnum & Bailey Circus moved its winter quarters to Florida, which proved to be a great asset for Venice, because wherever the circus performed, it advertised Venice and brought in people and traffic. Anxious to see both Venice and the circus, visitors arrived by the trainload. Residents would line up to see the circus animals disembark from the train and parade through town. (Courtesy of VMA.)

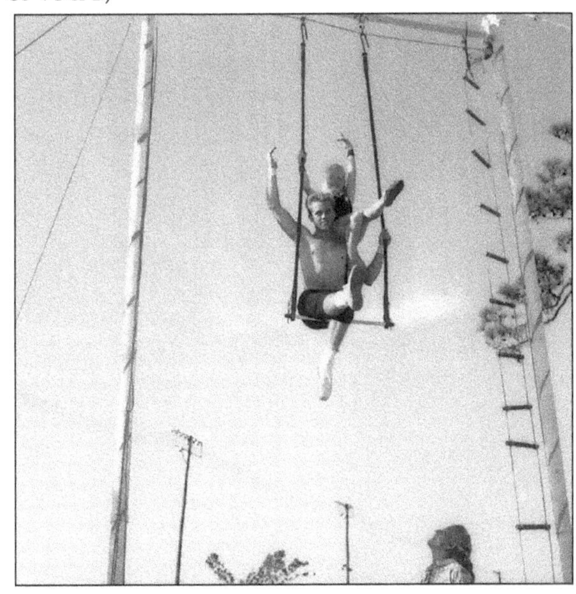

Although the Ringling Bros. and Barnum & Bailey Circus has not used Venice as its winter home for many years, trapeze equipment can still be found in the backyards of some homes. A couple of young people are pictured here practicing. They might have been part of the Sarasota High School Sailor Circus. John Ringling gave permission for the Sailor Circus to use the phrase "the Smallest Circus in the World." (Courtesy of SCHR.)

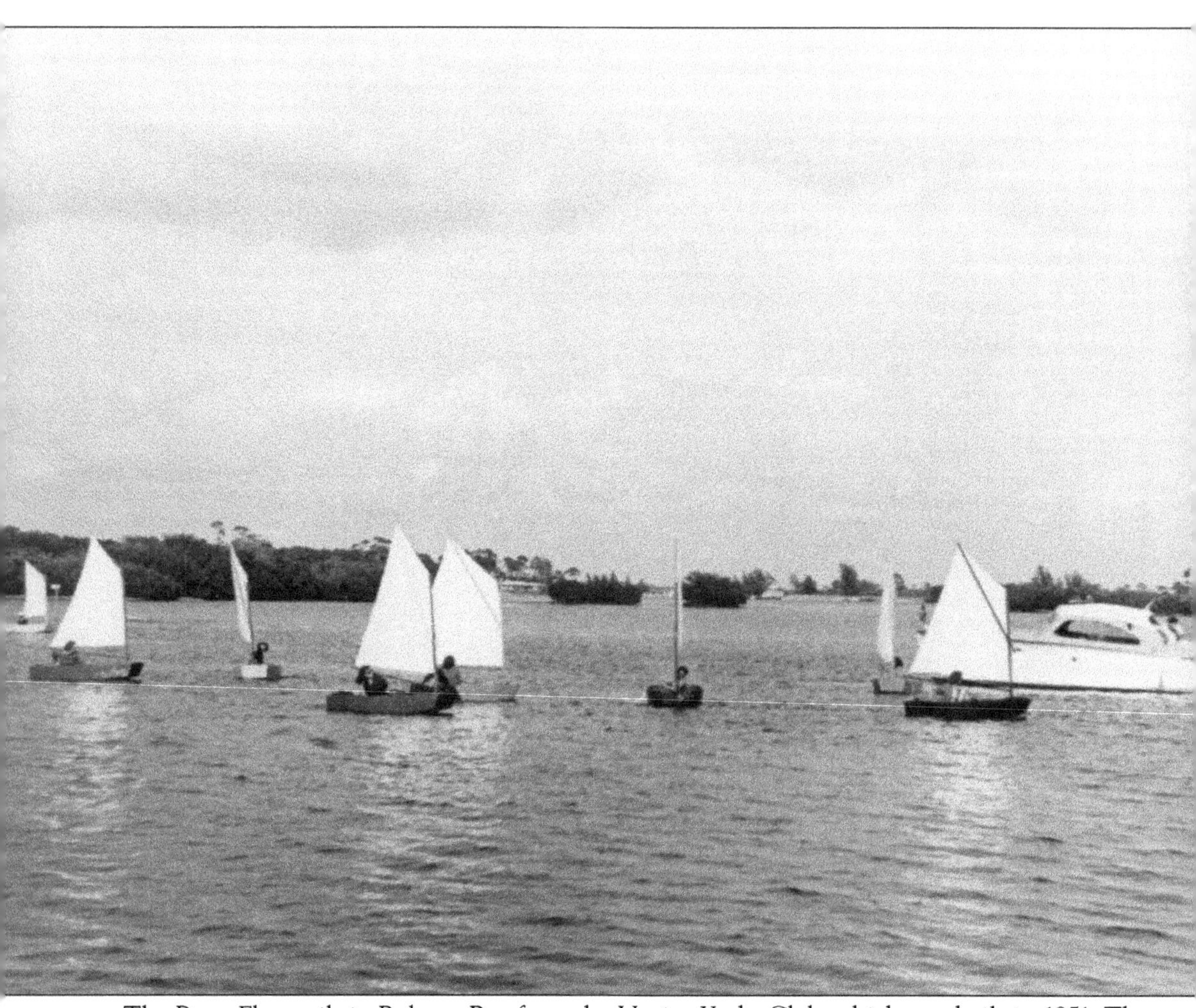

The Pram Fleet sails in Roberts Bay from the Venice Yacht Club, which was built in 1951. The Venice Youth Boating Association is sponsored by the Venice Yacht Club and gives children a chance to sail. For many years, the Crow's Nest Restaurant hosted a regatta to help support the program. (Courtesy of VMA.)

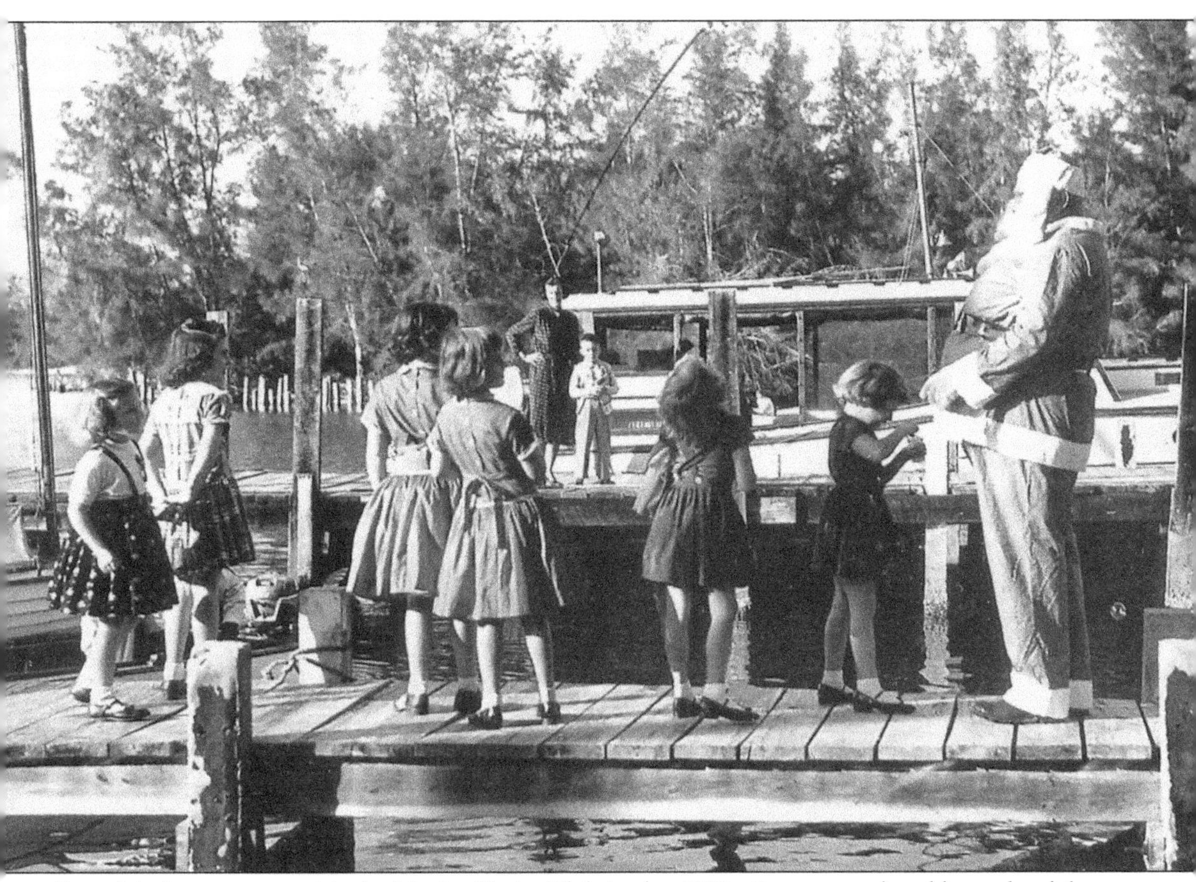

Santa's helper came to visit the Venice Yacht Club in the 1960s. Santa was played by yacht club member George Carruthers of Casey Key. The Venice Yacht Club was one of the 13 original members of the Florida Council of Yacht Clubs. (Courtesy of Ann Carruthers.)

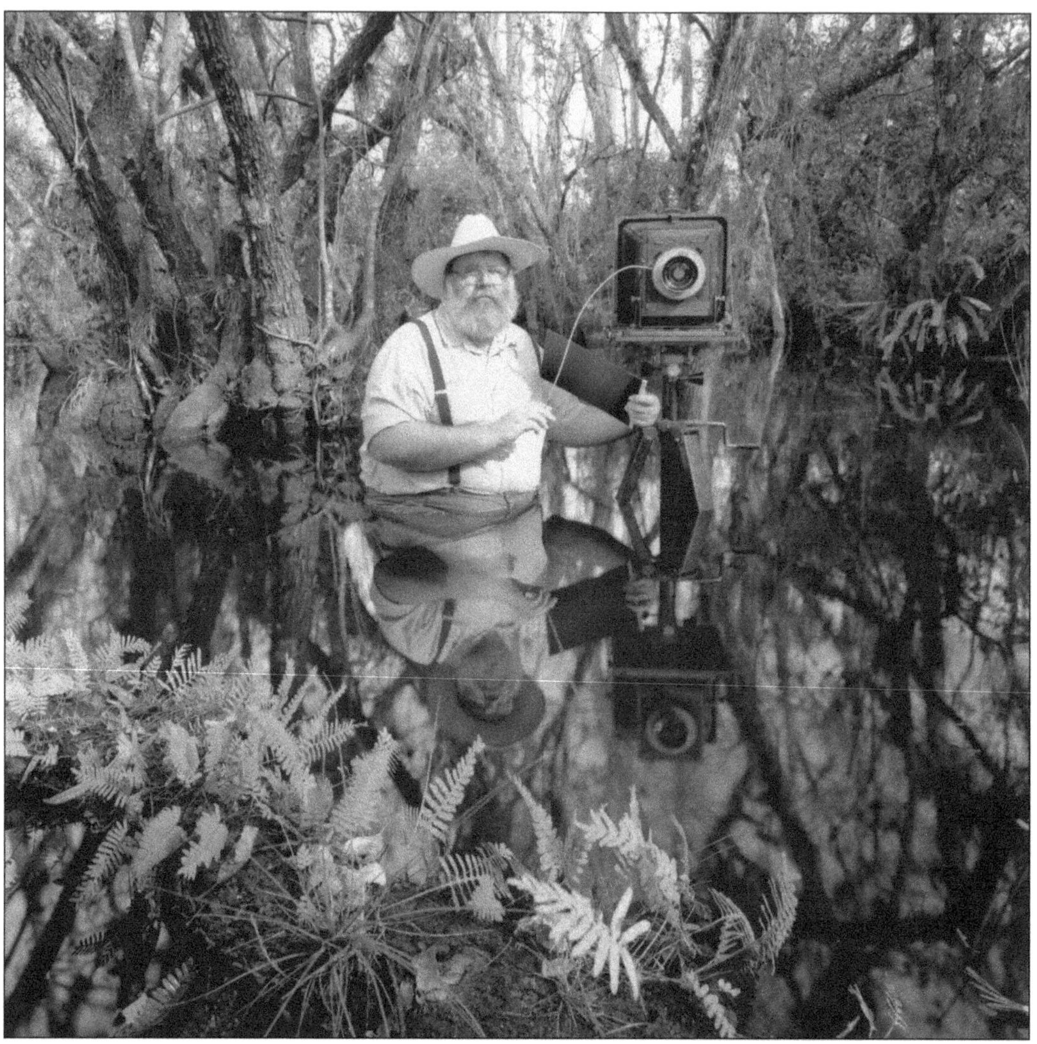

Clyde Butcher originally moved to the Everglades to escape life after his teenage son was killed by a drunk driver. There, he developed a relationship with the untamed wilderness that surrounds his home. Butcher says that his "powerful black and white photographs explore [his] personal bond with the environment," and he feels that "the pristine splendor of the wilderness is a healing sacrament." "Nature is messy," he told a group of aspiring photographers and guests at the Venice Chamber of Commerce. (Courtesy of Clyde Butcher.)

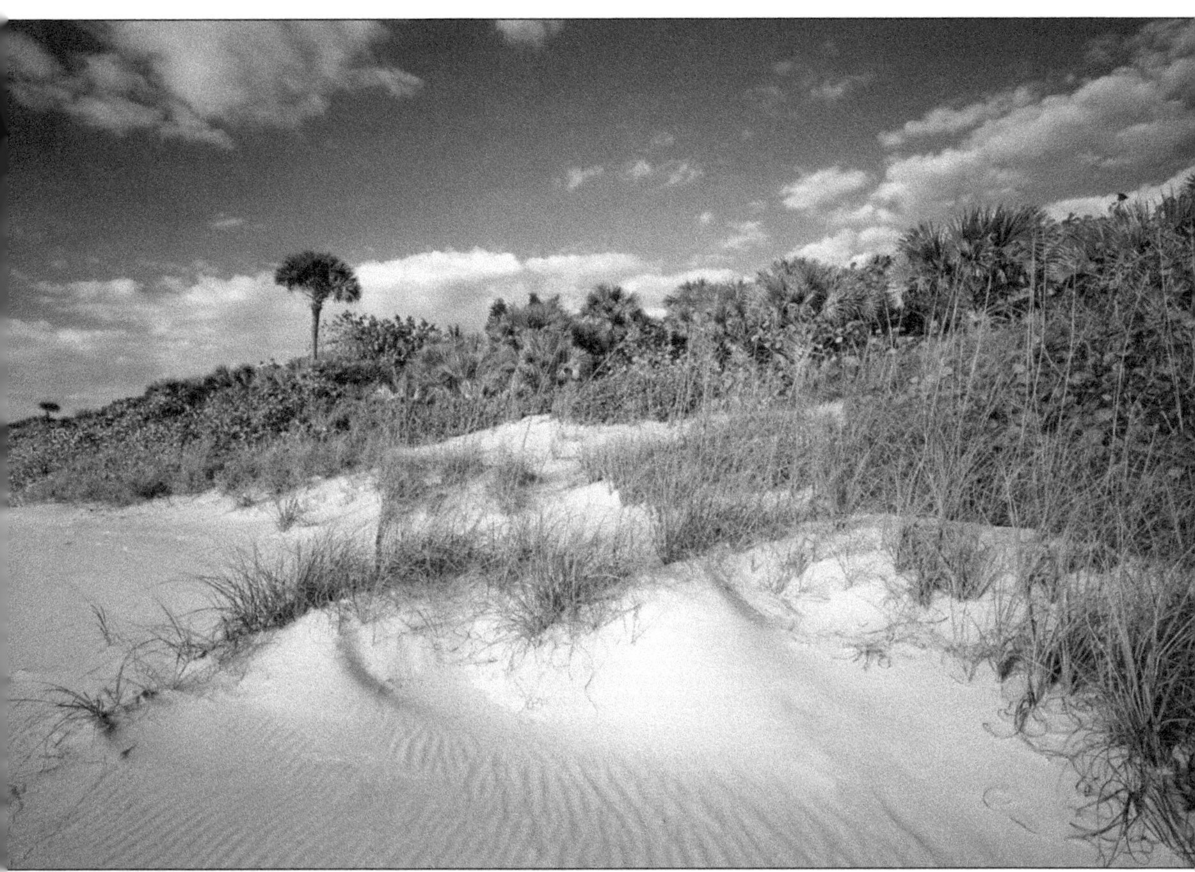

This Venice photograph was taken by internationally renowned photographer Clyde Butcher, an environmental activist who wants to help make the world a better place. Capturing the beauty of threatened natural landscapes with his black-and-white photographs helps preserve the environment. His pictures make people want to preserve the beauty he shows. Butcher also has donated his time and money to local organizations including Historic Spanish Point and Bay Preserve, both located in Osprey, Florida. His daughter Jackie Butcher Obendorf and her husband, Neal, work at the Venice studio and continue the philosophy of her father. (Courtesy of Clyde Butcher.)

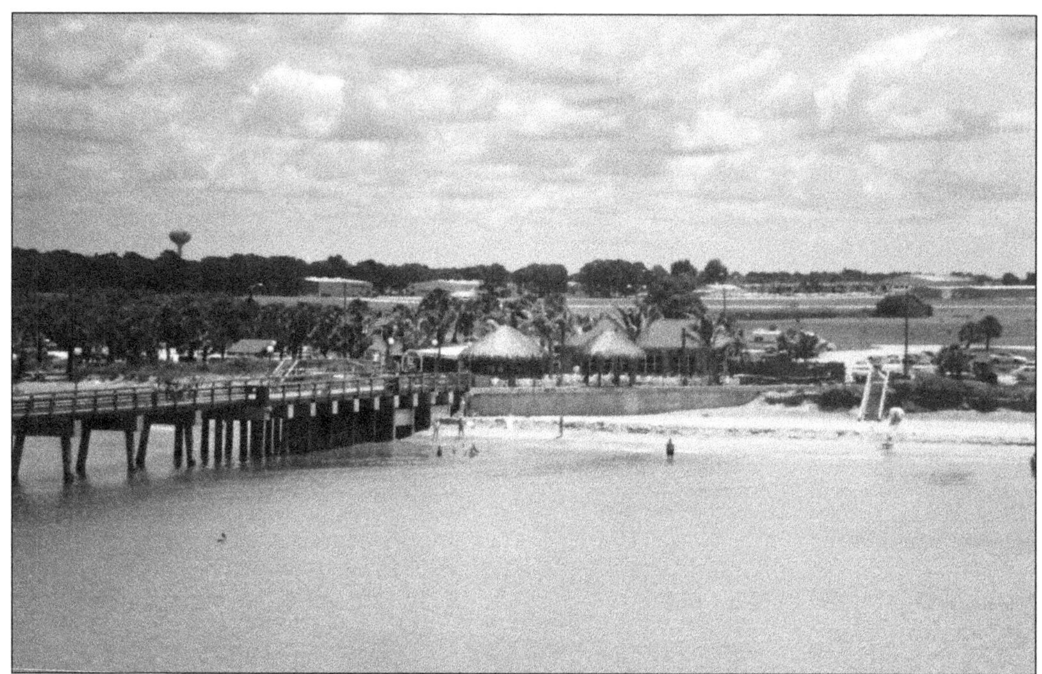

Sharky's on the Pier is pictured here in 1991. Greg Novack and Mike Pachota shared a business in Michigan before moving to Venice and starting their first restaurant, Patches, in 1982. Then, in 1986, Novack and Pachota won the bid to build a restaurant on the site of a dilapidated beach concession stand. They opened Sharky's on the Pier, a family-style restaurant, on February 10, 1986. (Courtesy of Sharky's on the Pier.)

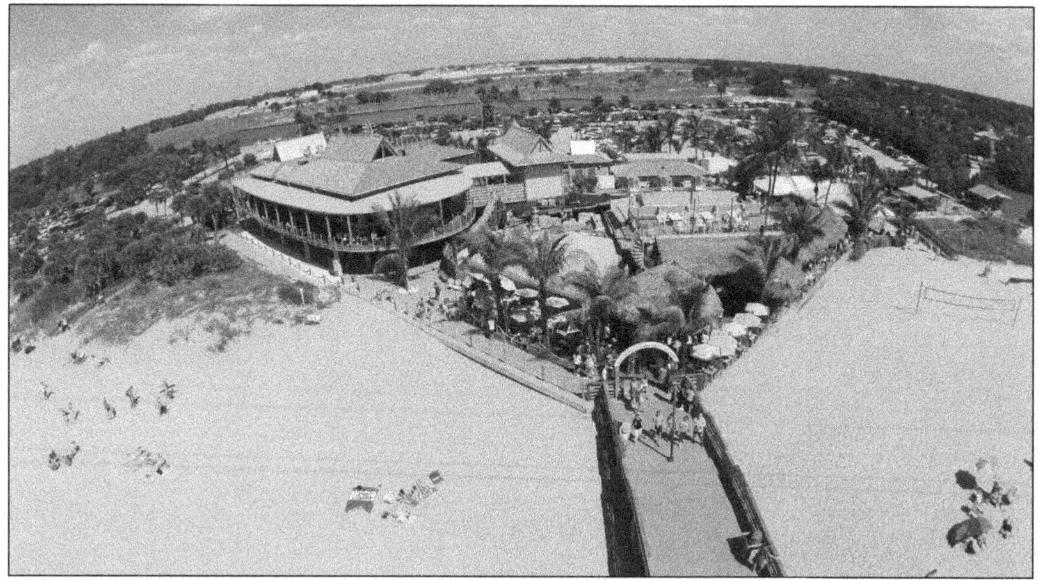

Today, Sharky's on the Pier has grown from a 78-person restaurant to expansive indoor and outdoor seating. On December 8, 2013, a new restaurant named Fins was added. An architectural delight, Fins serves fresh sushi, seafood, and steaks, along with wine and drink pairings. The restaurant participates in several local charities, and owner Mike Pachota is a founder of the Shark's Tooth Festival. (Courtesy of Sharky's on the Pier.)

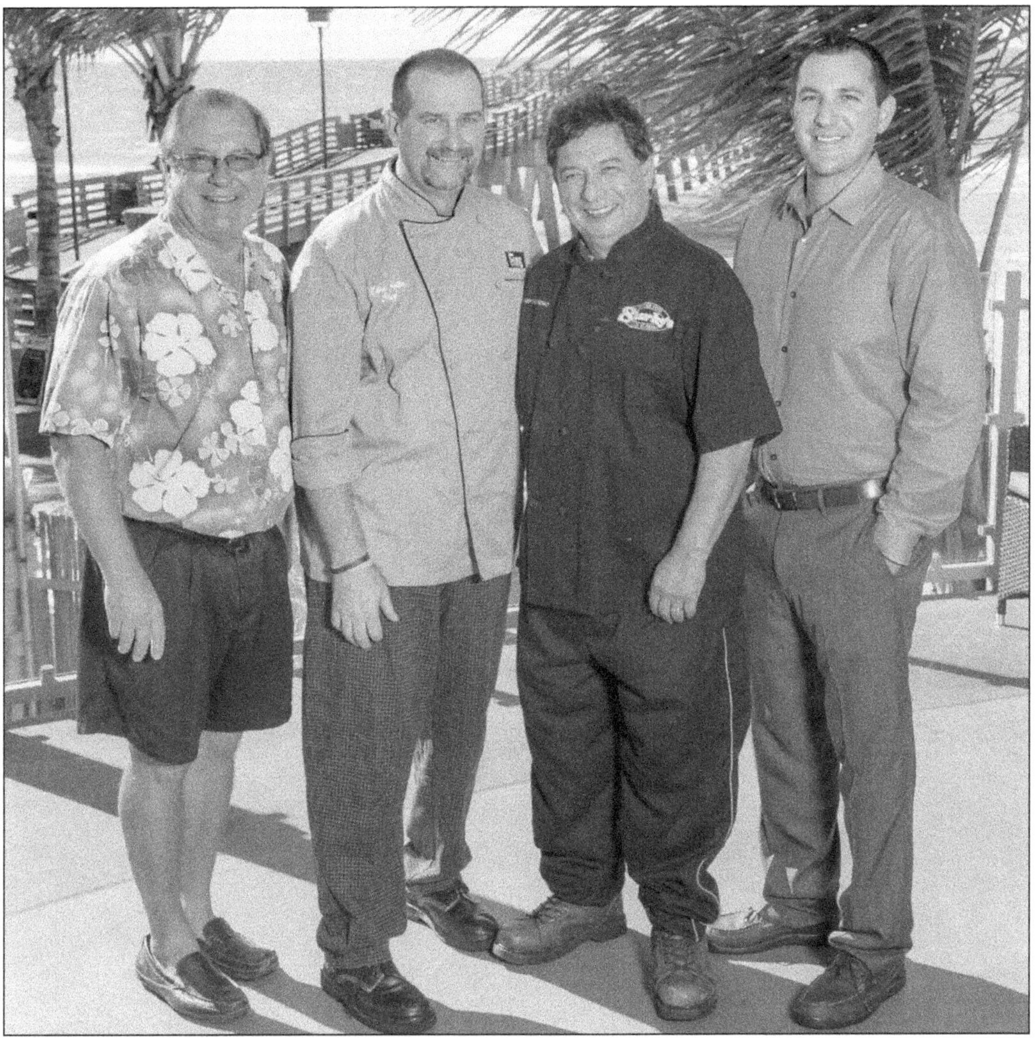

Pictured here are the co-owners and executive chefs of both Sharky's on the Pier and Fins. From left to right are Mike Pachota, co-owner; Marc Alton, executive chef of Fins; Homero Gutierrez, executive chef of Sharky's; and Justin Pachota, Mike's son and co-owner. (Courtesy of Sharky's on the Pier.)

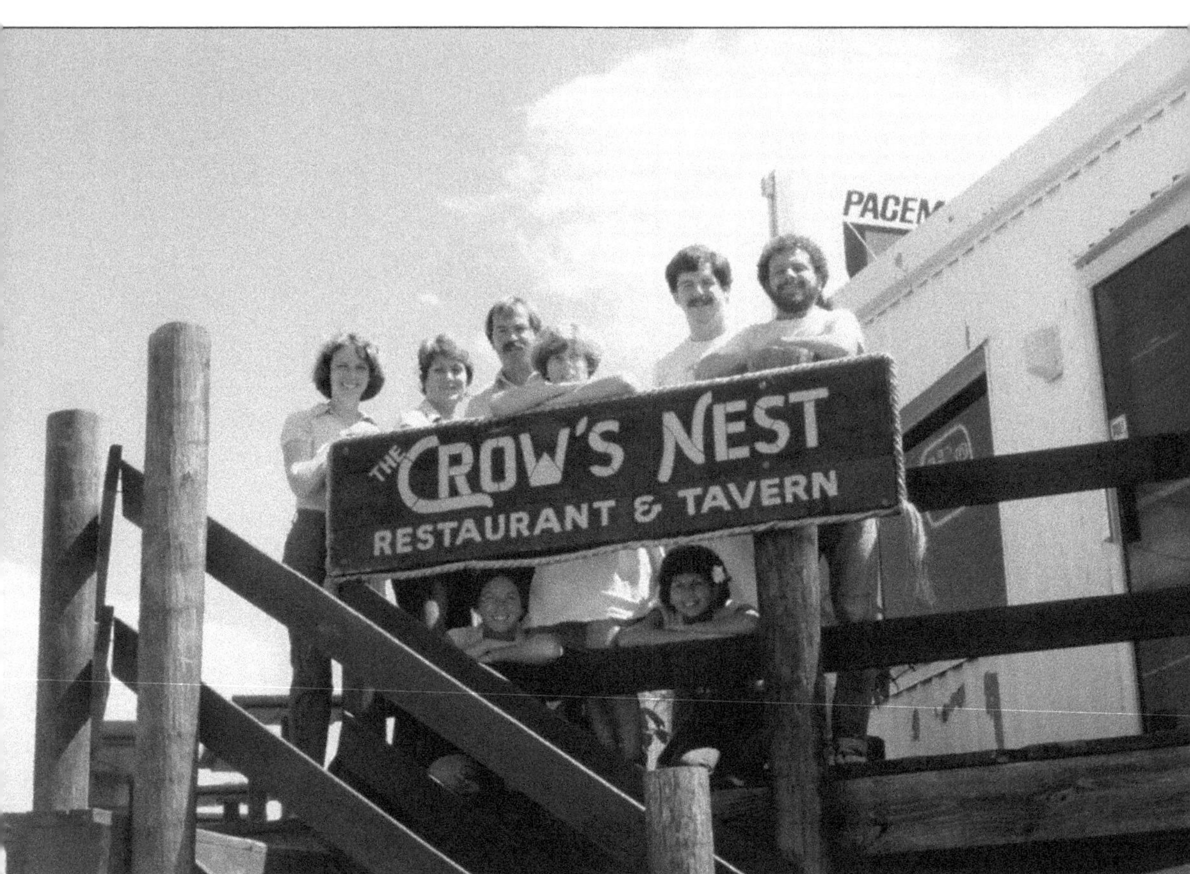


The Crow's Nest was founded by three owners in 1976. Today, it is solely owned by Steve Harner. In 1982, the Crow's Nest purchased the Tarpon Center Marina, which became the Crow's Nest Restaurant and Marina, with seating for 100 people on the second floor. Early on, the staff became like family as the establishment grew from a small eatery to a full-size restaurant and marina. For years, the Crow's Nest sponsored a regatta to raise money for the Venice Youth Boating Association. Pictured here is the small staff from the 1970s. (Courtesy of the Crow's Nest.)

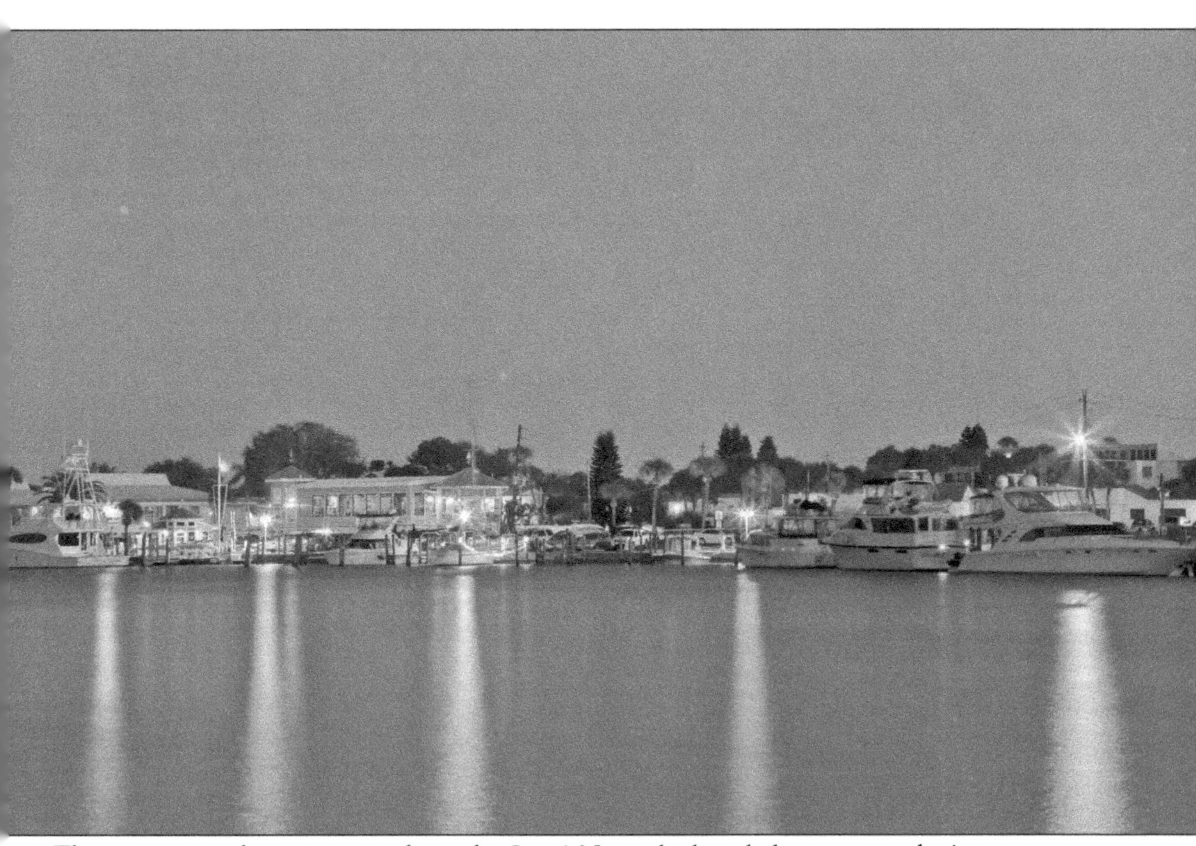

This stunning nighttime picture shows the Crow's Nest, which includes a marina, ship's store, wine cellar, and private dining room. Owner Steve Harner's philosophy revolves around "great people committed to hospitality and striving to please every guest." (Courtesy of the Crow's Nest.)

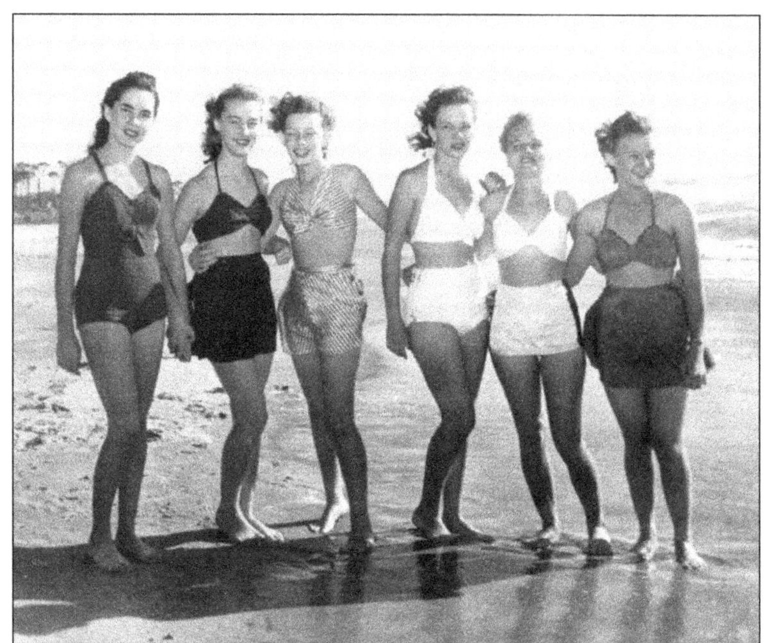

Students from the Venice-Nokomis High School spend a day together at Venice Beach around 1946. They dressed in bathing suits for this beautiful picture. The girls are, from left to right, Beverly Lanier, Mary Ann Lanier, Virginia Bowden, Ruby Rigby, Miriam Smith, and Gladys Underwood. (Courtesy of VMA.)

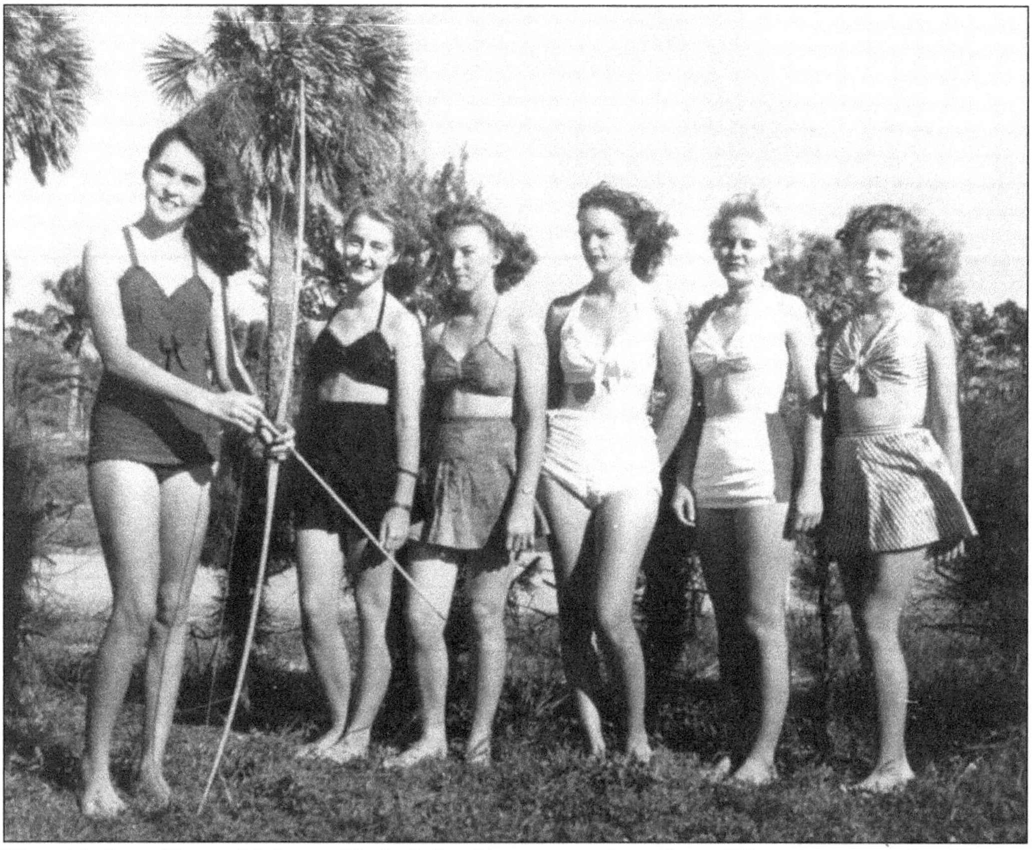

The girls from Venice-Nokomis High School prepare to do archery. They are pictured in Venice on the same day as in the previous photograph. (Courtesy of VMA.)

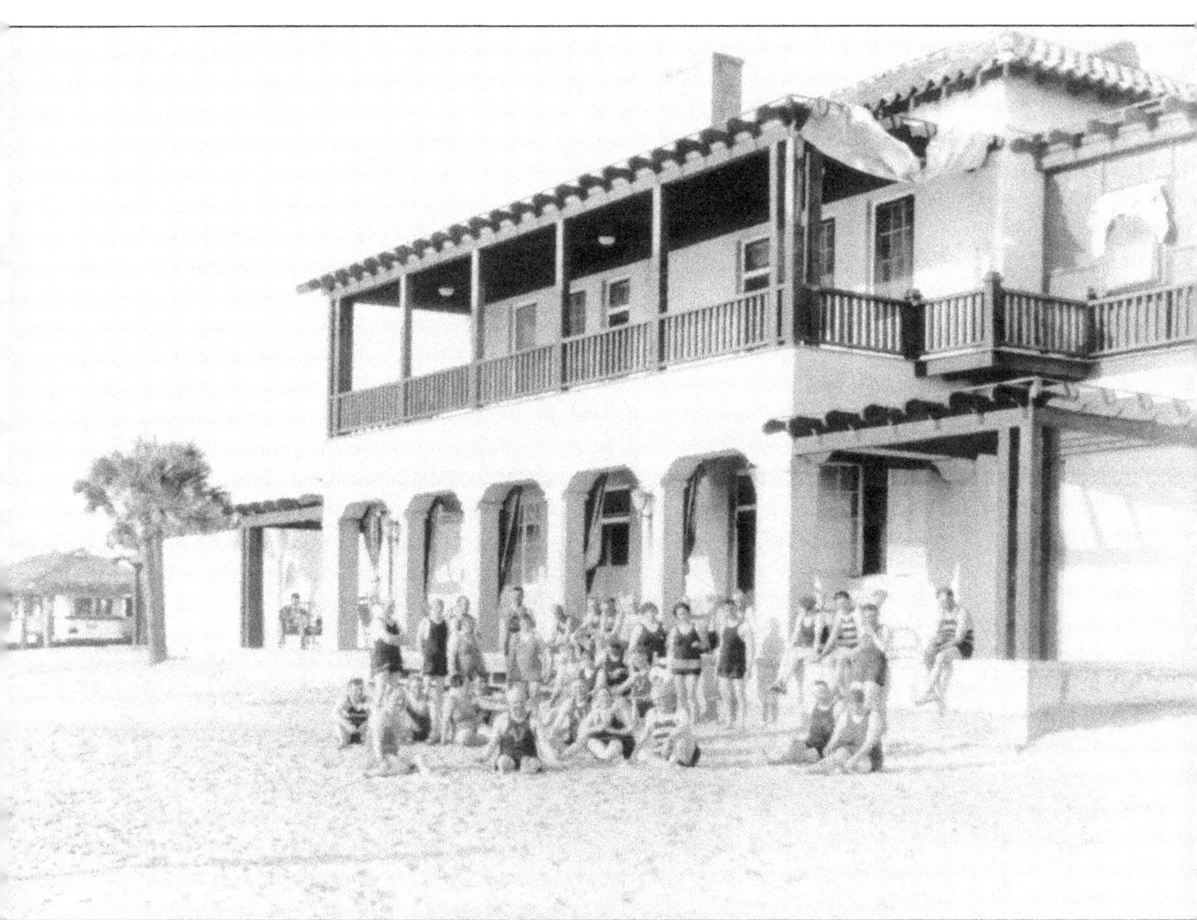

Dr. Fred Albee built this Mediterranean-style bathhouse and pier on the beach in 1925. He wanted to have a proper place for bathers to change to enjoy Venice Beach. The bathhouse was located at the intersection of Ormond Street and the Esplanade North. Unfortunately, the pier was taken out during a storm in 1926, and the bathhouse came down during a storm in 1932. (Courtesy of VMA.)

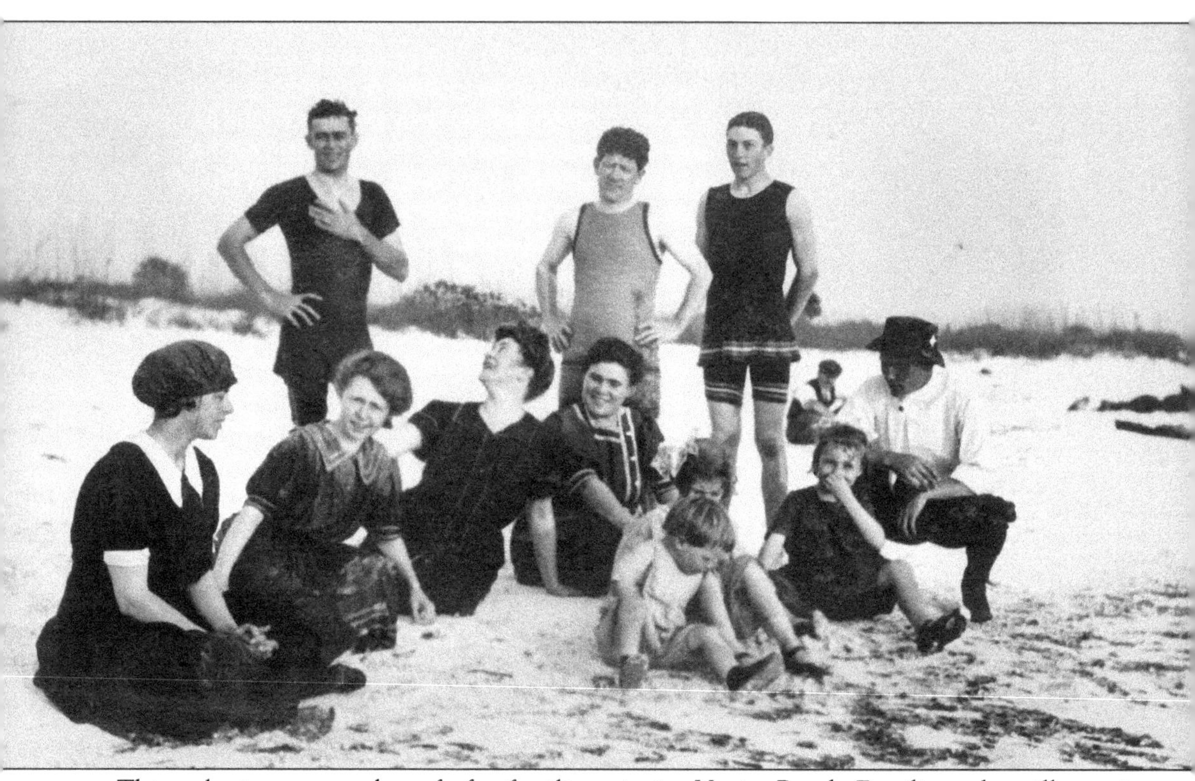

This early picture was taken of a few families enjoying Venice Beach. Families today still meet in Venice to splash in the water or look for prehistoric sharks' teeth at either Venice or Caspersen Beach. (Courtesy of VMA.)

# *Six*

# Manasota Key

## Lat 26.9333 N, Long 82.3667 W

Manasota Key is rich with history, natural vegetation, and beautiful beaches. The key, which straddles Charlotte and Sarasota Counties, is located in Englewood, Florida. Known as "the Gem of the Suncoast," the island is situated between the Gulf of Mexico and Lemon Bay.

The Smithsonian discovered artifacts from early residents dating back 1,000 years that historians believe might have belonged to the Calusa Indians, a tribe that was still in the area during the 17th century. The resourceful tribe built canals and constructed artificial islands. In the early 18th century, the tribe's population decreased, and it disbanded after being subjected to European diseases. Some of the survivors went to Cuba or joined the Seminole Tribe.

Englewood was incorporated in the 1880s by the Nichols brothers—Hubert, Howard, and Ira—who named the town in remembrance of their home in Illinois. They came to Englewood to grow lemons and filed a plan to develop the area with their Lemon Bay Company. Electric power was partially available in 1910. The great Florida land boom brought developers to Englewood in 1919, and the Tamiami Trail opened to Miami in 1928.

Walter Roberts was asked to write about his life on Manasota Key. When he first moved to the key in 1937, there were no roads. He would carry a shovel and boards to help get out of the sand when his car would sink. Few plants survived due to the fact that there was little soil. Native Florida plants, such as palm trees and live oaks, were common on the island. A man who owned a nursery planted 40 different species of plants to test what would survive, but unfortunately, he did not keep records. Manasota Key is a long peninsula that was transformed into an island by the Intracoastal Waterway. This waterway continues into Sarasota County. The key is only 2.8 square miles. In 2000, the population on the key was only 1,345 residents.

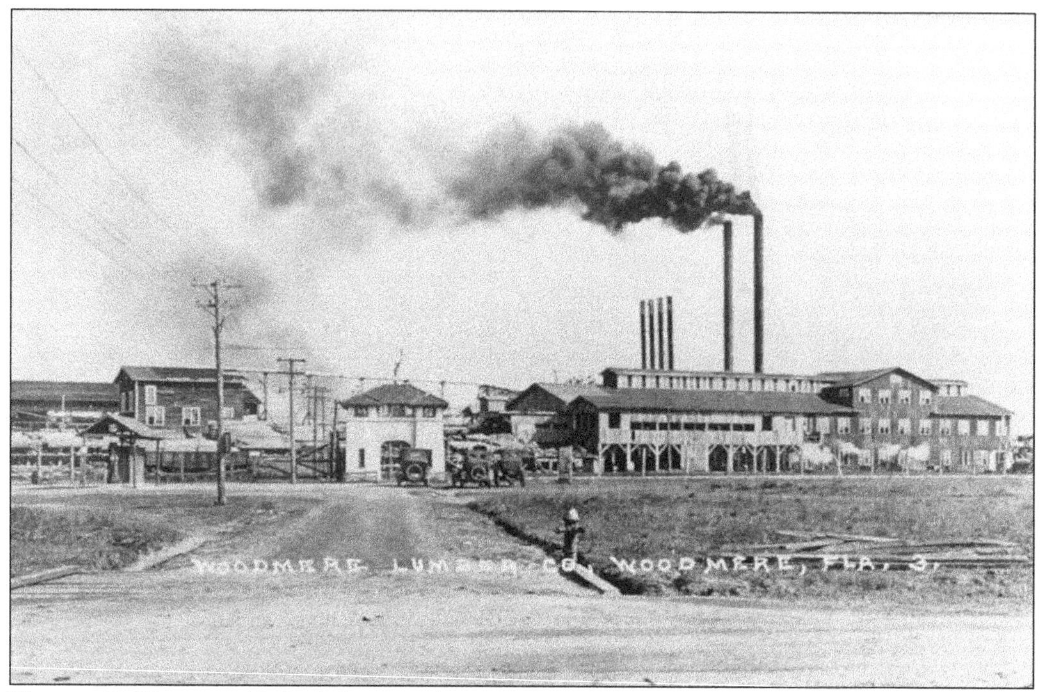


Herman E. Kluge established the Woodmere Lumber Mill in 1925. During the 1920s, the mill employed 1,500 people. Some men came with their families and lived nearby. There was plenty of business until the Great Depression, when many lost their jobs. (Courtesy of VMA.)

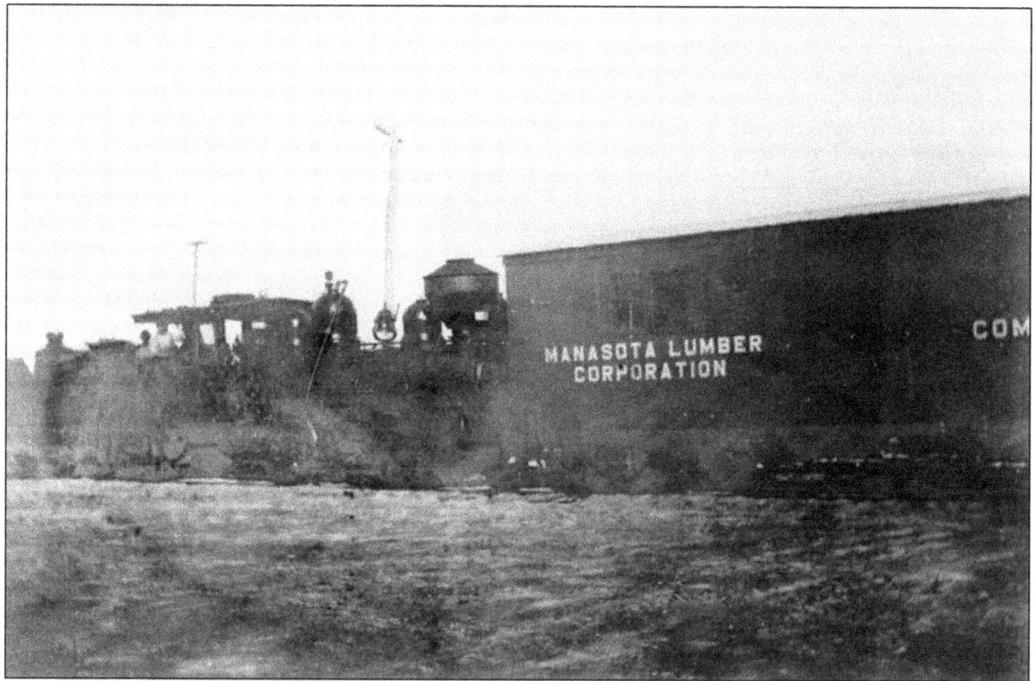


After the Gulf Coast Railway Company built the tracks from Venice to Nokomis, the Woodmere Lumber Mill could transport its wood by rail. The railway is pictured here with supplies from the lumber mill. (Courtesy of VMA.)

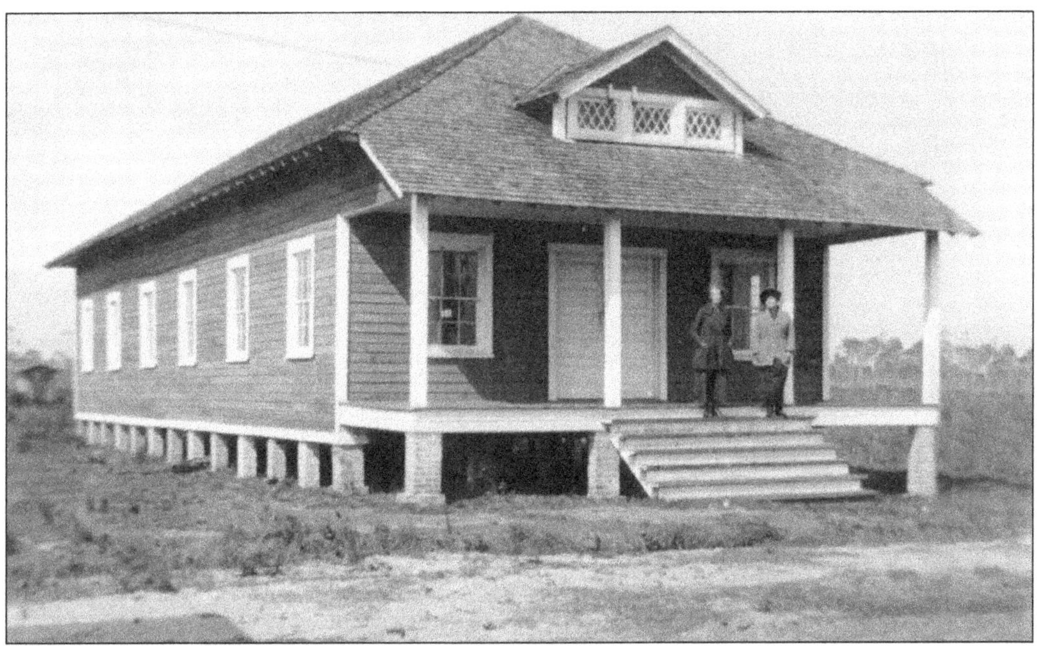

The Woodmere Lumber Mill provided a school for the children of mill employees. There was a one-room schoolhouse for children of all ages. The lumber mill was located on Route 776 in Englewood. At the time that the mill was operating, the town was called Woodmere, Florida, although it did not have its own post office. (Courtesy of VMA.)

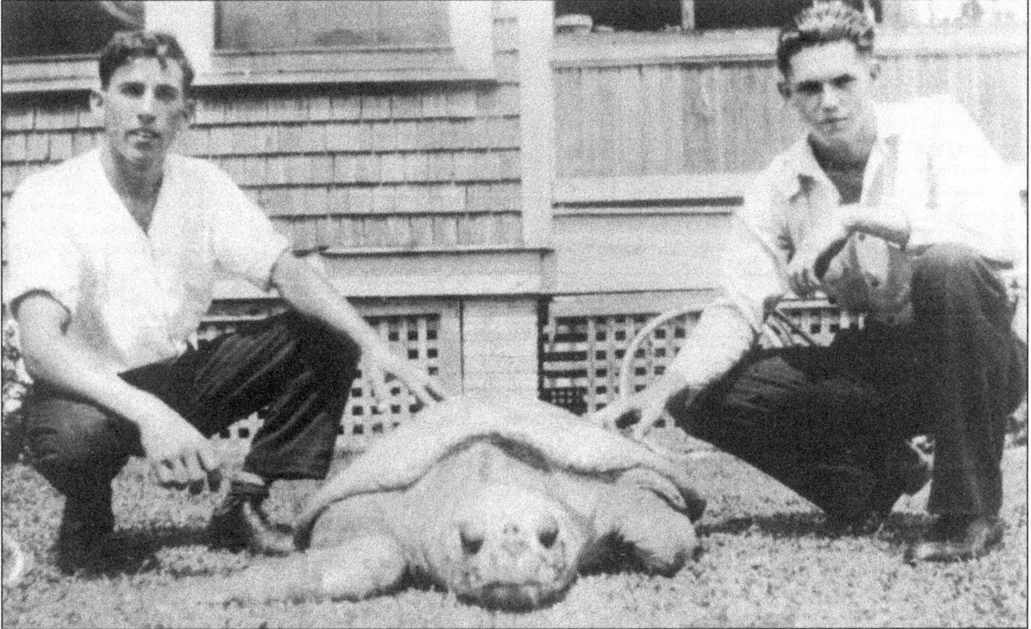

Robert W. Murray (left) and Harry Sjoblom are pictured with a loggerhead turtle they found on Manasota Key Beach in 1933. After catching the turtle, they canned the meat. Today, the loggerhead turtles are a protected endangered species. Residents who live along the Gulf of Mexico are asked to dim their lights during hatching season so that the hatchlings will migrate into the water. (Courtesy of VMA.)

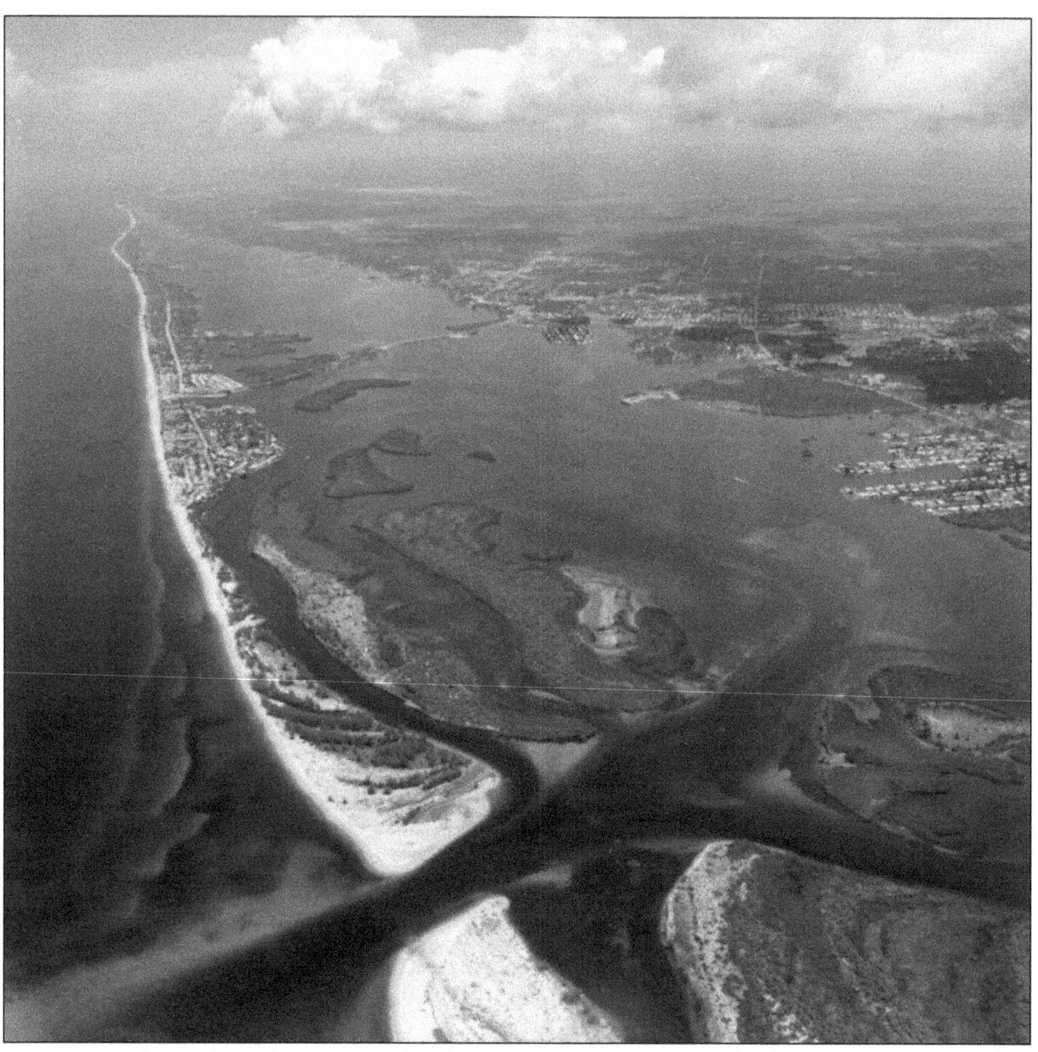

Stump Pass, located on the south end of Manasota Key, is constantly changing due to weather and tides. Therefore, the pass requires a lot of dredging maintenance to keep it navigable. Boaters have to use caution because of the shifting shoals. (Courtesy of VMA.)

Bob Buffum, former owner of the Manasota Beach Club, is enjoying a quiet afternoon after the January–April tourist season has ended. He is fishing on an inner tube on the Gulf. Bob and his wife, Sydney, purchased the club in the early 1960s. At the time, it was used as a camp, with only a few buildings. (Courtesy of the Manasota Beach Club.)

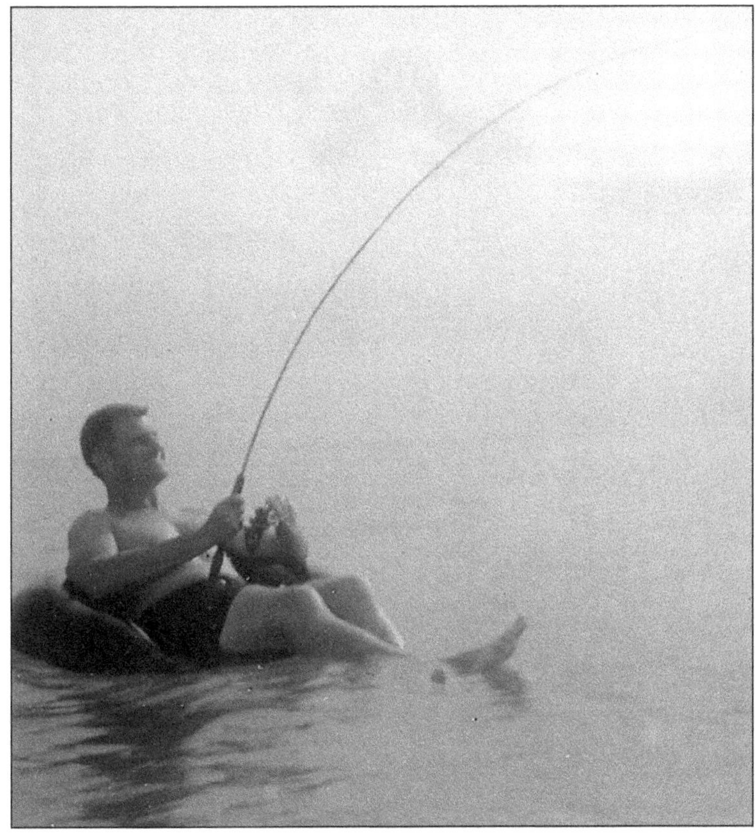

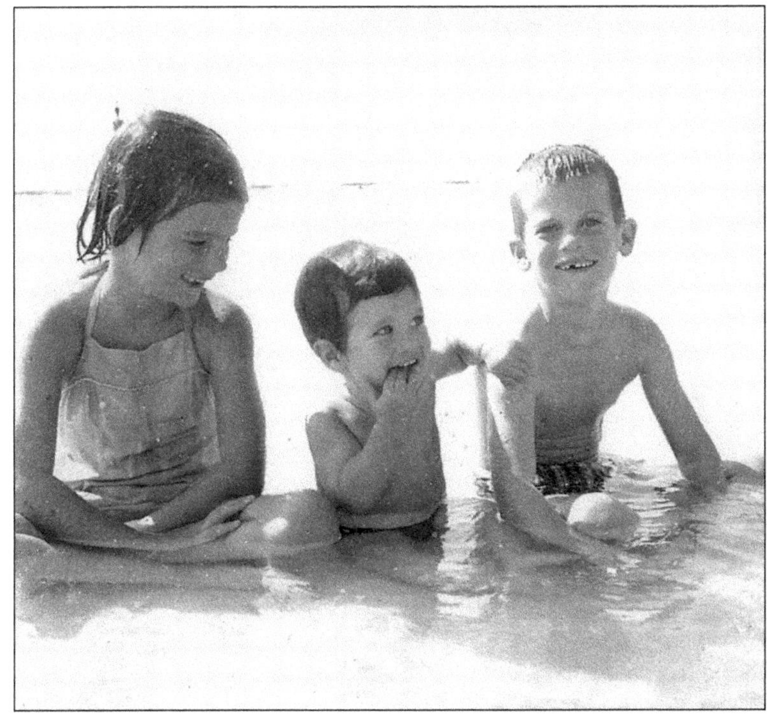

The Buffum children cool off in the water at the Manasota Beach Club. From left to right are Buffy, Jim, and Rob. When the family moved to Manasota Key, the two eldest, Buffy and Rob, were toddlers; and the youngest, Jim, was born at the Sarasota County Hospital. The Buffum children grew up in the hotel business. Today, Buffy runs the beach club, and her brother Jim is part owner of the family hotel, the Weekapaug Inn in Rhode Island. (Courtesy of the Manasota Beach Club.)

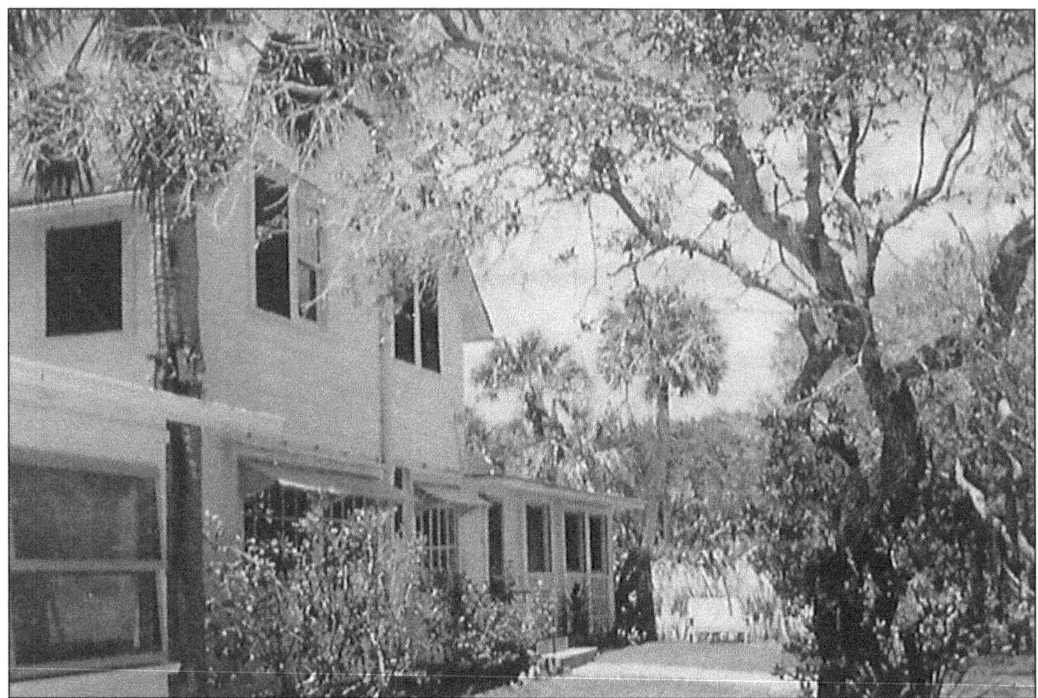

This is an exterior shot of the Manasota Beach Club's dining rooms and office. Guests look out at nature surrounded by sea grapes, live oaks, and the Gulf. The club provides a venue for weddings or other special events. The Buffums offer guests three meals a day, and the dress code requires gentlemen to wear a coat and tie for dinner. The club is also open for membership to residents in the area. (Courtesy of the Manasota Beach Club.)

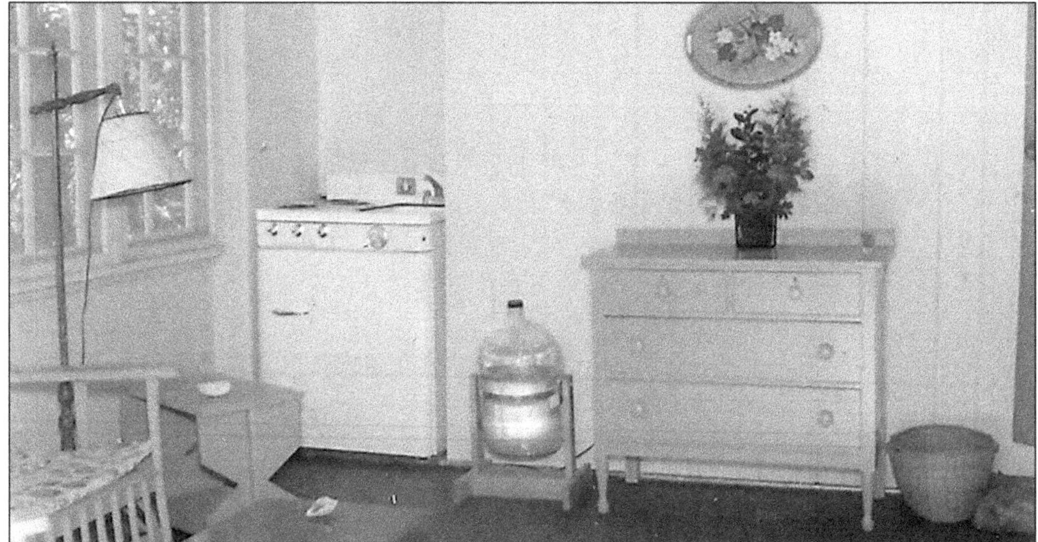

The cottages are quaint and homey with a mix of antiques and modern furniture, which provide simple comfort for the visitor, as seen here. The Buffums have built 14 additional cottages on the Gulf side over the years. Pictured here is the interior of a cottage with an antique rocker and a washing machine. The Buffums would advertise the beach club while working at their inn in Westerly, Rhode Island. (Courtesy of the Manasota Beach Club.)

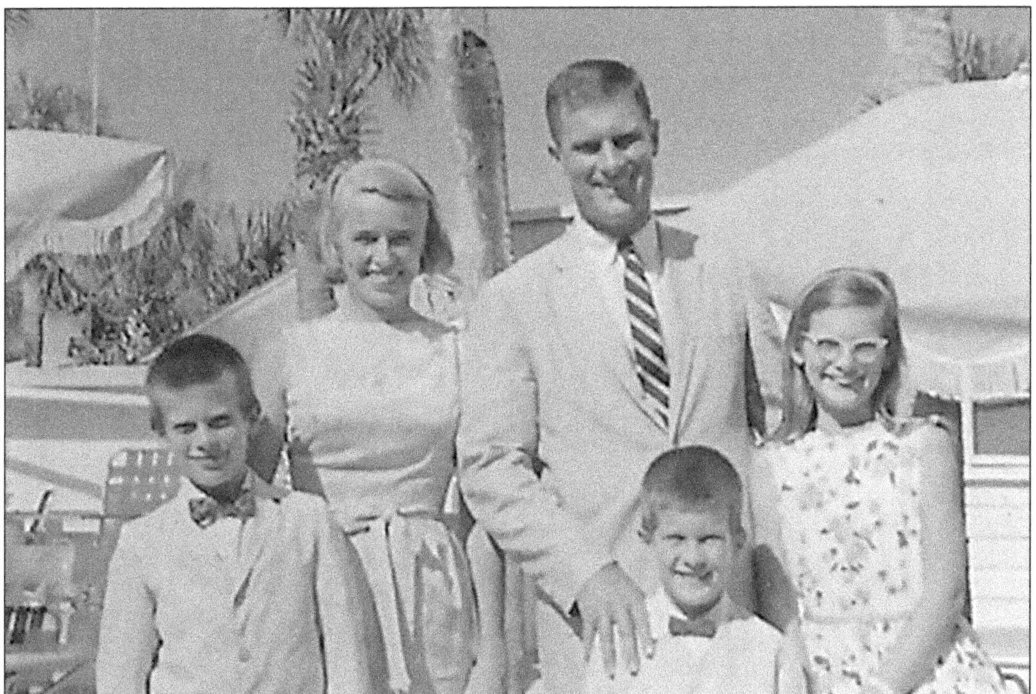

The Buffum family purchased the property in the early 1960s. Syd was expecting her third child, Jim, who was delivered at the Sarasota County Hospital. The Buffums were trained in the hotel business thanks to their family inn in Rhode Island. For many years, they worked hard traveling to Rhode Island in the summer and Manasota Key in the winter. From left to right are (first row) children Rob, Jim, and Buffy; (second row) Sydney and Bob. (Courtesy of the Manasota Beach Club.)

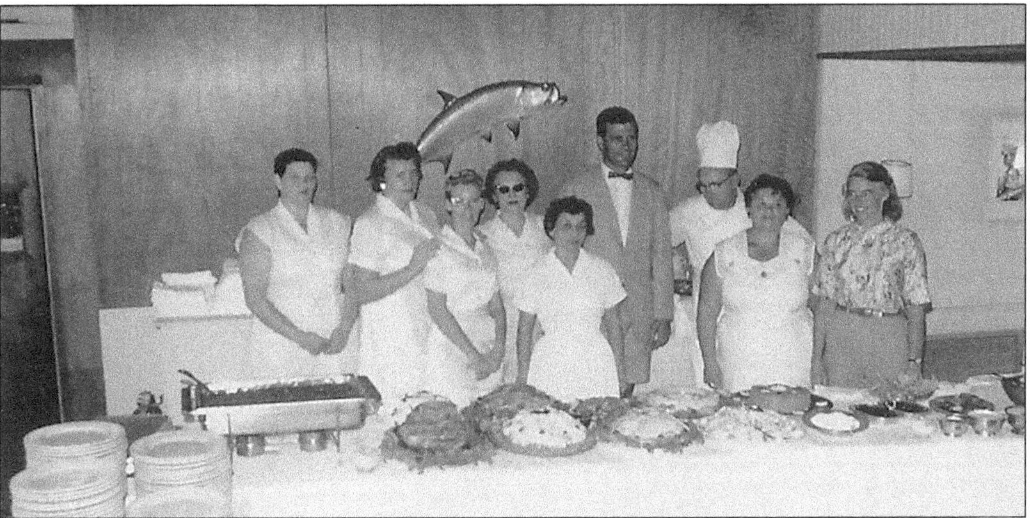

This is a picture of the longtime staff at the Manasota Beach Club. Here, employees become like family, and many stay on year after year. The club was first owned by a German couple by the name of Mr. and Mrs. Otto Pfunstine. During the 1930s, they ran the club as a nudist colony with two solariums for the men and women. Mr. and Mrs. Gwynne were the next couple who purchased the place and changed it to a more formal club, requiring guests to be fully clothed while on the property. (Courtesy of the Manasota Beach Club.)

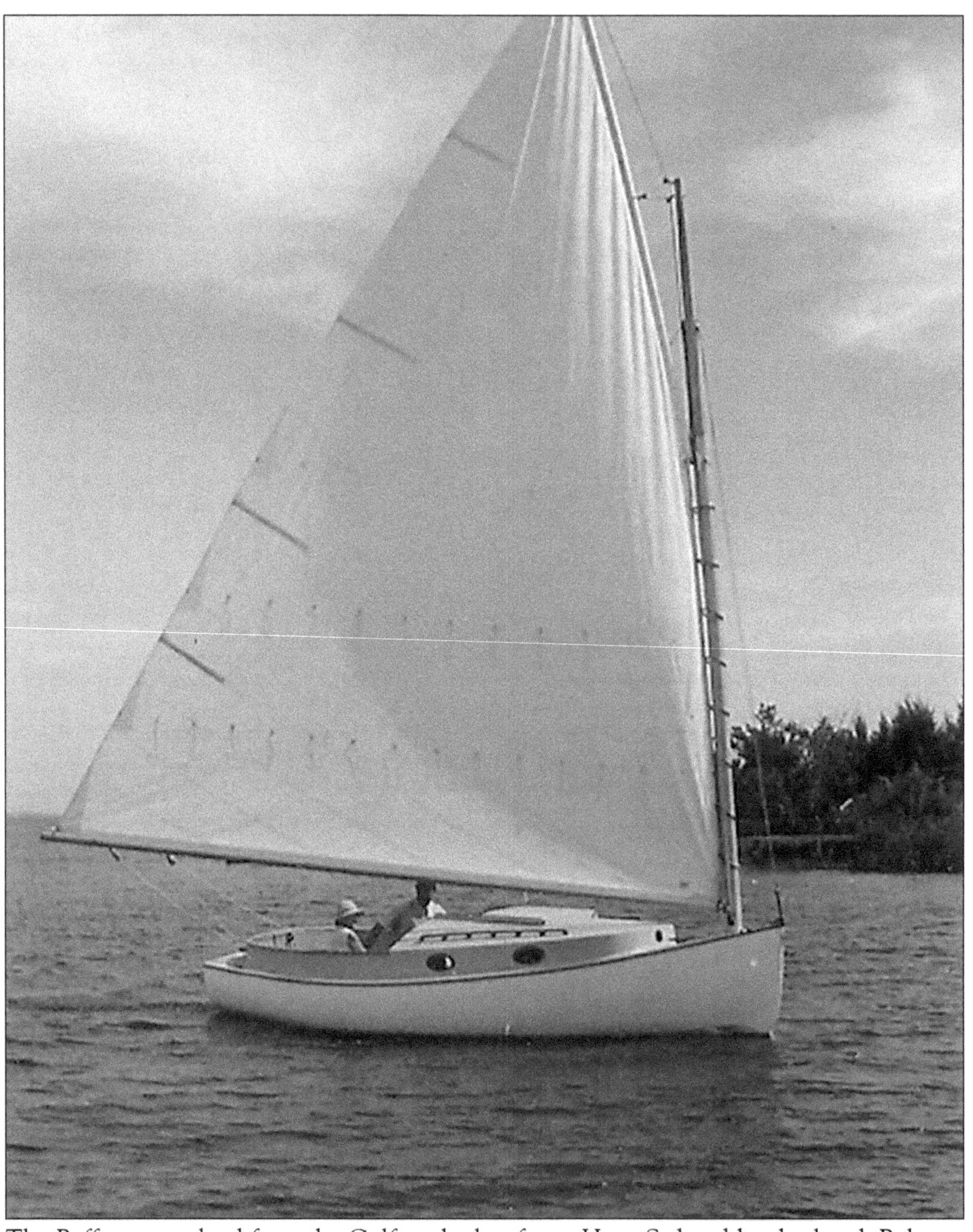

The Buffums own land from the Gulf to the bay front. Here, Syd and her husband, Bob, are sailing their boat *Half Hitch*. Sarasota County prohibits commercial buildings on the bay side of the island. Children love staying here and can swim in either the ocean or the club's pool. (Courtesy of the Manasota Beach Club.)

Pictured here are children dining outside at the Manasota Beach Club. Many parties are held on-site. The Buffums have preserved the beautiful trees and landscape. A canopy of branches spreads across the property, providing a picturesque site for marriage ceremonies, followed by pictures on the beach. (Courtesy of the Manasota Beach Club.)

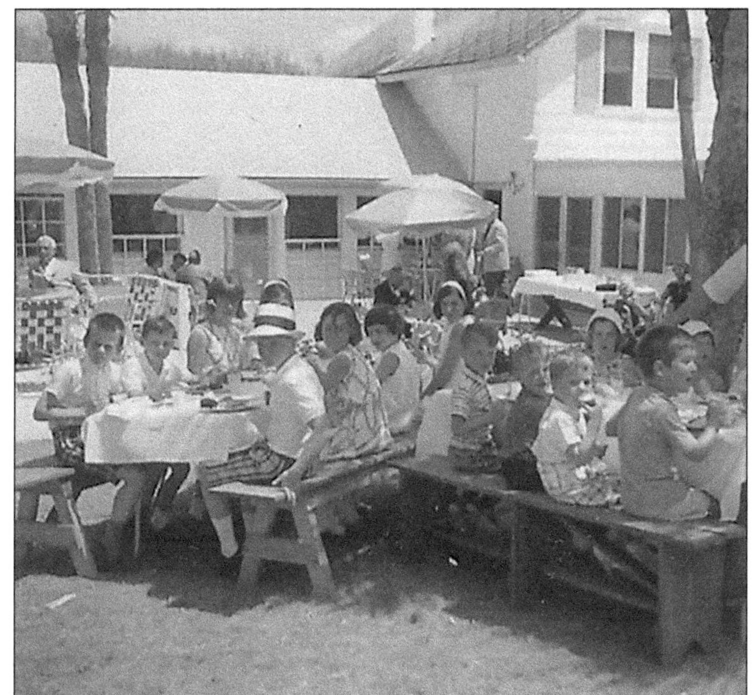

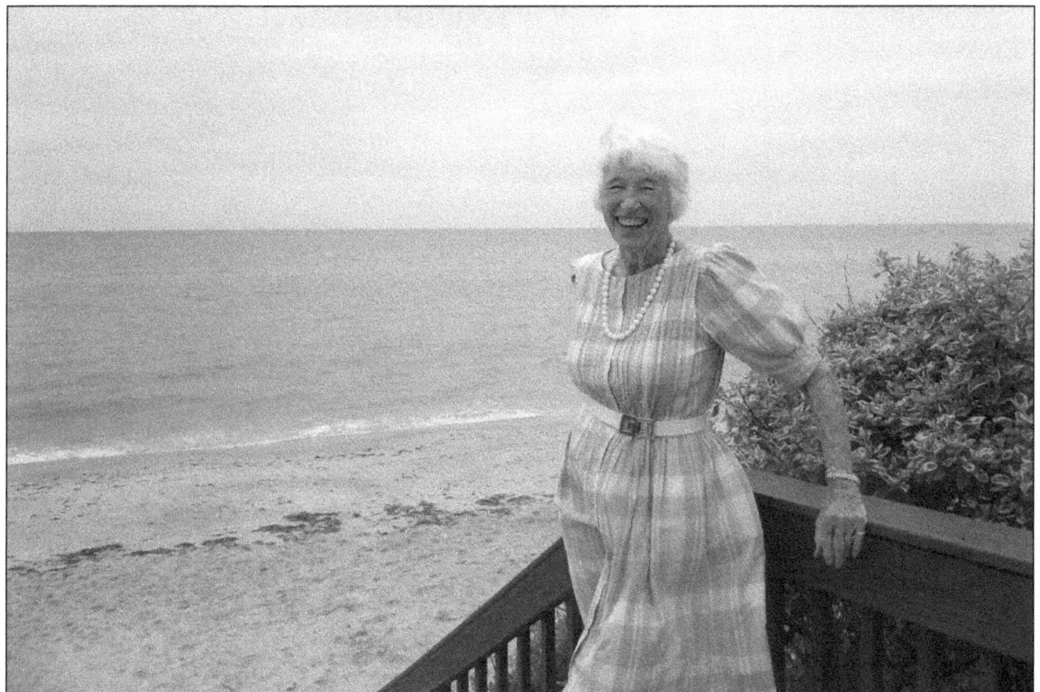

Sydney "Syd" Buffum still loves the place she has called home for the past 45 years. She graciously gave a tour of the Manasota Beach Club and explained how they would purchase property abutting their land when it would become available to expand their site on the Gulf. Proudly showing the entire property, she appeared to be happy to be deeply rooted like the trees. (Courtesy of the Manasota Beach Club.)

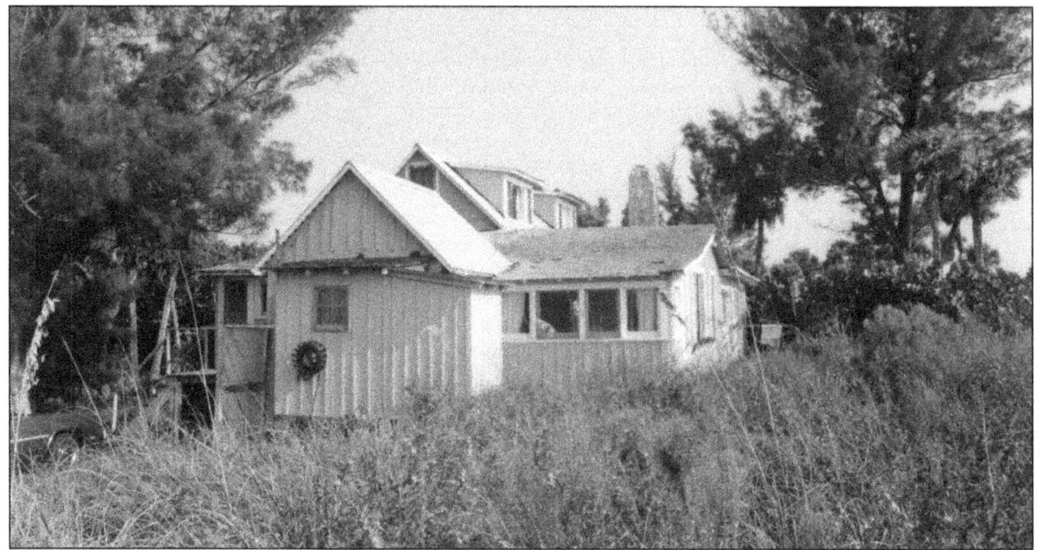

Pictured here is the Hermitage before it was moved and renovated. In 1907, Swedish immigrant Carl Johansen purchased land on Manasota Key from Giles Chapman. He and his wife, along with three of their 13 children, built a home for his family. They purchased lumber from across Lemon Bay and transported the wood across the water. The Johansens left the area in 1916. The house remained empty for 15 years, after which it had several owners. (Courtesy of SCHR.)

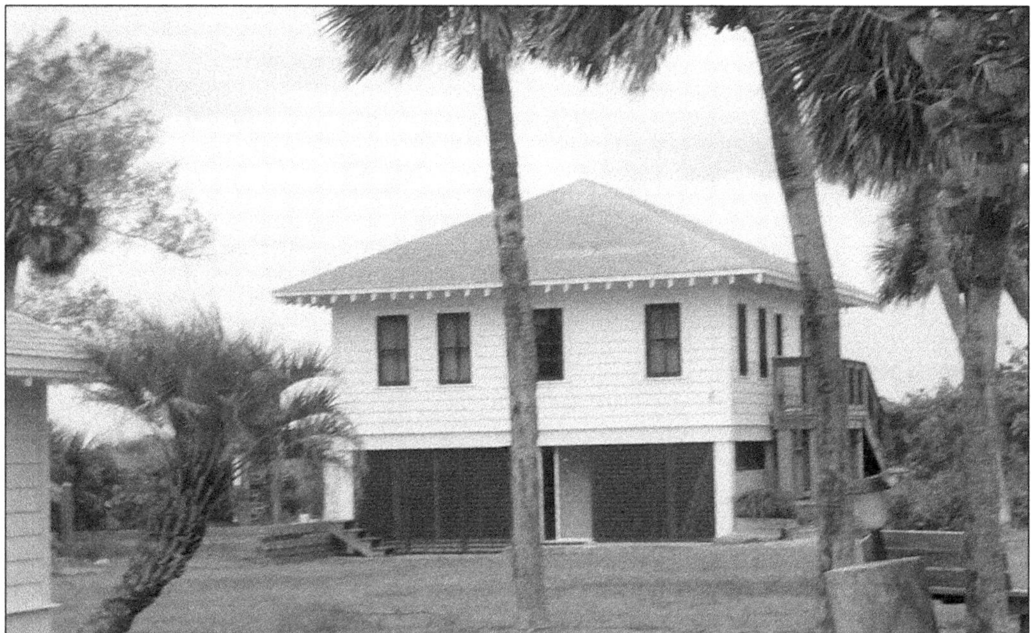

Pictured here is one of the current cottages at the Hermitage. In 1936, a brochure advertised the Hermitage as "The Sea Island Sanctuary," along with the following distinction: "The Isolation of our location permits the practice of nudism 24 hours a day if desired." In 1988, the Sarasota Parks and Recreation Department purchased the lot and buildings of the Hermitage with the plan to knock them down for parking. A group of concerned citizens stepped in to preserve the buildings. Syd Adler, Patricia Caswell, and the Sarasota Arts Council worked hard to earn money for the artist retreat. (Courtesy of SCHR.)

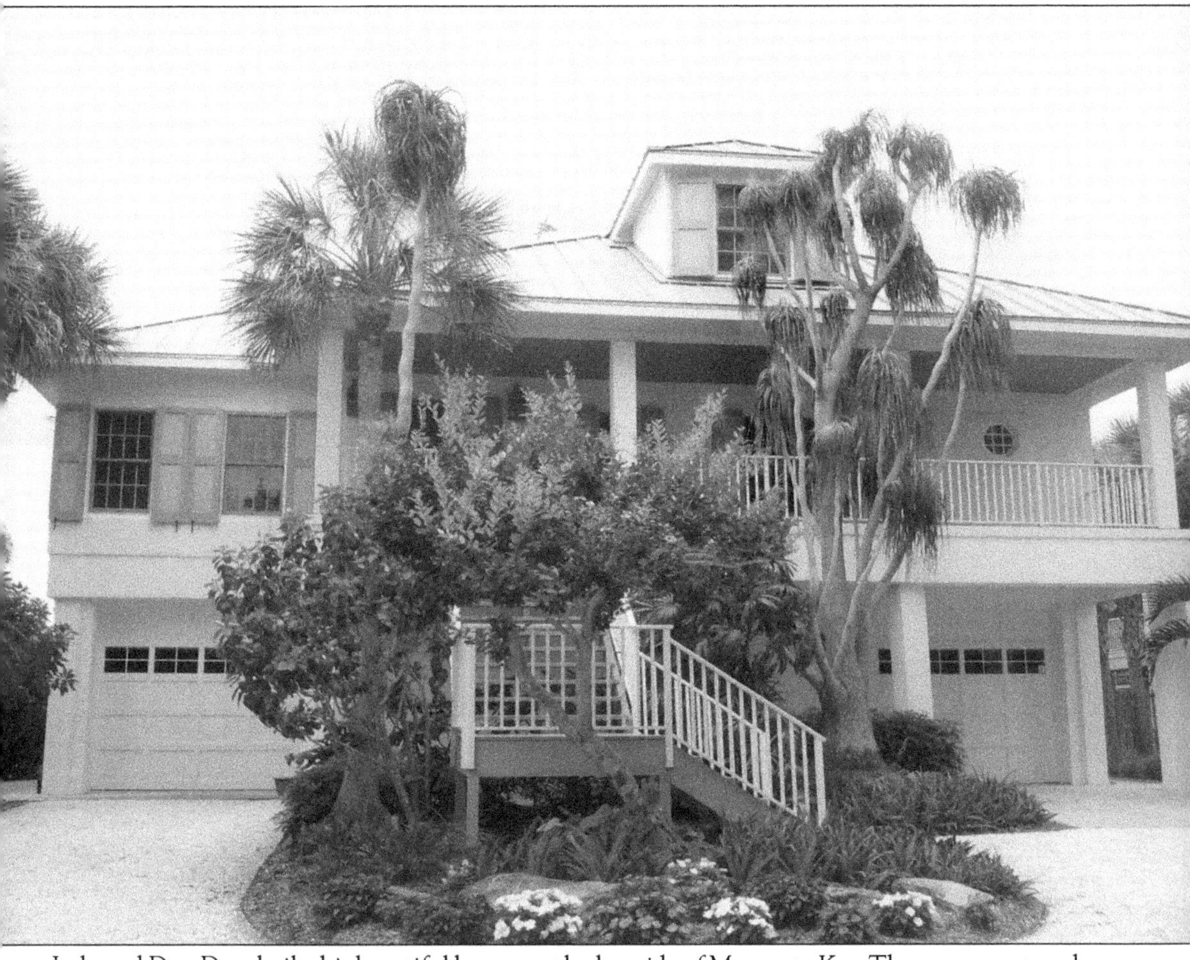

Judy and Dan Dees built this beautiful house on the bay side of Manasota Key. They once ventured out on their boat to have a picnic at the Don Pedro Island State Park (Palm Island), located between Knight Island and Little Gasparilla Island. Fog set in, however, and they were barely able to find their way home. With their competent boating skills, a little luck, and a flashlight, they made it home safely. (Author's collection.)

www.ingramcontent.com/pod-product-compliance
Lightning Source LLC
LaVergne TN
LVHW060626110826
845147LV00015B/946

* 9 7 8 1 4 6 7 1 1 4 8 6 8 *